Praise

uncovered editions
www.uncovered-editions.co.uk

Series editor: Tim Coates
Managing editor: Michele Staple

New titles in the series

Already published

uncovered editions

MR HOSIE'S JOURNEY TO TIBET, 1904

A REPORT BY MR A. HOSIE, HIS MAJESTY'S CONSUL AT CHENGTU, ON A JOURNEY FROM CHENGTU TO THE EASTERN FRONTIER OF TIBET

London: The Stationery Office

Applications for reproduction should be made in writing to The Stationery Office Limited, St Crispins, Duke Street, Norwich NR3 1PD.

ISBN 0 11 702467 8
First published in August 1905 as Cd. 2586.
© Crown copyright.

A CIP catalogue record for this book is available from the British Library.

Cover photograph: In Ladak, on the Leh–Yarkand road.
© Royal Geographical Society.

Maps produced by Sandra Lockwood of Artworks Design, Norwich.

Typeset by J&L Composition Ltd, Filey, North Yorkshire.
Printed in the United Kingdom by The Stationery Office, London.
TJ4360 C15 10/01

CONTENTS

About the series

Uncovered editions are historic official papers which have not previously been available in a popular form. The series has been created directly from the archive of the Stationery Office in London, and the books have been chosen for the quality of their story-telling. Some subjects are familiar, but others are less well known. Each is a moment in history.

About the series editor, Tim Coates

Tim Coates studied at University College, Oxford and at the University of Stirling. After working in the theatre for a number of years, he took up bookselling and became managing director, firstly of Sherratt and Hughes bookshops, and then of Waterstone's. He is known for his support for foreign literature, particularly from the Czech Republic. The idea for *uncovered editions* came while searching through the bookshelves of his late father-in-law, Air Commodore Patrick Cave, OBE. He is married to Bridget Cave, has two sons, and lives in London.

Tim Coates welcomes views and ideas on the *uncovered editions* series. He can be e-mailed at timcoates@theso.co.uk

GLOSSARY

aneroid	aneroid barometer, often used as an altimeter
argol	thin circular cakes of manure, dried and used as fuel
banyan	Asian fig tree
bere	barley
bract	leaf (bearing a flower in its axil)
brick tea	tea pressed into cakes
brinjal	aubergine
capsicum	pepper plant
caravansarie	unfurnished inn or extensive enclosed courtyard where caravans stop
coir	strong fibre of coconut husk, used in making rope or matting
debouch	emerge, flow from
dzo	offspring of yak and cow
freshet	a flood, or overflow of a river caused by heavy rains or melted snow
gutta-percha	a sticky, rubber-like substance
hermit kingdoms	those that were cut off from contact with all countries but China during the 17th, 18th and 19th centuries

hypsometer	instrument for measuring the heights of places on the earth's surface by observing the boiling point of water
lama	Tibetan priest
Lamaism	Tibetan Buddhism
lamasery	Tibetan monastery
lares et penates	household gods; the home
li-kin	provincial transit duty
loquat	common name for *Eriobotrya japonica* and for its fruit
mill lade	mill stream
mou	unit of measurement = 0.15 acre
obo	prayer-cairn
Om Mani Padmé Hum	Buddhist invocation (freely translated as "O, the Jewel in the Lotus, Amen"); used especially by the Lamaists of Tibet
pumelo	grapefruit-like fruit of tropical tree
sere	dry, withered
Taotai	provincial officer
tsamba	barley-meal; Tibetan barley dish
yamen	official residence or office
zareba	hedge providing protection against wild animals or enemies

COINS, WEIGHTS AND DISTANCES

1 tiao	1,000 copper cash = 2s. 3½d. (approximately)
820 to 850 copper cash	1 Ssuchuan dollar
1 Ssuchuan dollar	0.71 Chengtu tael = 1s. 11d. (approximately)
1 Chengtu tael	1.05263 Shanghae tael = 2s. 8⅜d. (approximately)
1 Shanghae tael	0.89766 Haikuan tael = 2s. 6¾d. (approximately)
1 Haikuan tael	2s. 10⅔d. (average value in 1904)
1 rupee, Chinese	0.36 Chengtu tael = 11⅗d. (approximately)
1 candareen	1/100th of 1 tael
1 mace	1/10th of 1 tael
1 oz, Chinese	1⅓ oz, English
16 oz, Chinese	1 catty = 1⅓ lb, English
100 catties	1 picul = 133⅓ lb, English
1 *li*	¼ statute mile★

★The length of the *li* differs according to the nature of the country, but in the west of China, 4 *li* may be taken as the average per mile in level and mountainous country combined.

In the early years of the 20th century there were several consular missions to remote parts of China. It isn't easy from the reports to understand what particular purpose was given to these expeditions, except to enlighten and enthral the members of the party. That in itself was sufficient to inspire some beautiful writing, with the apparent intention of conveying delight to the British Parliament.

Here, Mr Alex Hosie, Consul-General at Chengtu in the Province of Ssuchuan, describes a three-month round-trip (1,320 miles) from Chengtu to Ning-ching Shan on the eastern frontier of Tibet, undertaken around the time of the British invasion of Tibet. In addition to describing the perils of his journey he gives a detailed account of the countryside and its flora and fauna. To the west of Ta-chien-lu (now Kangding), the people — their houses, clothing, food, language and religion — are to all intents and purposes Tibetan, and Mr Hosie provides a fascinating description of their customs and way of life.

The reader may also be interested in Travels in Mongolia, 1902, *a description of a journey undertaken by Mr C.W. Campbell two years earlier, and also* The British Invasion of Tibet: Colonel Younghusband, 1904, *an event to which Mr Hosie refers in his diary. Both these books are available in the* uncovered editions *series.*

China and neighbouring countries, c. 1900

INTRODUCTION

The great highway connecting Chengtu, the capital of Ssuchuan, with Lhassa, the capital of Tibet, passes westward through the cities of Shuang-liu Hsien, Hsin-ching Hsien, Chiung Chou, Ming-shan Hsien, Ya-chou Fu, Jung-ching Hsien, Ch'ang-ch'i Hsien, and Ta-chien-lu T'ing, through Litang and Batang, and across the Chin-sha Chiang or upper waters of the River Yang-tsze to the Ning-ching Mountains, which at this point form the boundary line of the "Land of the Lamas" and her suzerain China. The distance by road from Chengtu to the frontier is reckoned at 2,400 and to Lhassa 6,105 *li*, equivalent to about 600 and 1,500 miles respectively. By this road travel the Chinese Imperial Residents for Tibet, occupying several months on the journey; along it devout pilgrims, eager to look upon

Mr Hosie's route from Chengtu to eastern frontier of Tibet, and back, 1904

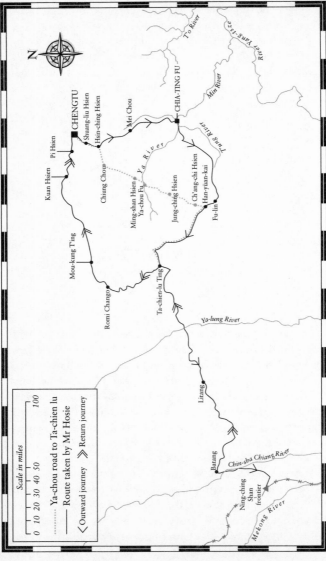

the face of the Dalai Lama, advance, some by continuous
genuflections and prostrations, taking years to reach their
goal; and over it dash Imperial couriers, who, by changing
horses at the post stations and travelling night and day, are
able to carry messages from Lhassa to the nearest telegraph
office at Ta-chien-lu—some 5,185 *li*, or 1,300 miles—in
less than 20 days. By this road, too, a considerable part of
the trade between western China and eastern and southern Tibet is slowly and laboriously conveyed on the backs
of pack animals. It is a road barred by numerous mountain
ranges, whose lofty passes inspire terror in the breasts of
the superstitious wayfarers, who at each successive crossing
give vent to their pent-up feelings in muttering the well-
known prayer, *Om Mani Padmé Hum*, and with joyous
shouts of "Hla solo, solo!" lay each a stone as a thank-
offering to the gods on the obo, Hla Dzi, or cairns which
dot the summits and represent the offerings of many weary
travellers. This road as far west as Batang has been traversed
by not a few Europeans; but, comparatively well-worn as it
is, it still possesses a charm, leading, as it does, to much that
is very imperfectly known. Mysticism is never wanting in
devotees; but a Consular officer is more concerned with the
material facts of trade than the arcana of Lamaism or the
religious system of government of the last of the Hermit
Kingdoms. In 1883 I journeyed along the Tibetan road
from Chengtu to Ch'ing-ch'i Hsien, and at Han-yüan-kai,
a few miles beyond, branched off and struck south through
the Chien-ch'ang Valley to Ta-li Fu in western Yünnan.
Little did I then dream that 20 years later I should again find
myself in Ssuchuan facing westwards.

It is monotonous to travel the same road twice in the
same direction, and I accordingly resolved, instead of following the Ya-chou road to Ta-chien-lu, to go south from
my headquarters at Chengtu to Chia-ting—a distance of
100 miles by road—thence proceed westward along the

valley of the T'ung or Ta-tu River, and strike the Ya-chou–Ta-chien-lu road at Han-yüan-kai, whence, as stated above, I had branched south on one of my previous journeys in western China. The easiest and quickest way to reach Chia-ting from the provincial capital is to take a boat outside the east gate and drop down that branch of the Min River which, made up of streams diverted 30 miles to the north-west for purposes of irrigation, and flowing east by south under the north, east, and south walls of the city, goes south to join the parent river at Chiang-k'ou, an important market town and trade depôt some 30 miles below Chengtu. It is, however, only from May to October that speedy transit is available, for during the rest of the year the stream is shallow, and small boats of the lightest draught find great difficulty in scraping their way over its pebbly bed. At high water Chia-ting may be reached in from 36 to 48 hours, and during freshets in even less; but, cooped up in a boat, one sees little of the surrounding country, and I determined to proceed overland, although it entailed a journey of four instead of two days. I had travelled by road from Chia-ting to Chengtu in January 1903; but, as tillage and trade change with the seasons, I wished to see the country, interesting even in winter, under other conditions.

The plain of Chengtu, some 90 by 40 miles, is the chief granary of the province of Ssuchuan. Naturally fertile, it has been rendered still more productive by the hand of man. The plain slopes from west to east and south, so that while the city of Kuan Hsien, on its western border, stands at an altitude of 2,280 feet above sea level, Chengtu★ which is situated to the east and distant 30 miles, has an elevation of only 1,700 feet. At Kuan Hsien the Min, or,

★ Lat. 30° 40′ 29″ N, Long. 104° 4′ 36″ E: His Britannic Majesty's Consulate-General, near north gate.

as it is also called, the Fu River, which rises in the north-west corner of the province, debouches from the mountains on the plain and by artificial rock-cutting and stone dikes is split up into two main channels, which are in turn sub-divided into a perfect network of streams and canals ramifying north, east, and south throughout the whole plain. So widespread are these ramifications that, by a northern channel, the Min connects with the T'o River to the east. Here there is rarely any danger of a failure of the summer rice crop from drought, for at that season water is usually abundant; but, in winter, the main eastern channel is annually cut off by a barrage above Kuan Hsien to enable the silt to be removed and the dikes to be repaired. Then it is that wheat, rape, poppy, barley, beans, and peas may suffer from a deficiency in the rainfall. These channels, with the exception of those which carry their contents into the T'o, meet in the south of the plain near the district city of Hsin-ching Hsien, with an alti-tude of 1,650 feet, where low hills close in from east and west. South of these hills the irrigation system recom-mences and is carried towards Chia-ting along the valley of the Min, which may be looked upon as a southern continuation of the Chengtu plain. Not only are all these streams and canals available for irrigation, but are they also utilized to generate power required in various industries. Here is to be seen a flour-mill driven by a vertical or horizontal water-wheel; there a similar mill is engaged in crushing rape seed preparatory to the extraction of the oil.

In winter, when the water is low in the beds of the streams, Persian wheels of light bamboo work are set up along the banks, and, unattended, silently pour, as they revolve, the contents gathered by their rim tubes into raised troughs, whence the water is led by bamboo gutters to the thirsty land.

The whole plain is full of agricultural and industrial life and activity, but it is only from the surrounding mountains that a good view of it can be obtained, for it is so thickly wooded that not more than a few hundred yards are visible from one spot. The villages and farmhouses are screened by bamboos and trees of various kinds, and these innumerable clumps of foliage bar any extensive view. Such is the nature of the country round Chengtu. From the city walls one looks across the densely wooded plain to the range of hills bordering it on the east, but the mountains to the west are rarely visible. Even from this vantage ground one sees little of the plain itself but a confused mass of greenery, lit up in February and March by the bright yellow blossoms of the rape, and in May and August by golden patches of ripening grain.

CHENGTU TO TA-CHIEN-LU

28th July 1904

At 8 a.m. on 28th July my caravan passed through the south gate of Chengtu, and we were fairly started on our journey to the Tibetan frontier. Some days had been spent in making the necessary preparations. Chair-bearers and porters had to be engaged; loads had to be duly weighed; and the many odds and ends connected with a several months' trip had to be attended to. All was now over, and I was again in the plain of Chengtu.

The description which I have given of the plain in general applies in every particular to that part of it which runs south-west from Chengtu. Shuang-liu, the first district city through which the high road passes, is 40 *li* distant; but

Chengtu to Ta-chien-lu, showing outward and return route taken by Mr Hosie

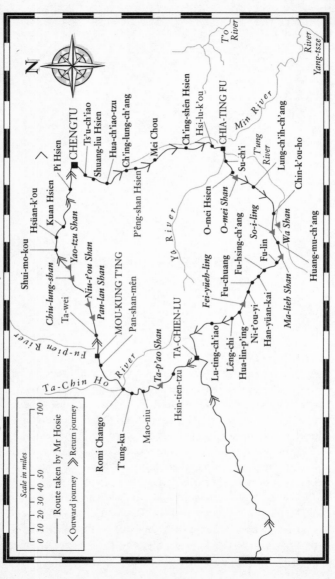

midway is the large and important market town of Ts'u Ch'iao, the great silk mart of the plain. Here, during the season—May and onward—the raw silk is brought from the country districts and disposed of to agents, who annually take up their residence in the numerous inns contained in the town. For some miles the road is paved with a double row of stone slabs, the whole a yard wide with mud between the rows; but at every 4 or 5 yards a blank or hollow of a foot is left to prevent it being used by the wheelbarrows which swarm on the level ground and would easily cut into the sandstone. The result is that the unpaved or wider part of the road is used for traffic, and the stone part neglected except by foot passengers, and that only during rain when the side mud becomes ankle-deep.

Shuang-liu is a small city, but has large suburbs outside two, at any rate, of its four gates—the east, which we entered, and the south, which we left. This is the third time I have passed through the city, and on each occasion I have found it crowded and the shops and street stalls hard at work. One gets only a peep at the city wall on entering the gates, owing to the surrounding suburbs. It is undoubtedly a prosperous place.

After passing the big bridge outside the south gate of Chengtu, the high road crosses numerous sandstone bridges, great and small, throughout the first day's stage as far as Têng-kung-ch'ang on the right bank of the Min River, 5 *li* south of Hsin-ching Hsien, and just below the junction of the two main branches coming from the plain. A small stream, the Nan Ho, from Chiung Chou, passing to the west of Hsin-ching, enters the Min River below the junction and under the town. The whole day's journey of 95 *li* lies over a country riddled with irrigating streams and canals, at present in full swing, as the paddy (rice) plants are now about $2\frac{1}{2}$ feet high, and require all available moisture to bring them into ear. With the exception of some patches of maize and beans (*Glycine hispida* Max.), there is nothing but paddy to be seen, and the plants, partly submerged, gave excellent promise. The alder (*Alnus cremastogyne* Burkill) was the most prominent tree, literally fringing every watercourse, and the dikes between the plots of paddy sheltered beans just coming into blossom. The reason why the plain of Chengtu looks less populous than it is may be explained by the fact that the farmhouses are concealed by clumps of bamboo, cypress (*Cupressus funebris* Endl.), and occasional specimens of Nanmu (*Machilus nanmu* Hemsl.) and *Pterocarya stenoptera* C.D.C. I saw one or two specimens of *Cunninghamia sinensis* R. Br., but this tree is commoner further north. A few miles before striking the left bank of the Min the mulberry (*Morus alba* L.) and the *Cudrania triloba* Hance, both used in sericulture, became prominent, and I heard once again from one of my Chinese escort the same story of the necessity of feeding infant silkworms on the leaves of the latter to ensure a larger yield and a better quality of silk.

During the afternoon a range of low, red-soiled hills was visible about a couple of miles to the east of the high road. By this range flows what I may call the Chengtu River, which joins the Min River on its left bank, 120 *li* from the capital and 50 *li* from Têng-kung-ch'ang, where I am now writing. Ferry boats were busy plying on the Min and the Nan Ho at the latter place.

There was an enormous traffic on the road, especially as far as Shuang-liu. Wheelbarrows laden with passengers, many of them asleep in spite of the jolting, trundled along. Huge bags of rice and black pigs were being similarly conveyed, the latter strapped in pairs on their backs, joining their squeals to the squeaking of the wheels. Horses and oxen were also engaged in the rice traffic, and there were porters with medicines, salt, timber, and fowls of every age.

There were also loads of raw sheepkins from Ta-chien-lu, but what interested me most was the baggage of the ex-Imperial Resident for Tibet, on its way from Lhassa or other places *en route*. What I saw of it was being conveyed by wheelbarrows and porters, and was packed in raw-hide boxes, bags, and carpeting. I imagine that I met only a part, but even that, had it consisted of trade products, would have cost an enormous sum in freight. Servants were scattered here and there in charge of it: one with a white button, dusty and tired, was being trundled along in a wheelbarrow, while another was sitting astride a diminutive pony, saddled with a Tibetan rug.

The street and roadside stalls were laden with cooked maize cobs, melons, brinjals, string beans, marrows, grapes, long red turnips, and other fruits and vegetables.

29th July
It rained heavily overnight, and was dull, but not raining when we trooped out of Têng-kung-ch'ang at 5.30 a.m. The road follows for some miles the right bank of a western branch of the river, and being simply of mud was not improved by the overnight rain. A fresh drizzle soon came down, and continuing as far as P'êng-shan Hsien did not mend matters.

I have said above that the streams from the centre and west of the Chengtu plain unite at Têng-kung-ch'ang, but the river is soon broken up again by islands into a number of channels, which afterwards meet at Ch'ing-lung-ch'ang, an important and busy market town on its right bank. The uniting is due to a range of low hills, which pushes its way from north-east to south-west as far as the left bank. East of this range, and between it and another range running in the same direction, flows the Chengtu River, which joins the Min on its left bank, between Ch'ing-lung-ch'ang and P'êng-shan Hsien from which

Chiang-k'ou at the junction is distant 10 *li*. The right bank of the river south of Têng-kung-ch'ang is rapidly being eaten away by freshets in spite of wedge-shaped groins built of boulders and stones heaped in bamboo baskets, and Ching-lung-ch'ang itself appears to be in imminent danger of disappearing into the river at no distant date. When I was at breakfast at this market town my chair-bearers, owing to the rain, pleaded with me to embark on one of the cargo boats lying along the bank, and descend as far as Mei Chou where we are spending the night, 95 *li* from our last night's quarters; but I was sorry to have to decline, as I had come to see the country not the river.

It was fortunate I did not comply with their request, for there was a sudden change in the products of the country. Fields of maize in all stages of growth, from ripe cobs to plants a couple of feet high, took the place of rice. Beans (*Glycine hispida* Max., and *Phaseolus mungo* L.) were growing on the same ground with the maize, and neighbouring fields were cropped with ground-nuts (*Arachis hypogoea* L.), some showing their yellow flowers, while others had already thrust their blossom spikes into the soil, and were developing the nuts underground. Several rows of millet (*Holcus sorghum* L.) were usually grown as a border to the maize fields, doubtless to make the passer-by believe that the whole field consisted of millet, with a view to prevent raiding the ripe cobs, and those who know the great resemblance between the two plants will appreciate the cleverness of the ruse; but even this did not satisfy the grower, for watch-stations, thatched with straw and accessible by ladders, were erected in almost every field and duly tenanted. I have heard the maize cobs of China frequently flouted as regards size by people of the new world; but nowhere have I seen larger specimens than in Mei Chou. There were also patches of white sugar cane about 6 feet high, and sweet potato shoots, which we also saw being carried to market, were planted in several places, usually after tobacco, whose old stalks still remained sprouting in the ground.

The road goes straight south from P'êng-shan Hsien to Mei Chou, a distance of 40 *li*, and half-way the cultivation of maize ceased and gave place to paddy, which was now in full ear. The country was a sea of paddy, with islands dotted here and there of darker green. These islands were the farmhouses concealed in groves of bamboo, cypress, and other trees. The alder still fringed the watercourses, the mulberry and Cudrania were fairly abundant, and amongst other trees I noticed *Pterocarya stenoptera*, *Melia azedarach* L., occasional large specimens of the banyan (*Ficus infectoria* Roxb.), a few willows, and the loquat (*Eriobotrya japonica* Lindl.).

There was little in the way of trade observable during the day. Rape seed, some bundles of wicks from *Juncus effusus* L., and loads of paper from Chia-chiang Hsien were going north. We also met a considerable number of water buffaloes, and I should be glad to know why it is that the white bands which cross the breast and neck of the young animals are lost in later years. There was very little to be seen of wild animal life. The coo of the wood-pigeon and his mate's reply were the only evidence of animal existence. Not even a sparrow, crow, or magpie was to be seen. The sound of the mill-wheel came repeatedly from the dark bamboo islands in the sea of paddy.

P'êng-shan Hsien and Mei Chou are both poor places, surrounded by red sandstone walls pierced by four gates. They are not far from the right bank of the river. The inn in which I am spending tonight in Mei Chou bristles with smells; but, as a hunt has revealed no better accommodation, I am obliged to blunt my nerves for the night.

30th July

We made an early start from Mei Chou, getting away at 5.45 a.m. On our way to the south gate we found that the southern part of the city is given up to the cultivation of vegetables, and mulberry trees were showing over the garden walls. Nanmu trees were also abundant, especially in the grounds of a large temple near the gate. A few hundred yards from the gate we struck the right bank of a western branch of the Min which bifurcates 5 *li* above the city at a place called Wang-chia T'o. The main branch lies to the east, and both reunite not far south of the city. Boats were coming down the eastern branch on their way to Chia-ting. The road follows the right bank for the most part, but frequently cuts off bends by striking across country. The general direction is south.

During a stroll in the early morning I caught up a middle-aged man with dishevelled locks, accompanied by a poor child of five or six in a similar condition of filth and disorder. I addressed and asked him what he was doing and where he was going. He replied that he was a native of Chihli who was visiting the Sacred Mountains of China and was bound for O-mei Shan. I pitied the child and said so, but the man persisted in saying that the infant was fond of the roving life. They were moving along very slowly, as the child could not possibly walk at any pace. The man said he was not a priest—Buddhist or Taoist. I offered him some money to help him on his journey, but this, to my surprise, he declined not quite indignantly but with needless reiteration, saying that he accepted money from no one, but that he and the child managed to subsist as best they could. It seemed to me that the man was either insane or trying to wipe out by sanctity the memory of some great crime. In any European country the police would have had the man up before a Magistrate for cruelty to the child. But we cannot judge Orientals by a European standard; for in China, at any rate, as soon as an infant is able to walk it becomes a breadwinner. Of this I had good evidence during the day, for at Chang-chia-k'an, 20 *li* from Mei Chou, where preparations were being made for market-day, tiny children, boys and girls, were sitting behind baskets or creels full of fir cones and needles expectant of purchasers, who were beginning to flock into the town.

We crossed the ferry of Huang-chung-pa, 12 *li* from Mei Chou, at 7.10 a.m. This, about 60 yards wide, appears to be simply water admitted from the river into a fold of the country. We followed down its right bank to the main stream. The country, so far, was full of maize, mostly bordered with millet, paddy, beans, and ground-nuts. The beans and the ground-nuts were growing amid the maize. There were the usual watch-towers; but where the millet border was absent it was a tempting of Providence to have the red-tufted cobs thrust across the roadway almost into one's hands—a temptation which I noticed some of my soldier-escort were unable to resist.

At 20 *li* from Mei Chou we breakfasted at Chang-chia-k'an, where a file of eight soldiers, armed with rifles, awaited me at the entrance to the town. The local military official expressed his intention of strengthening by this number my usual escort of five; but I had to decline the honour, as escorts have to be paid by the traveller. In the inn there were about 20 large earthenware jars of millet spirit fitted with bamboo stands. As millet was growing in the country I was surprised to learn that the innkeeper's supply came all the way from Chung-pai-sha on the Yang-tsze, a 20 days' journey. There was no doubt about it, for the labels on the jars bore out the innkeeper's statement. Each jar contained 350 catties, or $466\frac{2}{3}$ lb and the cost of a jar laid down at Chang-chia-k'an was 13 taels. Most things in China have their uses, and I found that the dried stems of the rape plant find a ready market and are employed for casing leaf tobacco.

Leaving Chang-chia-k'an, we struck south-by-west to the base of a range of low sandstone hills clad with fir. Hence the cones and needles above referred to. Here a western branch of the Min flows towards the hills and supplies a deep irrigation canal cut out of the sandstone at the eastern base of the range. The road lies along the embankment, between the canal and the river, as far as the hamlet of Hung-hua-yen, where are one or two fine banyans, 17 *li* from Chang-chia-k'an. Three *li* more brought us to the village of Hei-lung-ch'ang, distant 20 *li* from Ch'ing-shên Hsien. The country is now less level, and, although everywhere cultivated, I noticed that Persian wheels and endless chain pumps were in use for raising water to irrigate the fields. The mulberry, and especially the Cudrania, were the most prominent trees everywhere, and it will be understood that we are in a great centre of sericulture.

At 12.20 p.m. we entered Ch'ing-shên Hsien, 60 *li* from Mei Chou, by the north gate. Here it was market-day, and the streets were crowded as we left it by the south gate. But the city is not always so busy, as may be gathered from the following: one of my horses dropped a shoe during the day, but owing to the absence of the only farrier in the place, the unfortunate animal had to be left behind till his return. It lies close to the right bank of the Min. Here there is an excellent inn with a small compound, and I debated for a long time whether I should spend the night in it. Everything was in its favour, but, as it would mean 90 *li* to reach Chia-ting on the morrow, I decided to push on another 20 *li* to make sure of arriving at the latter place early in the afternoon, and enable me to make some necessary arrangements for my westward journey.

We left, and struck the river at the end of a long street outside the south gate. Before arriving at Ch'ing-shên

Hsien, a range of hills, running east and west, comes into view south of the city. For this range, along the north base of which the river flows from east to west before passing through it, we made in a southerly direction, skirting hedges of mulberry and Cudrania, which are now densely dotted about the fields, and through an avenue of *Cunninghamia sinensis*, to a ferry crossing a western tributary of the Min called Ssŭ-mo Ho, 16 *li* from Ch'ing-shên Hsien. Here I waited until all my caravan was safely across, when we passed on, and at the end of 20 *li* arrived at the market town of Liu-chia-ch'ang, which we reached at 4 p.m.

From Chengtu southwards I have passed through a country magnificent for the fertility of its soil, the variety of its products when the winter crops are included, and the tireless industry of its population; but with it all there is a lack of comfort that appears incredible to the European. I am writing this in a small room with a soft mud floor, in which, when I arrived, there was neither table nor chair. The only furnishings were a settle and a bare wooden bedstead, that would not be tolerated in a prison in England. There is a paperless wooden grating doing duty for a window, and yet, on a board underneath this grating, is written large, in red ink, the one character "T'ien", meaning Heaven! The son of Han is still much in need of education. It is to be hoped that the present rage which pervades the provincial capital in this direction, and is spreading beyond it, will have useful results.

31st July

We had a short stage before us today, and were not sorry to leave our mud room at Liu-chia-ch'ang at 5.15 a.m. We had only 70 *li*, about 20 miles, to accomplish to reach Chia-ting. The Chinese reckon the distance by road from Chengtu to Chia-ting to be 360 *li*, and, as a mile on the plain may be taken as the equivalent of $3\frac{1}{2}$ *li*, the result is practically 100 miles. In the mile which separated us from the right bank of the Min we passed through patches of tobacco, maize, ground-nuts, and soya beans, while the land was thickly dotted with mulberry and Cudrania. Following the right bank of the river for a distance of two miles, we struck a large shingle bank, which is formed where low hills draw in from the west and end in sandstone bluffs, and crossed it at the ferry of Hsi-lu-k'ou, the name of the few wretched eating-houses perched on the hills forming the left bank.

The river now makes a long bend west and northwest before resuming its southern course to Chia-ting, and the road takes a short cut across these hills, which are exceedingly interesting. They are under 500 feet above the level of the river and are thickly wooded, and I noticed specimens of the vegetable tallow and wood-oil trees (*Sapium sebiferum* Roxb., and *Aleurites cordata* M.Arg.). Fir and oak were also well represented, and my old friends the *Ligustrum lucidum* Ait. (large-leaved privet) and especially the ash, *Fraxinus chinensis* Roxb., were met with. The latter is the "Pai-la-shu", or white-wax tree, and a coating of white wax, about an eighth of an inch thick, covered the under sides of the branches. We worked our way over and through these hills, reaching the highest point at Kuan-tzŭ Mên, where the road is cut through the sandstone summit. In the small valleys between the hills, room was found for patches of paddy and sweet potatoes.

At 8.15 a.m. we again struck the left bank of the river flowing east soon to go south. We were now only about 100 feet above the river. At Pan-ch'iao-ch'i, a few eating-houses making up a hamlet, I was met by an escort from the Prefect of Chia-ting and the Magistrate of Lo-shan. When working our way through the hills, we had a good view to the west of O-mei Shan peeping out from clouds hanging on the mountain side. As we advanced, the hills on the left bank of the river fell away and gave place to a plain, sandy and uncultivated for a time, but soon covered with crops and trees of various kinds—especially mulberry, Cudrania, white wax, and *Pterocarya stenoptera*. The maize was nearly all gathered, and the cobs were drying in flat baskets and mats in the sun preparatory to the grain being removed by hand. The grain is again dried in the same way after removal, and the empty cores are used for stoppering jars. We had a meal at Mêng-tzŭ-ch'ang, having done about 15 miles (50 *li*) since morning. It is a poor-looking place, but being market-day, was crowded with people from the surrounding country.

Soon afterwards I noticed the first patch of Rhea (*Boehmeria nivea* L.) on the present journey. It was merely an edging for a field of beans. As we proceeded down the plain we passed two fine specimens of *Ginkgo biloba* L., giving their name, Pai Kuo Shu, to the small hamlet and roadside shrine where they were growing. They must have been 60 feet high, with fine dense foliage and straight trunks some 20 feet in circumference near the ground. There was little or no paddy in this plain, evidently owing to lack of means of irrigation; but the dense foliage, with the heat and the deafening music of the cicada, reminded me very forcibly of a day in Ceylon.

At noon we again struck the bank of the river, and were immediately met by an officer and a dozen soldiers sent by the Foreign Bureau (Yang Wu Chü) of Chia-ting. I may mention that the officer had the cuffs of his sleeves embroidered in silver, and the men were armed with Winchesters. At 12.25 p.m. we took a boat, our escorts another, and dropped down to His Majesty's ship *Woodcock*, where I received a warm welcome, and was besieged by messages from, and calls by, Chinese officials.

There was some trade on the road during the day. Yellow raw silk, packed in matting, was going north from Chia-ting to Chengtu, and I noticed several loads of what, in spite of all previous investigations into the products of the province, had escaped my observation. They consisted of compressed white cakes, beautifully rounded like cheeses, of the ground-up sawdust of the cypress. The stuff is compressed for convenience of transit, and is the chief ingredient in the manufacture of incense sticks.

1st August

The Prefectural city of Chia-ting lies at the junction of the Min and the T'ung Rivers, the former flowing under its eastern and the latter under its western wall. It is an important trade centre on its own account as the depôt of the great silk and white-wax industries of the Prefecture, and it also attracts for export a great part of the outward trade of Tibet from Ta-chien-lu through Ya-chou and down the Ya River, which flows into the T'ung, and from Sun-p'an, coming overland to Kuan Hsien and down the Min River. It is likewise the head of navigation for large native boats from the Lower Yang-tsze, bringing cargo for Chengtu and the west of Ssuchuan generally. It is, in addition, the place where one of His Majesty's ships of the Upper Yang-tsze flotilla is usually stationed for some months annually during high water from June to September.

Chia-ting, as I have already stated, was the point fixed by me as the starting-point of my journey to the Tibetan frontier. From this city it is reckoned 12 stages to Ta-chien-lu by following the road up the Ya River to Ya-chou; but as I had made up my mind to follow up the valley of the T'ung River to the same destination by what is known as the small road, I did not expect to accomplish it in the same time. Moreover, O-mei Shan, now the favourite summer resort of foreigners in western Ssuchuan, was a tempting bait for a short detour, especially as I had failed to see during my previous visit in 1884 the spectre of the Brocken—the famous "Glory of Buddha"—and I resolved to take the mountain on my way westward.

The Chinese authorities at Chia-ting were unremitting in their attentions to me during my brief stay there. Early on the morning of my departure they sent their cards to speed me on my journey, and when I left by the west gate at 7.30 a.m., on the 1st August, the soldiers attached to the Foreign Bureau awaited outside the walls, and, after a flare of trumpets, fired several volleys in my honour.

The high road follows the hilly ground along the left bank of the T'ung behind the city. On the bank timber was piled, and rafts that had recently come down were being broken up. From this centre timber for building purposes is distributed in all directions, and I understand that those acquainted with local conditions are able to buy and transport it to Chengtu cheaper than similar wood from Kuan Hsien can be purchased in the capital.

On leaving the hills we crossed a bank of sand and shingle little cultivated, and struck the left bank of the Ya River, a tributary of the T'ung, 15 *li* from Chia-ting. The Ya River, when in flood, rushes over this sandy plain. At the time we crossed by the ferry it was about 300 yards in breadth. Five *li* from its right bank we entered the important market town of Su-ch'i over a red sandstone bridge of 17 arches spanning the O-mei River. Small boys were swimming and diving in the broad shallow stream; rod-fishers were at work, although I did not see them catch anything; and it was to all appearances washing day at Su-ch'i, for a number of women were scrubbing their clothes on the right bank. The houses near the river are built on solid sandstone foundations about 12 feet high. It is a great silk-weaving centre, the industry having been attracted from Chia-ting owing to excessive taxation at the latter place. Two rafts with cormorants were being poled up stream as we breakfasted at an inn overlooking the bridge. The mulberry was a prominent tree in the gardens of the town.

Immediately to the west of Su-ch'i the ground rises about 100 feet above the O-mei River, and on the slope stand two small pagodas. The road passes west by north over this plateau covered with paddy, and soon enters low wooded hills, through which it winds to a second plateau with little but rice and a few plots of rushes (*Juncus effusus* L.) At the entrance to the market town of Chên-tzŭ-ch'ang, 30 *li* from Su-ch'i, I was met by an escort from O-mei Hsien, and amid the blare of trumpets and firing of guns I made my way to an inn for the mid-day meal. Only 20 *li* now separated us from the city of O-mei Hsien, and, passing over a beautiful plain resembling in many respects the plain of Chengtu, but thickly dotted, as the latter is not, with the white-wax tree. Much of the wax had already been harvested, and the branches had been lopped off to facilitate its removal.

There were fine clumps of bamboo, and alders were very prominent along the irrigation streams which flow down from the O-mei range of mountains lying approximately north and south. White wax, of which we saw loads in the shape of circular cakes about 1 foot in diameter and 3 inches thick, and weighing from 17 to 18 catties, being carried to Chia-ting, is one of the most important indus-tries of the O-mei district. Another valuable industry is silk. The mulberry and Cudrania were prominent trees from Chia-ting to O-mei Hsien. We also met loads of white paper manufactured in the district being carried eastwards by porters. This paper is specially manufactured for making paper cash, and finds its way to Chengtu for the purpose. Medicines dug from the O-mei mountains likewise form an important export from the district, and a certain quantity of O-mei tea is collected and fired principally for local consumption. We arrived at O-mei Hsien, which we entered by the east gate, a few minutes before 4 p.m.

2nd August

Early in the morning I left the city of O-mei Hsien by the south gate, accompanied by a few bearers and porters, to accomplish my second ascent of O-mei Shan. The atmosphere was clear, and a good view was obtainable of the three ranges which, running north and south, make up the Sacred Mountain, whose foot is some 20 *li* to the south-west of the city to which it gives its name. The road runs south-west towards the southern end of the nearer and lower range. It is bordered by white-wax trees, which are also dotted about in the fields, and by some magnificent banyans. The finest specimen of the latter I saw was distant 5 *li* from the city, opposite the temple of Shêng Chi Ssŭ. The circumference of the trunk a few feet from the ground measures about 30 feet, but it is made up of the original stem and many suckers, which have found their way to the ground and gone to form a single irregular trunk.

The temple, too, deserves a close inspection by the traveller. At the entrance is a low tower in which is suspended a bronze bell some 10 or more feet high and about 12 feet in diameter at the lip, which is scalloped, and about 6 inches thick. Some 50 yards beyond in the temple grounds a beautiful specimen of a bronze pagoda about 20 feet high rests on stone slabs and is surrounded by a wooden rail. It is thickly studded with rows of small single Buddhas in relief at the base, while the main body of the tower is varied with similar Buddhas mounted on tigers and elephants. It is a magnificent specimen of workmanship, but unfortunately, like the temple, it is falling into decay. It is slightly broken in one or two places, and the rail does not protect it from eager pilgrims who polish the base by rubbing thereon copper cash to be carried home as charms. Both bell and pagoda are said to have been cast during the Ming dynasty.

At the village of Hsiao-tien-tzŭ, 10 *li* from the city, the road divides: one branch, known as the small road, leading to the large temple of Ta O Ssŭ, much frequented by foreigners as a cool retreat in summer; the other, the main road, joining the small road below the temple of Pai Lung Tung, 40 *li* from O-mei Hsien. At the latter temple I spent the night. The three ranges are connected by spurs, some of them exceedingly narrow, and by these the road leads from range to range till the final or highest range is reached. It is simply heartbreaking, after a weary climb up stone steps, to find a long descent on the other side; but such is the road which the pilgrim to the summit of Mount O-mei has to follow, rising with the road as it twists and turns in its upward course.

No one who has climbed the mountain is likely to forget the long, all but perpendicular, climb to the temple called Hsi Hsiang Chih—the "Elephants' Bathing Pool". So narrow are some of the spurs that one looks down into an abyss on either side of the roadway; but the ranges and spurs are all densely wooded, and the danger to the unwary is thus considerably obscured. The lower slopes of the ranges were cultivated here and there, and maize and beans were the ordinary crops. The land is temple property, and is leased to small cultivators, who guard their property so religiously that foreigners living on the mountain are unable to procure the unripe corn. They will not listen to its being gathered till it is yellow and hard.

Higher up cultivation in the general sense ceases, small gardens round the temples taking the place of cultivated plots. The *Cunninghamia sinensis*, which is a common tree on the lower slopes, ends at about 6,000 feet, and its place, as far as the summit, is taken by the silver fir (*Abies* sp.), whose trunk and branches are moss-grown and frequently covered with creepers and young trees of various kinds, the seeds from which they spring having found a suitable germinating ground in the moss.

3rd August

I left Pai Lung Tung at 5.30 a.m. and, with occasional lifts by a mountain chair, improvised from the poles of my sedan, reached the summit at 4.15 p.m. Mr E. Colborne Baber's height of O-mei Shan—11,100 feet above the level of the sea—is usually quoted as the authority; but in giving this height he distinctly stated that it is open to an error of 500 feet. In one of the rooms of the temple, which is about 25 feet below the actual summit, I found the altitude by hypsometer to be 10,133 and, by adding 25, a total of 10,158 feet. As O-mei Hsien is 1,740 feet above the sea, the actual ascent from the plain to the summit is 8,488 feet. Five *li* above Pai Lung Tung I passed through the temple of Wan-nien Ssŭ (3,500 feet), in which the bronze elephant described by Mr Baber is still caged in stone bars. All these temples on the mountain side are very unimposing. Built as they are of wood grown on the spot, they suffer much from the dampness of the climate, which quickly gives them a brown decaying appearance. Since my previous visit, a pavilion has been built on the actual summit, and the precipice is guarded by an open-work stone wall, nearly 6 feet high, enclosing the three bronze pagodas. At the foot of the pavilion, the remains of the bronze temple are gathered together, and look like a heap of old iron. The abbot informed me that the arsenal at Chengtu had made an offer for the lot, which he had declined.

The sights to be seen from the top are the "Glory of Buddha"—the reflection of the sun on the clouds hanging in the abyss below the summit of the precipice; the "Myriad Lights", or lamps which are visible at night in the gulf underneath; and the Snowy Mountains of Tibet. I spent the 4th August on the summit, but although I saw a faint passing shadow of the sun on the edge of a cloud, I failed to recognize the actual "Glory of Buddha", as pictured to me by more fortunate visitors. Clouds hung around the summit, and were but rarely dispelled by occasional showers. On one of these rare occasions I was able to get a view of the Chengtu plain, with the Min, T'ung, and O-mei rivers looking like shining ribbons of light winding about on a green background.

At dead of night I was roused by a priest to see the "Myriad Lights", and looking down into the gulf I certainly observed many faint lights twinkling far below me. They were not the lights of houses or wayfarers, and I suggested to the priest that they must be the reflection of the stars overhead, but he scoffed at the explanation. They and the "Glory of Buddha" are the supernatural visions reserved by the priesthood for the superstitious pilgrims who annually throng the mountain. Clouds hid the Snowy Mountains of Tibet; but, as I hoped to make a personal acquaintance with them later, my disappointment was not acute. The pilgrim season was nearly over; but a few, including a solitary yellow-capped Tibetan, still clambered upwards, while others were being carried down on the backs of porters. I witnessed a night service held in the temple just under the summit for the benefit of the few pilgrims who remained there overnight. The abbot, in full canonicals, recited prayers, interspersed with the beating of drums and the clashing of cymbals, the pilgrims sitting on benches and standing around, with their eager faces lit up by the glare of many candles. It was a weird spectacle. On another occasion I heard the abbot expostulating with the pilgrims, who were rubbing cash on the pagodas. He said: "These cash which you are taking back to your homes as souvenirs of your visit are of no avail. Go into the temple, and listen to the preaching of the doctrine."

Potatoes were, as usual, growing on the summit, and there was a little stunted rape in flower; but the priests explained to me that the latter had been practically destroyed by the heavy rains which had recently fallen. There was, however, an excellent crop of white strawberries, small, but of good flavour. Medicinal roots and tubers of various kinds were exposed on stalls set up here and there on the mountain side for sale to pilgrims, and beggars with all manner of deformity were clamorous for alms.

White-wax trees and tea shrubs were prominent on the lower slopes, and the *Cunninghamia sinensis* was being felled and cut up into planks and boards for conveyance to the plain.

5th August
I left the summit and arrived at Pai Lung Tung drenched with heavy rain, which began to fall soon after our start. Next day I descended by the small road passing Ta Ssŭ, and returned to the city of O-mei Hsien to pick up the rest of my caravan, and prepare for my westward journey.

7th August
Nothing depresses the traveller in China at the end of the day more than the filthy accommodation provided by the ordinary Chinese inn. Quarters more than usually filthy are my fate tonight at Lung-ch'ih-ch'ang, the first stage south-west from O-mei Hsien, and 26 miles distant from that city. We passed through the south gate at 5.55 a.m., and proceeded as if once more bound for the summit of

the Sacred Mountain. But at the hamlet of Liao-po-lo, 5 *li* distant, and within 50 yards of the big banyan already referred to, the road bifurcates, one branch going south, the other to Mount O-mei. We followed the former, going south and south-west over a continuation of the plain. Irrigation is everywhere possible, owing to the streams flowing from the mountain, and although the country is occasionally broken by low spurs descending eastward into the plain, water is abundant. Except on the higher ground, where maize and yellow beans were growing, paddy, if a little backward, was to be seen on all sides. The alder was a very prominent tree by the banks of the streams, and the white-wax tree more densely fringed the paddy plots, and the fields themselves were thickly dotted with it. In some places women were rubbing off the wax from the young trees into large flat bamboo baskets without breaking the young branches.

In the case of the older trees, with stems 8 to 10 feet in height surmounted by branches springing from the gnarled tops, the branches are cut off for convenience of collection. I noticed many trees with withered leaves, in which the wax insects (*Cocci pela*) had been enclosed, still attached to the boughs with very little resulting wax, and I was informed that cold weather at the time of suspension had proved very destructive to the insects' life. In fact, for the last two years the production of wax in the district of O-mei has been on the decline, and is attributed not merely to the weather, but also to scarcity of insects. Establishments are annually opened in the city of O-mei for the sale of the insects; but, owing to a scarcity of the scales in the Chien-ch'ang valley whence they come, few, if any, establishments have been opened, and the farmers have had to get their supply as best they could. White wax in the O-mei district is sold at about 60 taels a picul of 100 catties; but in this case each catty weighs 24 Chinese ounces or 2 lb. It is carried to

Chia-ting, where the scale of weight is 17.3 Chinese ounces to the catty, or 1 lb 6⅔oz.

I have referred above to the milling of wood for the manufacture of joss or incense sticks, and I have been told that the wood used is the *Cupressus funebris*. The industry is carried on not far from the north gate of O-mei Hsein, and I am certain that the Cupressus is not used there for the purpose. The tree used is called the Shui Kua Shu, or "water-melon tree", which I have not yet been able to identify. The tree, whose wood is exceedingly light, is cut into round sections about 18 inches long. Two wooden wedges, one longer than the other, are driven a few inches firmly into two holes drilled in the circumference of the section. They are in a line, and fit into two eyes at the end of an 8-foot flat wooden lever, whose other end is fitted to the crank of a water-wheel. As the wheel revolves the section of the tree is drawn backwards and forwards over a roughened slab, behind which there is a tank in which the woody sediment settles. The latter is removed from the tank and placed in a fine bamboo basket which retains the sediment and allows the water to escape. The stuff is then placed in hempen bags and pressed into cakes of various sizes and weights; but before being made up into incense sticks it is disintegrated by soaking in water and mixed with the ground-up bark of a tree known as Hsüan Ma which evidently contains some adhesive substance.

The whole day's journey of 26 miles from O-mei Hsien to Lung-ch'ih-ch'ang consisted in attempting to circumvent at a respectable distance the O-mei ranges. The attempt was in vain, for at Lung-ch'ih-ch'ang we have still with us the southern outliers of the main range. The O-mei plain is bounded on the south by a range of low, well-cultivated hills, backed by a higher range. The road passes south-west over the plain, crossing several mountain streams flowing east, and spanned by good stone bridges, till reaching Kao-ch'iao-p'u, some 9 miles from the city, it runs up a valley along the right bank of a stream coming from the O-mei ranges. The valley bifurcates, and the road keeps to that lying to the south, ascending gradually to the water-parting at a height of 3,500 feet above the level of the sea. It then drops suddenly 400 feet to the village of Yang-ts'un-p'u, 20 miles from O-mei Hsien, and follows a stream flowing south-west. The road crosses and recrosses this stream many times, and several bridges have been washed away by floods; but the stream is shallow and is easily forded.

Most of the hill slopes, including the lower parts of the O-mei ranges, were covered with maize and beans, while the valleys, in arable places, were growing paddy. After the water-parting the white-wax trees decreased in numbers. The hillsides were well wooded, and the mulberry, Cudrania, *Eriobotrya japonica*, pumelo, vegetable tallow, *Pterocarya stenoptera*, and willow were to be seen here and there. The alder was very abundant.

There was considerable evidence of trade during the day. Salt was accompanying us on the backs of carriers, and was bound for Fu-lin. It is carried by water from Chia-ting as far as a place called Yen-chi-k'ou and thence overland. The salt porters move slowly with their loads of about 130 catties, accomplishing the journey from Yen-chi-k'ou to Fu-lin in from 15 to 20 days. They are paid for the journey at the rate of 2,000 cash per 100 catties, and I noticed many returning with hard cash. At Kao-ch'iao-p'u the road was alive with coal porters, who were bringing the mineral from a place called Erh Tao Ho, 50 *li* distant. It cost 120 to 130 cash a picul of 100 catties (1 catty = 16 oz Chinese).

Limestones were being extracted from the bed of the stream at Kao-ch'iao-p'u and burned. Timber and wooden balers were also being carried east. Coal was showing near the divide above the village of Yang-ts'un-p'u, and it is found near Lung-ch'ih-ch'ang. Iron is mined at a place called Wan-chia-shan, and iron cooking pots are cast at Li-shih-k'ou, 50 and 20 *li* distant respectively from Lung-ch'ih-ch'ang. We met many loads of the dried stems of a plant called Sun-kan. It is cooked and used as a vegetable with meat. Cones of soda packed in bamboo bracts and cased with woven strips of bamboo, each packet weighing 11 to 12 catties, were being carried east. It is manufactured at Chin-k'ou-ho and other places to the west, and I hope to hear more of it later. Each porter usually carries four cones slung at the ends of a carrying-pole. Huang Lien (*Coptis chinensis* Hemsl.) is found in the hills near Lung-ch'ih-ch'ang, and is valued at 3 taels a catty. Astibile and Angelica are also included among the medicinal products of the district.

As Lung-ch'ih-ch'ang is approached the road runs south along the high left bank of the stream and drops into the market town, which is a large and important trade centre. From the southern outliers a large flat plain runs down to the left bank of the stream opposite the town; it was covered with paddy. High up on the slopes of the O-mei ranges I saw smoke rising in several places during the day, and I came to the conclusion that charcoal burning was proceeding; but I learn that soda is also manufactured there. We dropped into Lung-ch'ih-ch'ang, altitude 2,900 feet, at 3.45 p.m. Ahead, hills and mountains seem to block the valley through which we have to pass on the morrow.

8th August
Leaving Lung-ch'ih-ch'ang at 5.45 a.m., we followed the road which strikes the left bank of our stream of the previous day south-west down the valley. At one time it is 300 feet above the stream, at another it descends to its edge. The hills on the left bank are well cultivated on their

slopes, and here and there open up into valleys, down which trickle rills to the main stream. The result is that irrigation is possible for paddy where there is sufficient land for the purpose; otherwise maize and beans occupy the sloping ground. The right bank is mountainous, unwooded, and precipitous, and only a narrow patch of maize may be observed not far from the base. Down in the actual bottom of the valley, where a ridge of limestone has retained a considerable quantity of soil, the ground smiled under patches of paddy. At the southern end of the long, precipitous range a valley runs up into the western mountains. At the end of five miles we entered the market town of Ta-wei-ch'ang lying at the end of the valley, which is blocked by a range of mountains running east and west. At the end of the valley, and on the right bank of the stream, there is a large, low-lying piece of ground given up to paddy and thickly dotted with white-wax trees.

Leaving Ta-wei-ch'ang we crossed the stream over an iron suspension bridge, consisting of six 1-inch iron rods, with superimposed crazy planking forming the roadway. There are side rails of similar rods stretched over three stone pillars on each side, and the rails are connected with the outside rods on either side of the roadway by iron bands. Rods and rails are built into solid masonry at both ends of the bridge. At the west end of the bridge we entered the white-wax-tree-dotted flat, and then south to the left bank of a stream which issues from a valley in the mountains to the west. This stream joins that of the morning below Ta-wei-ch'ang, and their united waters disappear south-east round a high rocky bluff on their way to join the T'ung River, some 12 miles distant from Ta-wei-ch'ang. We forded the second stream with some difficulty, owing to its depth and strong current. Moreover, its bed was full of slippery boulders, which gave very insecure footing, and the assistance of several local men had to be called in to get my chair across.

The range running east and west, blocking the valley, now faced us as we ascended it by a series of steep zigzags, which had to be accomplished on foot and seemed never-ending. It did not surprise me to find by the roadside in one of the turns a grave marked by a plain deal board, with the inscription, "This is the grave of a man who was found dead here. His name is unknown." At the top of the zigzags I thought we had reached the summit, at a height of 3,800 feet above the level of the sea, but I was mistaken, for above the road ran south-west, gradually rising to a height of 4,050 feet. At the summit nothing but a wilderness of mountains and mountain ranges lay to the south and west, right ahead of us. At 3,800 feet there was a gradual descent of 200 feet to the village of Yü-lung-ch'ang, but the ascent soon recommenced. On the slopes of the mountain were maize and beans, the usual crops where a water supply is not obtainable. The commonest tree was the alder, with occasional clumps of *Cunninghamia sinensis*, and some small peach trees in fruit were to be seen.

The descent from the highest point was gradual for a time, but we were soon favoured with a repetition of the zigzags of the earlier part of the day, now down, now up. My chair was abandoned, and at 12.55 p.m. I walked into Ts'ai-kou with my escort of soldiers, who had been sent by the Sub-Prefect of O-pien T'ing to see me safely out of his jurisdiction, for in descending the very narrow valley or, rather, gorge, through which a small stream flows eastward, I found myself within that Sub-Prefecture, the stream in the gully forming the boundary of O-mei Hsien and O-pien T'ing. Smoke was ascending in many places on the mountain slopes, and I was told that soda was being manufactured there. Mules and porters were both engaged in carrying soda during the day, a mule load being six and a porter's four cones. Porters with cakes of salt accompanied us as usual.

Sixty *li* or 17 miles may appear a very short day's work, but we welcomed the miserable hamlet of Ts'ai-kou after the zigzags and heat of the day. On this road inn accommodation is provided only for the porters engaged in the salt, soda, and Sun-kan trade, and Ts'ai-kou is no exception. Its altitude is 3,750 feet above sea-level. I am very glad that I sent back my two horses to Chengtu this morning; they have suffered considerably from these wretched roads. I have secured mules in their place. They alone seem to be fitted for work in this mountainous country.

9th August

I was assured today, before starting at 5.15 a.m. from Ts'ai-kou, that the day's journey, with the exception of the first $4\frac{1}{2}$ miles, which was up-hill, was perfectly easy. Had I my informant with me here tonight, I should be inclined to have him dragged over the road and ask his opinion again. What I do know is that the road for 20 miles has been well watered with the sweat of my brow. True, at the end of a climb up the valley in which Ts'ai-kou lies, we came to a more or less flat piece of ground a few acres in extent, but it was only on arrival there—Ch'un-t'ien-p'ing—at a height of 4,680 feet that the real work of the day began. An hour later we had reached an altitude of 5,400 feet, with mountains rising still 800 feet on either side. We were now with the soda manufacturers, for although the burning of the brushwood takes place on the higher slopes, the ashes are carried down to the houses by the roadside and placed in wooden vats fitted with sieve bottoms. Over the ashes boiling water is poured, and the liquid which drains into tubs is evaporated into soda. The elevation at which the road runs would be nothing were it not that the pathway—I will not call it road—is paved with irregular

stones, and the zigzags are so sharp that the greatest difficulty is experienced in getting a sedan chair round them.
The mountain sides, mostly green with little but grass and
brushwood, were cultivated where possible, but maize was
a poor crop, being in flower from 18 inches to 24 inches
above ground.

We then descended into a narrow valley with precipitous limestone walls to 4,900 feet, again to rise to 5,100
feet, striking the head of a deep precipitous valley
hemmed in by high mountains, and running south-west.
From this another steep descent brought us to the hamlet
of Lo-lo-p'ing (4,225 feet), round which I noticed walnut
and wood-oil trees. Lo-lo-p'ing was only 12 miles from
Ts'ai-kou, our starting-point, and it had taken us six hours
to reach it. Another descent to 3,650 feet brought us to a
wooden bridge spanning a brook flowing down another
valley to what we later discovered to be the T'ung River,
seen as a little speck of yellow at the end of the valley
cooped up by high mountain ranges. Before descending
we caught a glimpse of Mount Wa to the south-west. The
mountain side on our right soon became too steep for the
roadway, and we turned west, going down to the left bank
of the T'ung River, but at least 1,000 feet above it.

We then followed for 7 miles the left bank of the T'ung,
by a narrow path cut out of the mountain side, with many
a boulder projecting into it, and many a zigzag till we
struck the mouth of a stream, an affluent of the T'ung,
flowing from the northern mountains. As we threaded the
valley of the T'ung, which from the heights did not appear
to be more than a 100 yards wide, and in many places less,
we got a good view of Mount Wa-wu whose highest conical point in the range appeared to be much higher than
O-mei Shan. Following up the left bank of the Chin-
k'ou-ho, the affluent of the T'ung for over a 1,000 yards,
we put up for the night at a village called after the stream,

or dashing mountain torrent, as it is, built on its left bank. The village hems in the valley, and has precipitous cliffs rising about a 1,000 feet on both sides. How we are to get up the valley is a question for tomorrow.

Maize was thriving on the steep slopes of the valley of the T'ung, and I noticed some patches of tobacco still unreaped. The mulberry and Cudrania were also to be seen, and a certain quantity of silk is produced. There is a *li-kin* officer at Chin-k'ou-ho whose duty it is to collect a tax on white-wax insects coming this way from the Chien-ch'ang valley during the season, and precaution is taken that none shall escape, for I saw a slip pasted on a house before reaching Chin-k'ou-ho describing it as a white-wax insect tax station, and it was explained to me that the officer's duty was to intercept all that might escape payment at the regular station.

In this connection I may mention that in the T'ung River valley, I noticed during the day white wax being deposited on the large-leaved privet.

In addition to soda, we met several loads of the dried roots of the medicine known as T'u Huo, and the bark of the Tzǔ-chih tree, also used for the same purpose.

The marvel to me is that trade exists along such a route, and its existence shows the spirit of enterprise which makes the Chinese the born trader that he is.

Peach trees were common during the day, and the fruit was exposed for sale at the doors of the huts lying between villages, which were rare.

The T'ung where we struck is not navigable, but I was told that timber is floated down. Sha-p'ing, an important market town about 20 miles down, is the highest point reached by boats from Chia-ting in the winter months. The upward cargo is mostly salt.

I questioned the salt porters somewhat minutely today as to their business, and found that they are petty traders on their own account. They buy the salt at Yen-chi-k'ou for 4 taels 5–6 mace a picul of 100 catties, and earn a profit at Fu-lin of about 2,000 cash a picul. The price at Yen-chi-k'ou is about 54 cash, and at Fu-lin some 80 cash a catty. The total taxation between the two places is 68 cash a load. Loads differ in weight, running from 130 to 150 catties.

10th August

Chin-k'ou-ho reeked of opium when we started at 5.15 a.m. Proceeding up the left bank of the stream for a few hundred yards till after its junction with a roaring torrent, issuing from a high narrow gorge, on its right bank we crossed it by a frail wooden bridge of two trees. The stream is at present narrow; but the wide bed, covered with boulders and shingle, shows what it can be in flood. High limestone cliffs bounded it for a time, soon giving way to more tractable mountains capable of cultivation to near their summits. Maize and beans were the growing crops. We then began to climb, and at an altitude of 3,420 feet entered a valley which we threaded in a north-westerly direction as far as Pai-shih-kou, about 5 miles from Chin-k'ou-ho. Here we had breakfast, in a solitary house which did duty for an inn and a guard station. The petty officer of the guard, which so far as I could see did not exist, kindly sent his son, a bright young lad, to guide us to the end of the day's stage, for the road is a mere bridle path, and our escorts from O-mei Hsien and Ma-pien T'ing were not well acquainted with the country. As it was, we lost our way for a short distance, and had to retrace our steps to gain what is facetiously called the high road. There was an excellent crop of maize in the Pai-shih-kou valley, which with beans and potatoes forms the staple food of the people. My followers would have none of it, and had to wait until the rice which they had brought with them was cooked.

In the inn I came across a fine specimen of a blood-hound. With fine, brown, square head and drooping ears, brown legs, belly, and tail, and a darker body, he was looking after the crumbs that fell from the tables occupied by my men. At last he came and crouched under my table, but a piece of ship's biscuit did not appeal to him. Unlike Chinese dogs generally, he showed no fear of or ill-will to the foreigner. Seeing me examining the dog rather closely, one of my Shanghai servants came up to me and remarked that it was a foreign dog. Explanations followed, and I found that he had been brought from the Lolo country to the south of the T'ung River. When I first saw the dog I at once called to mind Mr Baber's story of a native chief in the valley of the T'ung River having gone hunting with a pack of hounds for the defilers of his ancestors' graves.

Before reaching our breakfasting-place, the bottom of my chair was completely knocked off by a boulder projecting from the roadway, and much time was spent in effecting temporary repairs. I had had a small chair specially fitted for the journey; but it is already rent and mangled by thorns and boulders. We proceeded up the valley from Pai-shih-kou in a northerly direction, reaching an altitude of 4,350 feet, where, in the garden of a solitary house, I noticed *Nicotiana tabacum* and *Nicotiana rustica* growing side by side. The valley was well wooded with the white-wax tree and privet, the latter in flower. I also saw a group of bananas, the leaves of which are used for covering a Chinese sweetmeat, and a solitary coir-palm— *Trachycarpus excelsus* H. Wendl.

We then descended to 4,000 feet, and seemed to be making for a high range of mountains right ahead; but after a time we turned from north to north-west, and actually retraced our steps on the opposite side of the valley, crossing a rivulet by a small covered wooden bridge. Had we held on we should have come in a little over a mile to a lead mine which was opened a few months ago at a place called Hui-lung T'ung. The miners to work it were brought from the district of Jung-ching Hsien, which is a great mining centre. We now commenced to ascend in a north-west direction, following the east side of a valley backed by a high mountain range on the opposite side, with steep cliffs near the foot of the range. Our highest point was 5,480 feet, when we looked down upon a village—Shou-p'ing-shan—dotted on a fine piece of land sloping from the range just mentioned with a spur seemingly broken off from the range and dropped into the south of the valley. A white ribbon, a rushing streamlet, on the right bank of which lay the village, was flowing eastward to join the Chin'k'ou Ho before the latter enters the T'ung River.

A steep descent of 500 feet brought us to the left bank of the stream, over which we passed by bridge into Shou-p'ing-shan, or Shou-yung-ch'ang, as it is also called. The village elders welcomed me, and four soldiers met me before commencing the descent. It was during the descent that Mount Wa burst upon our view in all its majesty. It lay from our position north-west and south-east, flat on the summit with a fringe of trees distinctly visible; a high sheer precipice at the south-east, and two steps at the north-west end rising from the range of which it forms the culminating point. It is by these steps only that it can be ascended, and against them are placed three wooden ladders, each 300 Chinese feet in length. The summit is placed at from 50 to 60 *li* from Shou-p'ing-shan, and I am told that the ascent can be made in about 10 hours. A priest, in whose temple I am spending the night for want of habitable quarters, visits the temple called Pu-tu-ssŭ on the summit once a year. He says that on the flat summit, which has an area of over 10 *li*, three streams take their rise and fall into the T'ung River.

There was no sign of trade on the road during the day; but I believe the salt and other porters take a shorter and more difficult route from Chin-k'ou-ho direct to Ta-t'ien-ch'ih, where we ought to be spending the night, and do not pass through Shou-p'ing-shan. Our baggage carriers did not turn up till 4 p.m., and it was then too late to proceed another 15 *li*. We had had enough of climbing and steep descent for one day.

11th August

Today has been a day of valley and mountain climbing. We were off at 5.15 a.m., and began ascending in a north-westerly direction the sloping ground at the foot of which lies the village of Shou-p'ing-shan. As we descended we had an excellent view of Mount Wa, with its limestone cliffs, rising sheer up from its range on our left as the sun peeped over the mountain tops to the east and lit up its face. Mountain spurs are tossed about in the valley to the north-east of the mountain. At 5,600 feet we descended into a small valley, which we crossed and zigzagged up a hillside to a height of 6,130 feet, when we looked down on the village of Ta-t'ien-ch'ih, lying in a hollow at the foot of a bare limestone mountain, a northern continuation of the Wa range. The hollow is cooped up by mountains on all sides, and in the lowest parts there was much standing water, which escapes by underground filtration. By my aneroid Ta-t'ien-ch'ih is 6,050 feet above the level of the sea. In the hollow, maize was being cultivated in places, but most of the land was waste, and was being used as grazing ground by cattle. Before descending to Ta-t'ien-ch'ih I noticed a patch or two of poor buckwheat. The road finds its way through a gap in the hills to the north-west, the pass rising 350 feet above Ta-t'ien-ch'ih. This leads to another small hollow called Hsiao-t'ien-ch'ih with still more water. Higher up lies a valley bounded by hills covered with brushwood, which was being burned for the manufacture of soda. Enquiries made here elicited the information that the manufacturers dispose of the soda at some 46 cash a catty of 16 Chinese ounces.

Now began the day's toil—the ascent of the So-i-ling by a zigzag stone road in a north-by-west direction. I pitied the salt porters toiling up the mountain side with their heavy loads of 130 to 150 catties, resting overy 50 paces by placing a crutch under the load. Some of them had wooden frameworks arched over their heads to which the salt blocks were lashed, while others had heaped creels of bamboo or simply a board on which the salt covered with matting rested. Some, again, had the blocks suspended at the ends of carrying poles, and rested by placing the end of a wooden rod against and underneath a pad of twine or cloth bound round the carrying pole a short distance from the centre, while the butt-end of the rod rested on the ground. I was glad to reach the summit of the pass empty-handed. Here I tested the height of the pass by hypsometer, and found it to be 9,146 feet.

A short but steep descent of a few hundred feet on the other side brought us to the couple of houses making up the hamlet of Hua-hsiang-kou, where we had a meal, and I do not think that I ever tasted better-flavoured potatoes than those just dug from the garden patch by the side of the house. The flavour was really excellent, and they were fine big tubers, costing 10 cash a catty. Hunger may, however, have added to the flavour which I experienced.

Just after we had surmounted the crest we met about 30 carriers with loads of opium from Ning-yüan Fu, in the Chien-ch'ang valley. They were making the journey to O-mei Hsien in 15 days. It was last year's opium, and cost 20 taels per 100 Chinese ounces, and a load weighed 1,000 oz or $82\frac{8}{9}$ lb. The taxation per 100 oz between

Ning-yüan Fu and O-mei Hsien amounted to 7 mace 6 candareen, made up of two *li-kins* of 3 mace 3 candareen each and a levy of 40 cash at each of three guard stations *en route*. A small herd of cattle were grazing round Hua-hsiang-kou, and there is evidently some horse-breeding carried on in the country, for I noticed a considerable number of foals during the day.

Descending into the usual valley we kept along the north side, and at 8,000 feet came upon fields of oats, wheat in excellent ear and with good length of stem, buck-wheat, hemp (*Cannabis sativa*), potatoes in flower, peas in flower and pod, and *Nicotiana rustica* from 2 feet to $2\frac{1}{2}$ feet high, giving promise of a good harvest. We passed down south and south-west, crossing into another valley with high and precipitous cliffs bearing a strong resemblance to Mount Wa, and which I at first took to be the back of that mountain. The walls of the cliffs reminded me of a city full of battlemented towers. This, however, I was informed was Mao-ko Shan, and that Mount Wa will not again come into view until the day after tomorrow.

Still descending, we crossed into and passed south-west down another valley, which ultimately became a deep glen hemmed in by steep limestone cliffs, leaving little or no room for cultivation; but a wealth of wild flowers and creepers lined the road, and I have no doubt the English botanist who recently passed over this road has reaped a rich harvest. The glen ultimately opens out into a culti-vated valley with several cross mountain ranges showing a long way ahead to the west; but after threading it we turned north for a few hundred yards to the village of Lêng-chu-p'ing lying in a fold of undulating ground hemmed in by precipitous cliffs. Here we put up at 4.30 p.m. after a hard day's work. It is a small place, and the inn in which my caravan is stowed away is only half-roofed. It is in process of building or reconstruction, and the room which I occupy is well papered with Chinese texts. One of these says: "I think of the men of old." This is just what the Chinese *literatus* does, and if he would think less of the past and more of the present and future, his country would not be a loser. Lêng-chu-p'ing is at an altitude of 6,720 feet above the sea.

12th August

No one, not even the keenest sportsman, could have longed more earnestly for daybreak than I did, but for very different reasons. He was anticipating sport in the field, while I was having my sport in bed with the usual pests of Chinese inns. Finally, I was completely routed at midnight, and had to abandon my bed for a chair, where I spent the rest of the night. It was with a feeling of great relief that I heard the head coolie rousing his men at 4.30 a.m., and we were quite ready to start at the usual hour.

On the whole, we spent a very curious day in a very extraordinary country. In the first place, we descended from Lêng-chu-p'ing in a northerly direction into a deep limestone gorge or chasm hemmed in by precipitous cliffs. Deep down we could hear the rushing of a stream in the direction opposite to that which we were going. It was another of those streams that go to make up the T'ung River. We descended by a narrow footpath of small slippery limestones till we reached a wooden bridge spanning the stream. Ascending the opposite cliff by a similar footpath, we found ourselves where we had started, but on the opposite side of the chasm, which, at its mouth, was far too wide to admit of bridging. The result was that, although Lêng-chu-p'ing and Huang-mu-ch'ang are distant only a couple of miles in a straight line, we spent three whole hours in reaching the latter, having to round the chasm and several gullies and to rise to a height of 6,450 feet above the level of the sea.

The country to the west of Huang-mu-ch'ang reminded me forcibly of a number of Highland crofts reclaimed from the mountain slopes, but they were covered with maize, barley, beans, melons, buckwheat, and tobacco (*Nicotiana rustica*). There were also plots of cabbages here and there. The resemblance to Highland crofts was accentuated by the stone dikes surrounding the fields. There was much grazing land, and I noticed herds of cattle and ponies away upon the mountain slopes far to our left. The country was almost treeless, but peaches were for sale in the streets of Huang-mu-ch'ang and I noticed some specimens of *Cunninghamia sinensis*.

The road followed the north side of a high mountain range running north-east and south-west, and in following it we had to round eight gullies. As we advanced we kept ascending, and at a height of 7,230 feet dropped west into a valley whose slopes were clad with brushwood without the least sign of cultivation. A few goats were browsing just below the summit, and we descended by a steep road to 6,100 feet. A streamlet was flowing southward down the valley. The ascent again began and found us at 1.20 p.m. at the hamlet of Ts'ai-tzŭ-ti, where, had I known the nature of the remainder of the day's journey, I should have undoubtedly spent the night, uninviting though it looked. However, off we went upwards and upwards till we reached an altitude of 7,850 feet over a fairly good unpaved road. We had been climbing the Ma-lieh Shan. Here we turned north down into a steep valley, bounded on the north side by ranges of mountains, among the peaks of which a thunderstorm was spending itself. On the way up we caught two glimpses of the T'ung River flowing east and south respectively at two different places. They were small brown stretches of water. On descending northwards to the range running east and west we again caught sight of it over the low western tail of the range, to the east of which, on a level piece of ground, lay the village of Hsin-kai-tzŭ, or Ma-lieh, as it is also called.

There was little or no cultivation on the Ma-lieh Shan, while the easier slopes of the northern range were fairly well cultivated and dotted with small farmhouses. Cattle, sheep, and ponies were grazing on the northern slopes of the Ma-lieh Shan. We were exactly 13 hours on the road from Lêng-chu-p'ing to Hsin-kai-tzŭ, and, although little in the matter of actual distance was accomplished, the day was exceedingly hard as the greater part of the stage had to be done on foot. To the lover of nature in its wildest state I can confidently recommend the two stages from Shou-p'ing-shan westwards. Mountains and valleys appear to be thrown about in the most glorious and imposing disorder, and any attempt on my part to describe them would be futile. They are, in my opinion, beyond description, and it would be necessary to take up individual mountains or valleys to do justice to one of nature's grandest scenes. In my previous journeyings in western China I have seen nothing in the least approaching it in rugged grandeur.

There was nothing now in the way of trade. The salt porters still accompanied us, while others were returning with the results of their speculations in hard cash. There were, in addition, a few carriers with Chien-ch'ang opium and medicines. The altitude of Hsin-kai-tzŭ is 5,500 feet above the sea.

13th August

As we had only 40 *li*, or about 12 miles, to accomplish to reach Fu-lin, I delayed our start till 7 a.m., thinking to arrive before noon, as, generally speaking, 10 *li* can be made in an hour. I thought we had little to do but cross the low outliers of the range we faced yesterday on descending the northern slopes of the Ma-lieh Shan and drop into Fu-lin, but I soon found that I was very much mistaken. The foot-hills rose to a height of only 150 feet above Ma-lieh, but we kept descending zigzag a red-soiled mountain side covered with a splendid crop of maize and beans and very thickly studded with privet. At 4,700 feet we reached the bottom of a valley, down which flowed a streamlet with a fine waterfall in a south-westerly direction. A part of the streamlet had been cut off to form a mill lade, and we followed it rushing south-west and west into other smaller valleys.

At T'ien-pa, 3 miles from Ma-lieh, I noticed that the branches of the privet were thickly coated with white wax and that the insects had been suspended as in the case of the Fraxinus, but, as a rule, much lower down on the stems of the tree. I set about questioning a cultivator, and learned from him that white wax and insects were being produced simultaneously on the same tree. The bare branches above the coating of wax were studded with the female insects in the course of growth and development of their scales to contain the young insects for use during the following year. In no case are young insects produced on trees on which white-wax insects have not been suspended. This is only natural. I have tried to explain elsewhere★ that wax and insects are not produced in the district of O-mei Hsien, for the simple reason that in the process of melting down the wax the latter are destroyed. This, however, would apply equally to the privet, which here presents the same pollard appearance as the ash. One would think that, if the insect could be produced on the ash, a certain number of trees would be set aside to enable reproduction to take place, and save the cultivator the expense of buying fresh supplies from the Chien-ch'ang valley or elsewhere. It is possible, however, that the females will not thrive on the ash, or it may be (I throw out the suggestion with diffidence)

★ *Three Years in Western China*, Chap. xi. London, 1897.

that the milder climate of the Chien-ch'ang and neighbouring valleys, such as we have passed through today, is
better suited for their growth and development. There can
be no doubt that O-mei Hsien is much colder in winter,
and, as privet trees grow in many parts of the province
besides the Chien-ch'ang valley, it is almost certain that if
the conditions were suitable some attempt would be made
to bring the industry to a success. The cultivator, to whom
the matter was inexplicable, told me that about 100 loads,
each of 66 packets weighing 18 Chinese ounces of insects
apiece, were annually yielded by the privets in his neighbourhood, and that each packet was worth 6 mace 7
candareen.

From T'ien-pa we descended to the bottom of the valley at an altitude of 3,420 feet. There is a stream flowing
south down the valley to join the T'ung River, 10 *li* distant. This stream, which we easily forded, was once
spanned by an iron suspension bridge, of which the stone
tablets recording its existence alone remain. The bridge
itself was swept away by a flood. A village, also called Pai-
ai-ho, after the stream, lies on the north bank. We ascended
westward the north bank to a height of 4,150 feet, and
then descended into a valley. On the way down we saw the
T'ung River flowing south, backed by high mountain
ranges, but the market town of Fu-lin was still concealed
by low, well-cultivated rising ground in the valley. A black
spot, like ploughed land, lay below us, and into this we
soon dropped, to find it the stony bed of a mountain torrent about a 100 yards in breadth. A little yellow rill from
the north was at the moment its only tenant, and this we
now followed, fording and refording it to the substantial
lime and stone walls built to the north and east of Fu-lin
to keep the town from being swept away.

The slopes of the Pai-ai-ho and T'ung valleys were
under splendid cultivation. On the steeper slopes were

excellent crops of maize, beans, tobacco (*Nicotiana tabacum* and *Nicotiana rustica*), capsicums, millet, and melons, while the level ground was everywhere full of paddy well advanced towards harvest. Nor was this all. The privet, wood-oil tree, mulberry, palm, and vegetable tallow tree— all sources of valuable economic products—were exceedingly abundant, the last named especially in the T'ung valley. The bamboo was also there, but not particularly abundant. Of fruit trees I noticed the pear, peach, plum, loquat, and walnut. The alder was common, and here and there grew a few willows. Large, well-shaped pears were selling on the streets at 3 cash apiece, and well-formed purple plums were also abundant. When we left Ma-lieh at 7 a.m. the thermometer stood at 70°, but in the valley of the Pai-ai-ho it rose to 90° Fahrenheit, and walking up and down the steep mountain sides was not a pleasure.

One hears much of the floods of the T'ung River, which, better known as the Ta-tu at Fu-lin, enters the Min at Chia-ting; but when one considers the steep mountains which hem it in during its eastern course, and for which it is the only means of drainage, there is little cause for surprise that it is liable to sudden rise and fall, for heavy rainstorms sweep with remarkable suddenness down these steep rocky slopes, and swell its water with great rapidity.

Nearly all the inhabitants of the mountainous country through which we have just passed—men, women, and children—wear turbans, blue or white, and many of them undyed woollen or goat-skin coats. This costume gives them a somewhat non-Chinese appearance, and I felt sure they were not of Chinese type; but on questioning one man with a long, thin face and somewhat un-Chinese appearance, he told me that his ancestors had come from O-mei Hsien. The women, as a rule, affect large silver earrings and brooches. They have quite an oval type of face—at any rate, when young.

Fu-lin, which is at an elevation of 3,100 feet above the level of the sea, is an important market town over half a mile in length, and about the same distance from the north bank of the T'ung River. A short distance from its western end flows the Liu-sha River southwards to join the T'ung. Fu-lin is the meeting-place of several roads—that which we have just traversed from Chia-ting by way of O-mei Hsien and Yen-chi-k'ou; through it passes the main trade road between western Ssuchuan and western Yünnan along the valley of Chien-ch'ang or Ning-yüan Fu; and a small unimportant road joins it south of the T'ung with Ta-chien-lu. The main road from Fu-lin to Ta-chien-lu goes north for some 12 miles to the market town of Han-yüan-kai, whence it branches off north-west from the Ch'ing-ch'i–Ya-chou road to the north-east.

The T'ung River is navigable during seven months of the year (i.e., at low water) in a westerly direction from Fu-lin as far as Tzŭ-ta-ti, and by this route much of the salt which has been accompanying us to Fu-lin is sent for consumption in the interior. The Chien-ch'ang valley itself is mostly supplied by the salt wells of Yen-yüan Hsien to the south-west of the city of Ning-yüan Fu. The neighbourhood of Fu-lin, where, curiously enough, there is no *li-kin* station, draws its supplies of foreign goods from the Yang-tsze, Min, and Ya rivers, and from Ya-chou Fu they are carried overland by way of Jung-ching Hsien and across the Ta-hsiang-ling Pass. I am told that the consumption of grey shirtings amounts in value to about 7,000 taels, that the value per piece of 16 lb at Ya-chou is 4 taels 4 mace and in Fu-lin 5 taels 4–5 mace, the cost of the carriage per piece between Ya-chou and Fu-lin being 200 cash. Cotton-weaving is not an industry of this part of the country, and little or no foreign cotton yarn is imported. The value of miscellaneous foreign goods imported is given as 3,000 taels, or a gross total of 10,000 taels.

14th August

Fu-lin had hardly begun to awake to the business of the day when we passed through it westward into the valley of the Liu-sha flowing at the foot of high well-cultivated red-soiled hills on its western side. The valley at the entrance is about 1,500 yards in breadth, and the road runs up its eastern side in a north-westerly direction. It is not of uniform width, for spurs drop into it from the high hills on the east, and repeatedly contract it to little more than the wide shingly bed of the river, at present a mere streamlet. From valleys on the east mountain torrents have here and there washed down shingle and boulders, rendering part of the main valley uncultivable; but where cultivation is possible no ground is wasted.

To the immediate north of Fu-lin the ground is stony and not under crop, but it is densely covered with mulberry and *Cudrania triloba* trees for the feeding of silk-worms in season, and a fair amount of both yellow and white silk is produced. Part of this ground is also utilized for a graveyard, and here we are introduced to the horseshoe-shaped grave built up of stones coated with lime. The top of each grave was green with grass. In the mountainous country which we have just left the graves were heaped with circular cairns of loose stones.

We had not reached Lung-tung-ying, a village 5 miles from Fu-lin, when we were made aware that we were now traversing a great trade highway, for we met caravan after caravan of ponies, donkeys, mules and porters laden with bales of Hupeh cottons, paper, joss-sticks, palm-coir ropes, water-pipe tobacco, hemp, coarse chinaware, and a little salt. Native cotton cloth and paper were, however, by far the most important articles. I may safely say that we met about 500 animals during the day. Just to the north of Lung-tung-ying, where a spur drops in from the east and causes the road to zigzag 500 feet above Fu-lin, we met some loads of lump coal going south, and several accompanied us north during the rest of the day, so that the mine lies in the hills to the east some 5 miles from Fu-lin. Four animals laden with foreign cotton yarn, and flying the flag of the Ning-yüan Mining Bureau, passed us going south, and I learned on enquiry that the yarn is used for lamp-wicks in the mines. The road which we followed as far as Han-yüan-kai was in an excellent state of repair as Chinese roads go, and must have been recently put in order. My bearers were grumbling that the road tired their legs very much, but I attributed their feeling of tiredness to the close and hot atmosphere of the valley, the thermometer showing 79° Fahrenheit when we left Fu-lin and 90° Fahrenheit during the forenoon.

Where land was available it was well cultivated, and in many places the stones had been collected and diked in the bed of the Liu-sha to admit of the soil being cropped. Maize, sugar-cane about 4 feet high, paddy, millet, beans (Chiang Tou), *Panicum miliaceum*, ground-nuts, sesamum, sweet potatoes, and tobacco were all in evidence, while the mulberry, *Cudrania triloba*, willow, bamboo, orange, wood-oil tree, walnut, loquat, cypress, and jujube (*Zizyphus vulgaris* Lam.) were all to be seen, the mulberry, *Cudrania*, and wood-oil trees being especially abundant. Pears, plums, and peaches were for sale on every roadside stall. The only industry I noticed in the valley was the manufacture of large, wide-brimmed straw hats for summer wear.

At noon we arrived at Han-yüan-kai, 45 *li*, or about 13 miles, from Fu-lin, where our road branched off to Ta-chien-lu, and my followers were determined that we should put up there for the night, but I was equally determined that we should do another 25 *li*, or 7 miles, and lodge at Fu-chuang. They expressed themselves as simply horrified at spending the night at Fu-chuang, where they assured me that rice would be unprocurable and that there was no inn accommodation. Their plan had been carefully elaborated, for none of my baggage had turned up; but I told my bearers that when I went on a journey I did not allow them to dictate to me what I was and what I was not to do, and we went. I had waited two hours for my baggage, and the porters were amazed and angry to find me leaving as they entered the town. There was no help for it, and they had to follow.

We struck north-west along the left bank of the Liu-sha through beautiful country, the red-soiled hills opening out and admitting of cultivation to their summits. The road was excellent—level, and paved with flat stone slabs in the centre—and what was very refreshing after the Fu-lin valley, a fresh breeze met us as we advanced. The road did not continue in the same good condition, however, for parts had been washed away by mountain streams from the east, and in other places large boulder beds had been deposited by similar streams when in flood. Numerous gullies had to be rounded, and, although Fu-chuang had been in sight for some time, we did not arrive till 5.30 p.m., to find that rice was abundant, and that it contained three good inns, one of these almost new, in which we are now comfortably settled. The cultivation is the same as in the Fu-lin valley, but the country houses, externally at least, look far more prosperous. There is a new tree, which I have not seen before. It looked like a Melia, and is called in Chinese Huang-lien, but I hope to learn more of it later. It has fronds of small, dark, paired leaves, and the ruddy young fronds lit up the darker green. Some trees had bunches of fruit about the size of peas. The only articles of trade we met were coffin wood in the rough and thin boarding. Fu-chuang is 4,000 feet above the level of the sea, so that we have gradually risen 900 feet during the day.

15th August

It rained heavily overnight, and was still raining at our usual starting time on the morning of the 15th August. For a time there was considerable doubt as to whether we should proceed, my men showing no desire to begin the work of the day, and I, myself, half-inclined to take a rest; but, as luck would have it, the weather somewhat cleared at 8 a.m., and we were off at 9. We still kept to the left bank of the stream, with its wide, shingly bed frequently forming islands, green with plots of paddy surrounded by stone dikes and dotted with alders. Side valleys soon open out, each contributing its quota of yellow, muddy water, coloured by the soil of the red sandstone hills which bound them. Our road, however, always keeps to the left bank of the most westerly branch, now down to its bed and again high above it, as the ranges which run down to it on either side contract the valley or give the bed of the stream plenty of room. At times cultivation is confined to the hillslopes, which are not well wooded; but wherever it is possible to utilize the land in the valley it is done, and paddy is the crop. Maize was abundant on the slopes, but millet, well in ear, was becoming more prominent. I may state here that only in its lower reaches is the stream called the Liu-sha, and the branch we followed is known as the Ni Ho from the market town of Ni-t'ou-yi where we are spending the night. The road was bad going, muddy and slippery: in many of the gullies it had been practically washed away, and we had great difficulty in rounding them. Mountain torrents, knee-deep, had repeatedly to be forded, and the road was frequently lost among boulder beds of sandstone. It took us three hours to accomplish the 7 miles between Fu-chuang and Pan-chiu-ai or Tou-liu-tzŭ, the hamlet where we had our mid-day meal.

In the courtyard of the inn mat-weaving was being carried on on the upright loom in the manner which I have described fully elsewhere.* The rush used was the three-sided one. A man was weaving, and a woman, presumably his wife, was feeding each rush. Under the eaves of the inn hung the leaves of *Nicotiana rustica* undergoing the process of drying, and the landlord told me that the process would be complete in seven or eight days, dependent, of course, on the dryness of the atmosphere. He named a tree, a branch of which I had gathered, the hsiang-yeh (fragrant leaf), from the fact that the leaves take the place of the cypress, which, when slowly burned in ropes, drive away mosquitoes. Further enquiries led to the statement that the porters we had met on the road returning with their pack frameworks and rests, were the carriers of rice to Ta-chien-lu from Han-yüan-kai, through which we passed yesterday, and that the heaviest individual load carried for the seven days required to complete the journey was 150 catties, or 200 lb. The carrier gets 400 cash per 30 catties for his labour.

To the north of Pan-chiu-ai where the river valley contracts, the eastern hilly bank opens out, and cultivation became more general. The river soon divides, a branch coming from the west; but the valley of the eastern branch at once contracts, and the road crosses a ridge 4,780 feet above the sea to get back to the stream. A few hundred yards to the south of the hamlet of San-ch'i-k'ou, which is 15 *li* from Ni-t'ou-yi, we struck the telegraph line from Chengtu to Ta-chien-lu, and at the hamlet itself the great tea road from Ya-chou Fu to Ta-chien-lu. Like the telegraph line it crosses the hills, and saves the carriers a distance of a few miles. At the hamlet itself we saw our first tea carrier resting. He had a load of nine whole packets and three half packets at the bottom, but I shall have more to say on this subject later. Salt and paper were also being carried by porters to Ta-chien-lu. Descending from

* See *China No. 5 (1904): Report on the Province of Ssŭ-ch'uan*, p. 40.

San-ch'i-k'ou we saw ahead of us a beautiful valley well watered, and in a high state of cultivation, backed by uplands sloping gently up from the left bank of the Ni Ho, and the large and important market town of Ni-t'ou-yi resting on the edge of the stream.

The sloping uplands presented a magnificent picture of greenery—fields covered with every variety of green, and the still darker green of many kinds of trees. On our way down to the valley we passed a veritable orchard with pear, persimmon, plum, peach, walnut, and crab-apple trees, and a tree with dark green ovate-pointed leaves about $1\frac{1}{4}$ inches in length, with bunches of brown round fruit, at present about the size of peas. The fruit of the latter is not ripe till November, when it becomes dark, almost black, in colour. The privet was a common tree during the day.

Ni-t'ou-yi stands at a height of 4,900 feet above the level of the sea, and is graced at its southern entrance by a small white five-storied pagoda with pictorial representations. It is said to contain over 400 families, and what appeals to the traveller more than anything else, it has a splendid inn, the best I have met with in China. Behind the sloping uplands rises a range of mountains which we have to cross tomorrow by the Fei-yüeh Ling Pass.

For the second time during the present journey the bottom has been knocked out of my official chair by bumping against boulders, and it is now in the carpenter's hands being refitted to withstand the four days' journey that has still to be made to reach Ta-chien-lu.

16th August

I omitted to mention yesterday that the inn in which we were quartered last night had, in addition to its other embellishments, a stone tank containing a number of gold-fish. My bedroom was also adorned with the parts of two beautiful massive coffins, evidently intended for the landlord and his wife in due season. The lid of the larger coffin, made of *Cunninghamia sinensis*, as, indeed, was the whole of the wood, I was scarcely able to lift. It was curved, and measured 94 inches in length. The width at top and bottom was $26\frac{1}{2}$ and $21\frac{1}{2}$ inches, and the thickness at head and foot $3\frac{3}{4}$ and $2\frac{7}{8}$ inches respectively. The inn also contained a stack of excellent-looking lump coal. It is mined at a place called Hsiao-kou-t'ou, about 5 miles to the east of Ni-t'ou-yi, and cost 50 cash per 100 catties at the pit's mouth, and 70 to 80 cash laid down at Ni-t'ou-yi, or about 1 tael per ton.

We left Ni-t'ou-yi at 5.45 a.m. on the morning of the 16th August to face the Fei-yüeh range (9,022 feet) to the north-west, but soon found that many another hill lay between us and the valley of the main range, and that the road wound about them in a very tantalizing fashion. Now it lay along a rocky valley, and again over a hill-top. Finally we succeeded in reaching the main valley, and, after a long weary pull, reached the summit of the pass at 3 p.m. There is no great difficulty in surmounting the range until the summit is approached, where its steepness necessitates many a weary zigzag. Cultivation ceases about half-way up, and the hills bounding the valley to a height of 500 to 1,000 feet, are densely covered with brushwood, in which bloomed many kinds of wild flowers. The road is well paved with stones, which have been polished by the san-dalled feet of myriads of tea porters, who have also left their mark in the shape of inch-deep round cavities, made in many stones by the iron spikes projecting from the ends of their T-shaped rests.

We left Ni-t'ou-yi in the company of many tea porters, and I had the opportunity of examining their loads with some care. Not a single carrier had a wooden framework for piling his packages of tea, but as I have seen them attached to such frameworks between Ya-chou and Ch'ing-ch'i Hsien, the absence may be accounted for by the fact that many of the porters are changed at Ni-t'ou-yi, where there are six branch establishments of tea factories in Ya-chou, and a different system may be followed by the new men. At any rate, the packages were all tied together by ropes, and two shoulder straps were inserted between usually the fourth and fifth package from the bottom and the bottom package. Each porter, however, seemed to have his own way of carrying his load. Some carried the packages vertically, but the great majority preferred them horizontally. Many had two half-length packages at the bottom, and most had two whole packages tied together at the top, so that one projected inwards over the carrier's head. In every case the packages rested on the porter's back and shoulders—that is, the main body of the load. The largest load I saw consisted of 13 packages, each containing four bricks, and I asked the carrier the weight of a package. He replied 18 catties, which would give him a load of 234 catties or 302 lb.

That there might be no mistake about it I had one of these packages brought from a tea establishment to my inn at Ni-t'ou-yi and weighed in my presence. The result was exactly 18 catties. I believe, therefore, that the man whom I questioned carried the weight he declared to me. A full-sized package, which, as I have said, contains four bricks, measures $39\frac{1}{2}$ inches by 8 inches by $4\frac{1}{2}$ inches, and is cased with matting woven of flat strips of bamboo. The tea is first covered with two layers of paper, red inside, and frequently at the ends of half-packages protected by the bracts removed from the joints of the bamboo. The following information, collected at Ni-t'ou-yi, on the subject of this brick tea for Tibet may be of some interest.

In Ya-chou two qualities of brick tea are manufactured—coarse and fine. The net weight of a package of coarse tea is 17 catties, and is valued at 2 mace. A carrier gets 200 cash a package from Ya-chou to Ni-t'ou-yi, and 2 mace from Ni-t'ou-yi to Ta-chien-lu. The standard of sale at Ta-chien-lu is the sum of 50 taels, and the average number of packages purchasable by this sum is 48. Fine teas are made up in 18-catty packages, valued at 5 taels 3 mace to 6 taels per 100 catties. The carrier from Ya-chou to Ni-t'ou-yi gets 220 cash for each package as the price of his labour, and 110 cash for a half-package of two bricks. From Ni-t'ou-yi to Ta-chien-lu he is paid at the rate of 2 mace 3 candareen and 1 mace 2 candareen for each whole or half-package respectively. From 22 to 24 of these packages are purchasable at Ta-chien-lu for 50 taels. At Jung-ching Hsien, another centre of the brick tea man-ufacture, the weights and prices are different. A package of coarse tea weighs only 15 catties net, valued at 200 cash. The freight to Ni-t'ou-yi is 100 cash, and from Ni-t'ou-yi 200 cash; 50 taels in Ta-chien-lu will buy 50 of these packages. A package of fine tea weighs 19 catties net, and is worth 1 tael 1 mace. The freight to Ni-t'ou-yi, and from there to Ta-chien-lu, is 130 cash and 2 mace 4 candareen respectively; 50 taels at Ta-chien-lu will purchase 29 to 30 of these packages.

Porters with paper, rush mats, dyed native cottons, and salt also accompanied us, but few in number as compared with the tea carriers.

After crossing the Fei-yüeh Ling Pass, the descent on the north side is much steeper, and the road leads down into a deep valley, through hedges of wild roses, the branches of which were armed with closely set, flat, red spines, and covered with golden hips. We dropped, after a descent of 1,950 feet and a turn to the north-west, into the sleepy looking hamlet of Hua-lin-p'ing for the night (7,225 feet).

Cultivation, except on the Fei-yüeh range, was general, and I noticed maize, beans, tobacco, hemp, potatoes, buckwheat, and broad beans (a winter crop in the more temperate parts of Ssuchuan). Peas were also in flower and in pod. The broad beans were to the north of the Fei-yüeh range, as also a few patches of Tang-kuei (*Angelica* sp.), a well-known Chinese medicine. The plants of the latter were about a foot in height. The roots of the plant are the source of the drug. The seeds are planted in May, and when the plants are a couple of inches high they are taken up and placed in trenches, where they are covered over with dry soil to prevent growing. In March of the following year they are removed from the trenches, and planted out about a foot apart. In the end of the year the roots are dug up and sold for from 90 to 100 cash a catty, and sent to Chiung Chou and Ya-chou Fu. The freight per 100 catties to these two places is 1,200 to 1,400 cash. I am told that they are disposed of there at from 30,000 to 50,000 cash per picul, according to quality and season.

Among other trees the privet, palm, oak, fir, walnut, peach, and willow were seen during the day. There are two fine willows, with branches drooping almost to the ground, in the lower part of the valley leading to the Fei-yüeh Ling Pass, and there is another similar specimen in the village of Hua-lin-p'ing. In this valley, too, were many rushing brooks and graceful waterfalls.

17th August
We left Hua-lin-p'ing at 6 a.m. in a dense white mist which obscured everything except in the immediate neighbourhood of the pathway. Down and down we went northwards into a deep valley with a rushing stream going in the same direction. There were evidences of coal mining as we descended, the road being black with coal where the mineral was extracted from the pits, and maize and beans were growing in plots of black dust. This valley led us into another larger valley with a much bigger stream,

which we followed on its left bank, gradually descending from the hill slope to its bed, and fording and refording the rushing torrent as the road wound about in its boulder bed. Soon the valley runs east and west, closed in by limestone ranges, leaving little but room for the stream and its bed. Shortly after leaving Hsing-lung-p'u (5,020 feet), a miserable-looking market town, we finally crossed the stream and left the valley to enter the valley of the T'ung flowing from north to south, and joined soon afterwards by the stream we had just left. At the point above the junction the land was a beautiful picture of paddy plots; but instead of approaching the T'ung we ascended the high left bank and looked down on the river, a miniature Yangtsze, with its swift, muddy, swirling current and white, foaming rapids. From the heights it looked about 100 yards in breadth, but this is probably an underestimate, for the high precipitous mountains bounding it seemed to destroy the power of even an approximate estimate. At the market town of Lêng-chi (4,750 feet), which lies at the mouth of a valley and stream joining the T'ung on the left bank, the population was somewhat inquisitive, and gave me ample opportunity to make a close examination. The women wore very fine large silver ear-rings, bracelets, brooches, and chains with two clasps for suspending an over garment, which was also fastened at the neck with round silver buttons.

The road after we joined the T'ung was good, but the accommodation was very inferior, and my servants who had gone ahead could not find a suitable inn for the midday meal until 3 p.m. This was at Ta-pa or "Large Flat", which boasts of some paddy land watered by a stream from the east; but the lower mountainous slopes of the right bank were much better cultivated. We were overtaken by a rainstorm just to the north of Ta-pa (5,100 feet). We took shelter in a Chinese house for a time; but as the rain showed no signs of ceasing, we resolved to go on and endeavour to reach Lu-ting-ch'iao before dark.

The road soon led us down to the left bank of the river, and the bank was thickly strewn with boulders. The river here, flowing from north to south, makes a sudden bend west, and as it is obstructed by immense boulders lying off both banks, the seething foaming mass of water makes a deafening noise. At the bend from south to west on the left bank the mountain is high and precipitous, and here I had a by no means comfortable experience.

I happened to be in my chair at the time when I saw boulders rushing and whizzing down the mountain side across our path to the river. I lost no time in leaving my chair where I should have been perfectly helpless, and my bearers got into a fearful state of panic wishing to abandon everything for safety. There was a very long stretch of this avalanche ground; but amid the rushing of earth and stones we managed to get through safely. After I thought we were out of it a large stone about the size of my head passed close between the heads of my rear chair-bearer and myself, and crashed into the river, for I was behind my chair and determined that it should go through with my men first. Just beyond this point we came upon a man lying dead, and his weeping wife and friends trying to remove his body without endangering their own lives. He had fallen a victim to a crashing boulder. Much of my baggage was behind, but the carriers carefully watched their opportunity, and we are all safely quartered in a temple at Lu-ting-ch'iao on the left bank of the T'ung River.

This danger is quite recent. The road ran along the mountain side until last month, when the whole of the mountain side, road included, slipped down to the river, and in rainy weather the soil is loosened, resulting in showers of earth and boulders such as we had just experienced. At another place passed during the day before entering Lêng-chi a similar process is proceeding. The road has been swept away, and a road repairer is constantly at work maintaining a narrow track. The people of Lêng-chi have erected a stone tablet in honour of the Sub-Prefect of Ta-chien-lu who supplies and pays the caretaker.

In addition to the usual crops of maize, beans, buck-wheat, paddy, tobacco, and tall millet, I noticed both *Setaria italica* and *Panicum miliaceum*, and in one lonely spot opium not completely harvested. The stalks were still on the ground, and the capsules only half-bled. The alder, peach, persimmon, loquat, and privet were frequently met with, and the mulberry and walnut were particularly abundant. The cactus (prickly pear) was seen in many places on the banks of the T'ung, especially on the approach to Lu-ting-ch'iao.

In addition to the tea carriers a few porters, with iron-ware, principally hoes, accompanied us.

We met a Chinese official and his family coming out of Tibet. His baggage was distributed over a large number of carriers, and the party, which included one or two Tibetan girls, had an armed escort. The official, his wife, and young child with nurse had three chairs. The others, except three other children carried on the backs of men like packages of tea, either walked or rode, for several ponies and mules formed part of the caravan.

18th August

The town of Lu-ting, or Lu-ting-ch'iao as it is generally called, stands on the left bank of the T'ung, and contains a population of about 2,500 inhabitants. The Chinese esti-mate is 500 families. It is important as the place through which the great bulk of the trade between Tibet and Ssuchuan passes. When we left the town at 6 a.m. we at once faced the famous bridge which spans the T'ung and gives passage of the river to the many porters engaged in the trade. It is the finest suspension bridge I have seen in China. A square pier or tower of solid masonry stands about 30 feet above the level of the river on either bank. The ends of nine chains are built into the masonry on both sides of the river, and over each pier rises a pavilion. The links of the chains are $5\frac{1}{2}$ inches long, and the diameter of each link-rod is 1 inch. These nine chains are stretched 1 foot apart, and cross-boards, projecting a couple of inches on each side, are laid on the chains to form the roadway. Every few yards one of the planks or boards is attached to the chains underneath, and other boards are nailed at right angles on the cross-planks to keep them in position. On each side there is a rail of two similar chains 1 foot 4 inches apart, the lower chain being about a foot above the outside chain on either side of the roadway. Rods of two long links connect the lower and upper chains of the rail at intervals of 5 feet 3 inches, and similar rods connect the lower rail and the outside road-chains at the centres of these intervals. The ends of the rail-chains pass over two iron pillars rising from the piers on each side of the bridge and disappearing in the masonry underneath. There are thus nine road-chains, four rail-chains, and four iron pillars. The length of the bridge is 301 Chinese feet, and the breadth is 9 feet 4 inches English. There was very little dip in the centre of the bridge and no vibration to speak of.

Great care is taken of the bridge, and it undergoes annual repairs. For this purpose a tax is levied on all tea passing over by a collectorate located in the pavilion at the east end, for at the bridge the river flows due north and south. The tax amounts to 18 cash for every five packets, irrespective of quality and weight, and the annual receipts amount roughly to 1,500 tiao—that is, 1,500,000 copper cash. I have good reason to believe that this is the amount which reaches the hands of the official in charge, who complained that the amount had fallen off by half owing to the introduction of Indian tea into Tibet!

It, however, would be an unheard of thing in China if the official's accounts, as presented to him by his subordinates, were scrupulously exact. Let us take the official's figures of 18 cash per five packages, i.e., $3\frac{3}{5}$ cash per package, and dividing the total receipts of 1,500,000 cash by $3\frac{3}{5}$ will give the number of packages of tea passing over the bridge. The result is 416,616.6 packages, which, multiplied by 16—probably the average weight of each package in catties—gives 6,666,660 catties, or 8,888,880 lb. The only thing perfectly certain about these figures is the amount of the tax, for I questioned many porters on the road with exactly the same result—18 cash per five packages. I may be able to obtain corroboration or correction of these figures later.

The river filled the whole channel from pier to pier, and flowed like a mill race. Crossing the bridge we passed northwards through a short street on the other side and up the right bank of the river. The highest point reached was 5,500 feet or nearly 1,000 feet above the bridge, which is 4,620 feet above the level of the sea. The T'ung is here cooped up by high mountain ranges, little wooded and very little cultivated, and it is only where the valley at all opens out that there are signs of cultivation. The journey up the valley is very impressive. A stream here and there joins the river from the west, rushing through a boulder bed to bury itself in the T'ung. These streams have, as a rule, to be forded, for remains of wooden bridges lie scattered about. High mountains on either side and higher mountains ahead cloy the eye with majestic scenery, and the impression is deepened by the knowledge that a false step would lead one into the T'ung from a height of many hundred feet. In some places the roadway is cut through granite, for the passage of the T'ung has changed the geological formation, with overhanging cliffs, and cracks in the cliffs, after our experience of yesterday, did not inspire us with over-confidence.

My followers talked of nothing but their hair-breadth escapes of the previous evening, and, Chinese-like, magnified them to an alarming extent. Each one had his story of impending destruction, and as I sat in my chair while they were resting in a tea-house, I certainly could not but admire the rival claims to notoriety. They were all famous men in their own estimation, and it was a pleasure to me to think that they were able to divert themselves and their minds from the hard daily toil they are now undergoing.

On crossing the T'ung we entered the jurisdiction of a native chief, called the Tsa-li T'u-ssŭ. The chief himself, a young man of 25 to 26 years of age, resides at the village of Tsa-li, 15 *li* from Lu-ting-ch'iao, and on the high road. The villages along the road consist for the most part of the ruins of stone-built houses, the floors of which are now not unfrequently under cultivation. Tobacco I saw growing between the four ruined stone walls of one house in a wretched hamlet, where wooden Chinese houses had been set up among the more substantial ruins.

There can, I think, be no doubt that the inhabitants along the road are not pure Chinese. The women especially look so different. They have broad foreheads, oval faces, and wear the queue, round which a white turban is bound. They have certainly oblique eyes, but are much better looking than the Chinese. I was anxious to get a photograph of one of these maidens got up in all her finery and jewellery, but money was powerless to make her look at my camera. She retreated into the dark recesses of the house, and declined to reappear. The men said they and theirs were Chinese, but one of my escort tried to explain that, although they were nominally Chinese, they were really civilized savages. As a matter of fact, I much preferred the civilized savages, for whom he seemed to have nothing but contempt.

The Lu River, a wild dashing torrent whose better acquaintance we are to make tomorrow, enters the T'ung 60 *li* from Lu-ting-ch'iao, but a few miles to the south of it, and north of the village of Lêng-chu-kuan, another stream of white dashing cascades joins the latter from a deep narrow valley to the west. After rounding this valley and looking back, we saw to the south the snow-clad summits of a high mountain—the Hsüeh Shan—peeping out from thin fleecy clouds.

We met carriers during the day with sheep's wool, goat- and sheep-skins, deer horns, musk, and narrow strips of hide to be converted into glue, while tea and some iron cooking pans accompanied us. The lightest load of tea I saw during the day was carried by a small lad of ten. It was made up of three-and-a-half packages. He had come all the way from Jung-ching Hsien, and was bound for Ta-chien-lu. The heaviest load I saw was 15 packages of 16 catties each, or 320 lb. I measured the Jung-ching packages; they were $8\frac{1}{2}$ inches by 5 inches by 39 inches, and weighed, including casing, 20 catties each. The scanty crops met with during the day were paddy, maize, beans, *Setaria italica* and *Panicum miliaceum*. The peach, pear, mulberry, walnut, orange, and apple were the most prominent trees. The cactus was abundant, and frequently bearing its ovate fruit, which was exposed for sale with peaches, pears, and apples.

On approaching Wa-ssǔ-kou we left the valley of the T'ung, and proceeding north-west and west, dropped into another valley, down which a goodly-sized stream, called the Lu, rushes west to join the main river. There is an iron suspension bridge across the Lu at the east end of the town, leading to the State of Yü T'ung, under a native chief. I am told that respectable Chinese settling there are each allowed to take a temporary native wife on payment to the chief of a sum of 3 taels. They are free to leave the country when they choose, but the wives and children must remain.

Wa-ssŭ-kou stands on the right bank of the Lu above its junction with the T'ung, at an elevation of 4,780 feet. On the way to our inn I met a fisherman with rod and line and a couple of fine, big, live fish, which he had just taken from the Lu. I became the possessor of one of them, 7 catties in weight, which turned out to be a female, evidently on its way up the stream to spawn. It had been hooked in the side, not the mouth, and the captor brought his rod and fishing gear to the inn for my inspection. The rod was a bamboo, 16 feet long, with a fixed iron ring at the tip. The line was wound round a hollow section of a large bamboo, which when in use was strung on the angler's left arm above the wrist. The end of the line passing through the iron ring had a couple of large unbarbed hooks attached to it about a couple of feet apart, with a small lead sinker a little higher up. No bait is used. The angler evidently watches the fish ascending the falls and sweeps them out with his hooks. The size of the fish, however, necessitates the use of a gaff—a large iron hook, with a short wooden handle—with which he was provided. Had it not been for its blunted snout, the fish might have been mistaken for a salmon.

19th August
On leaving Wa-ssŭ-kou the road at once strikes the right bank of the Lu River, a mad, milk-white, seething torrent, dashing through and over boulders in its haste to join the Ta-tu. The 19th August has been the weariest day we have yet experienced. We started at the usual early hour, in the hope of covering the stage of only 60 *li* early in the

afternoon, but we were 12 hours on the road. The Lu River is hemmed in by steep treeless mountains, covered with short grass and brushwood, and here and there presenting bare rocky faces. There is very little room for cultivation of any kind. Maize, beans, tobacco, and cabbages were to be seen occasionally in small patches in the neighbourhood of solitary houses and wretched hamlets, consisting for the most part of dilapidated stone foundations, with wooden upper storeys, remnants of another race. A patch of poppy in flower showed the lateness of the season in these mountainous regions, for in the plain of Chengtu this crop is harvested in April.

The inhabitants are certainly of mixed blood, and the further west we go the more they approach to the Tibetan type. The road was paved with smooth boulders from the bed of the Lu, sometimes wide, and again narrowing, with large blocks of granite detached from the mountain sides encroaching upon it. Hour after hour we ascended, always hoping on turning the next corner to catch a glimpse of Ta-chien-lu, but that city, which lies in a narrow valley hemmed in by mountains, does not come into sight until the traveller is almost upon it, and even then only a part of it is visible. At the east end of the town two streams meet and form the Lu, one coming from a valley to the north-west, the other from the south-west, and Ta-chien-lu is built along the right bank of the former, and is cut in two by the latter. It is a small city, occupying the whole of the valley, squalid and extremely dirty. It has three gates, on the east, north, and south sides, with a short length of wall in the neighbourhood of each gate. Four wooden bridges span the bisecting rushing stream, and the two main streets run along the latter's banks.

The town is paved with stone throughout. The houses, built, as a rule, of brown-painted wood resting on solid stone foundations, are mean-looking and disappoint one's expectations regarding the principal depôt of Chinese and Tibetan trade. Small shops are numerous, but even the largest in the main streets are by no means imposing. Nearly every house flies its prayer-flag on the roof. Of the trade I shall speak later. The principal building, lying in the north-west part of the city, is the residence of the Ming-chêng Ssǔ or native chief of the State of Chala, which is bounded on the east by the T'ung and on the west by the Ya-lung rivers. It consists of a large compound, surrounded by a high stone wall enclosing lofty semi-Chinese buildings with sloping roofs and curved eaves, surmounted by several gilded pinnacles. The yamen of the Sub-Prefect, who is also charged with the duties of Commissary, lies near the chief's residence, but is small and poor-looking in comparison.

The population has been estimated to number 9,000, which, I presume, must include the floating population of caravan drivers and visitors, for I was informed officially that it is made up of about 700 Tibetan and 400 Chinese families. There are eight lamaseries in and near the city harbouring about 800 priests. The inhabitants are very mixed, including pure Tibetans, half-breeds (for most of the Chinese have Tibetan wives), and pure Chinese. I was fortunate enough to see them in their everyday life as well as on the occasion of a performance given, the day after my arrival, by lamas in the courtyard of the large lamasery of Du Jih Cha, about a mile outside the south gate, to which nearly the whole population of the city flocked. The richer Tibetan families even pitched their tents on the grassy lawns near the lamasery, and remained there during the two days of the performance.

The everyday life of Ta-chien-lu has a charm for the resident of a purely Chinese city. Mingling with, but exceeding in numbers, the usual blue cotton and silk-clad inhabitants are the dull-red and grey woollen-gowned

Tibetan men and women, moving with that free-and-easy gait unknown to their Chinese neighbours. In place of the thick-soled shoes and deformed feet, there is the long Tibetan boot reaching to the knee, with sole of soft hide and uppers and tops of grey and coloured woollen cloth respectively. Not unfrequently, however, the whole boot is made of soft hide with the hair inside; but in either case the tops are slit down the back a third or more of their length, and bound with coloured woollen garters just below the knees. The gowns, which hang to the ankle, are sometimes replaced by goat- or sheep-skin of a similar pattern. They are loose and capacious, so that the upper part of the gown above the girdle which encircles the waist is, in the absence of pockets, used for stowing away the inevitable wooden teacup or bowl, and other odds and ends of daily requirement.

The usual head-dress of the Tibetan male is a queue wound round the head and ornamented in front with white rings of stone or glass in addition to large silver rings set with coral. He often wears a large silver ear-ring with long silver and coral pendant in his left ear. His queue is frequently stuffed with other hair than his own. The woman's hair is usually parted in front, made up into a number of small plaits which are gathered into a queue bound at the end with bright-red cord and wound round the head. She is further adorned with large silver ear-rings set with coral, chains, brooches with coral and turquoise, rings with coral setting, and silver bracelets. This refers to Ta-chien-lu itself, for in the native states to the west the fashions and ornaments are different.

I must not forget the lama or priest, with his shaven or close-cropped head and red woollen garments, consisting of a plaited skirt, a waistcoat, and a long piece of cloth wound round his person and the end thrown over one of his shoulders, after the manner of the Scotch plaid. He may be seen in the streets of Ta-chien-lu during the day waiting for employment as temporary chaplain to a Tibetan family. Most families, with any pretensions to affluence, keep such a priest on the premises to perform by proxy their religious duties. He usually lives in a small room on the flat roof of the house, where, in seclusion, he chants his sacred books and beats a drum, the servants of the household attending to his wants in the way of refreshment and carrying out the other religious duties, such as the burning of incense on the house-top in the early morning and the changing of the holy water or butter in the metal cups placed before the idols in the special room or shrine allotted to them.

The large, square, stone-paved courtyard of the lamasery, in which the performance above referred to took place, was surrounded on three sides by two-storied buildings—the rooms of the priests—given up for the occasion to invited guests. The fourth side formed part of the main building, with balconies overlooking the courtyard. These were reserved for the chief of Chala and his household. The verandahs of the buildings were crowded with women and children all arrayed in their best. Many of the Tibetan and half-breed ladies wore long silk or satin gowns held in by silk sashes, usually of a yellow colour, and long, red-topped boots. In many cases gold had taken the place of the usual silver ear-rings, chains, brooches, rings, and bracelets, and added to the charms of the many beautiful women there assembled, for Tibetan ladies, when clean and well-dressed, as they were on this occasion, will take rank with their European sisters. Level, dark-brown eyes, finely cut features, an excellent carriage, and sprightliness of manner distinguish them from the timid and insipid Chinese. The Tibetan woman is not afraid or ashamed to give vent to her feelings in peals of merry laughter. The half-breed, too, has inherited much of the good looks of the Tibetan, and follows her mother as regards dress and manner, while even the Chinese woman has been infected with the thirst for jewellery.

The floor of the courtyard, with the exception of the centre, which was reserved for the performers and kept clear by lamas armed with bunches of nettles, was crowded with Tibetan and Chinese men and boys. It was a very motley assemblage. My ignorance of Tibetan and Lamaism prevent me from saying much of the performance itself. It was evidently a religious ceremony, with a certain amount of comedy thrown in. Dancing and posturing by parties of lamas dressed in fine embroidered garments were a main feature, and there were processions in which artificial elephants and horses, worked by men, were included. In some of the dances the performers were masked, and in one the skirts of the coat were embroidered in front with a row of five white skulls. A band of yellow-capped lamas accompanied the dancers with drums and long brass trumpets. I was invited to take a place on one of the verandahs, and the chief of Chala and his brother paid me a visit, and insisted on supplying me and some friends with refreshments.

TA-CHIEN-LU TO THE TIBETAN FRONTIER AND BACK

25th August

I left Ta-chien-lu (8,349 feet) at 10.20 a.m., after spending five whole days in arranging transport for Batang, and enquiring into the trade passing through the city. Ta-chien-lu is not itself a producer to any great extent. Guns and jewellery are manufactured for Tibetans occupying the country to the west, and there is another small industry in the town—the manufacture of borax from the raw material imported from Tibet, and on rarer occasions, it is said, from Nepal. Seventy-two catties of the raw borax are placed in an iron pan, which is then filled up with water. From this a cake of pure borax the shape of the pan and weighing 40 catties is evaporated. The raw material costs 2

Ta-chien-lu to Ning-ching Shan, on the Tibetan frontier

Map labels:

TA-CHIEN-LU
Ta-Chin Ho River
Cho-to Shan
Ka Ji La
Ho-K'ou
Ya-lung River
Ra-ma-la
Dé-rib-ka La
Do-zé-la
Wong-gi La
Li Chu River
LITANG
Nga-ra-ka
La-ma-ya
Mount Nenda
Hsiao-pa-chung
J'rah La Ka
Rung-sé La
D E R G É
Y U N N A N
BATANG
Chin-sha Chiang River (Yang-tsze)
Chu-pa-lung
K'ung-tzu-ting
Ning-ching Shan
Pang-mu-t'ang
Mekong River

N

Scale in miles
0 10 20 30 40 50   100

— Route taken by Mr Hosie
< Outward journey >> Return journey

mace, and the manufactured article is worth 4 mace a catty. It is exported eastward to Chengtu and other centres, where it is used in the refining of gold and silver, and in certain other industries.

Passing through the south gate, we soon came upon the first obo west of Ta-chien-lu. It lies in the middle of the broad roadway, and is made up of slabs of slate inscribed with Tibetan writing. It is a peculiarity of this obo that Tibetans entering Ta-chien-lu pass it on one side and on leaving on the other. They never pass and repass it on the same side.* There are two other obo a short distance beyond on the east side of the road, for the latter lies south and south-west on leaving the city.

The stream which bisects Ta-chien-lu is soon spanned by a one-arch stone bridge, known as the "Gate of Tibet". Over this goes the road, and leads past the parade-ground and lamasery, surrounded by tall poplars, where I had witnessed the performance on the 20th August. Here it enters a valley, a continuation of the valley to the east by which we had entered Ta-chien-lu, bounded by lofty, steep, grass-covered mountains, leaving little room for cultivation. Ruddy patches of buckwheat and a few plots of oats, wheat, and barley or bere (Ching Ko), were to be seen, but human habitations, usually single houses, are few and far between. The main road ascends the west side of the valley, while a branch road descends to the left bank of the stream, crosses it by a wooden bridge, and leads up a valley to the summer residence of the Ming-chêng Ssŭ, or native chief, of the country, to whom I have already referred. This road also connects with the Chien-ch'ang valley by way of Mo-hsi-mein and Tzŭ-ta-ti. The latter place is really no longer in existence, having been demolished by an avalanche last year.

* This applies to all obo.

On approaching the solitary house known as Ta-p'ing, 20 *li* from Ta-chien-lu, we met a large caravan of yak and dzo (the offspring of the yak and cow) laden with yak hides, sheep's wool, and Tibetan undyed cloth, known as Mu-tzŭ. The drivers told us that they were from Kanzé, and had been a month on the road. Kanzé lies on the northern road from Ta-chien-lu to Tibet, which branches from the Batang road after passing the Cho-to Shan, a task which is in store for us tomorrow. It is said to be a much easier route than that through Batang, as fewer ranges have to be crossed and pasture is more abundant. The caravan we had met had been taking it leisurely, as Kanzé is reckoned to be only 14 stages from Ta-chien-lu. At Ta-p'ing the main road strikes westward up the valley of a branch stream joining that flowing down the valley we had just left. Steep mountains covered with brushwood slope up from the stream, and their tops were capped with clouds. Rain quickly set in, and continued during the rest of the stage as far as the hamlet of Cho-to where we are spending the night, distant only 40 *li* from Ta-chien-lu.

Soon after entering the western valley, and after rounding a number of bends, we caught a glimpse through an opening in the bounding ranges of the Cho-to range to the west and right in our path. Ascending the valley, we crossed the stream, churned into white foam by the boulders in its bed, by a small stone bridge, and keeping for a time by its right bank and passing a small tributary, recrossed it by another small stone bridge, and followed up its left bank till it issues from a wider valley, well cultivated. The hamlet of Cho-to, consisting of three of four houses, including two inns, lies on the north side of this valley, which runs north-east and south-west. It is the meeting-place of two roads, that which we are following and another leading south-west down the valley and south to the Province of Yünnan, through the native State of Mili, or Muli, better known as

Huang Lama ("Yellow Lama"), and Yung-ning Fu. By this latter route Yünnan merchants bring opium for sale to Ta-chien-lu, taking back Indian rupees usually packed in bales of native cloth from central China. As a rupee in Yünnan is said to be worth 5 mace 5 candareen, while in Ta-chien-lu the value is only 3 mace $6\frac{1}{2}$ candareen, it will be readily understood that the business is a lucrative one.

This southern road to Yünnan connects with the Mo-hsi-mien–Chien-ch'ang valley road, as well as with the Batang road after the crossing of the Cho-to Pass. The ascent of 2,298 feet from Ta-chien-lu (8,349 feet) to Cho-to (10,647 feet) is gradual, and lies, for the most part, over a wide granite-paved road in glorious disorder, up and down which pack animals have to pick their way in the most careful manner. My caravan now consists of 13 pack animals—mules, six riding ponies, four mounted soldiers, and a mountain chair with four bearers, and two sets of relief bearers, for I found it impossible to take a chair with-out 12 bearers. Everything—clothing, stores, and the like—had to be repacked in hide boxes, and rice for all my followers had to be taken along with us as far as Batang, provisions being unobtainable *en route*.

It rained overnight before we left Ta-chien-lu, but cleared up sufficiently to enable us to start, as already stated, at 10.20 a.m. While waiting, I spent the morning in watching from the windows of my room in the inn cara-vans of yak, dzo, ponies, mules, and donkeys bringing into the city loads of wool, hides, and deer horns, and passing out with brick tea, the better quality sewed up in raw-hide packets, and the coarser packed loosely in bamboo baskets, pannier fashion. Yak, dzo, men, women, and children were also carrying into the city bundles of firewood, for coal has not yet been found in the neighbourhood.

The road was bordered with many shrubs and wild flowers in bloom, and here and there edgings of turf were decorated with small red berries. Besides a few poplars, scrub hazel coming into fruit, juniper and firs were the principal trees; but the country is scantily wooded, the mountain sides being clad with grass and brushwood.

We arrived at Cho-to at 4 p.m., where I watched other caravans going into Ta-chien-lu. In addition to the usual yak-skins, wool, and deer horns, I noticed packages of salt from the west which competed with eastern salt from the Wu-tung-ch'iao wells near Chia-ting.

Soon after leaving Ta-chien-lu two well-dressed Chinese standing by the roadside, accosted and told us that they had lost their passes (Lu P'iao). They are workers in silver bound for Litang, have tacked themselves on to our caravan, and are staying at our inn tonight. Their story is that they lost a package from their baggage containing their passes, without which they are not permitted to cross the ferry of the Ya-lung River. Such passes are granted by the Commissary at Ta-chien-lu to Chinese proceeding to Litang and Batang, and a charge of 2 taels odd is made for each.

26th August

Leaving Cho-to at 6 a.m., we soon left the valley along which runs the road to Yünnan, and struck north-west up another valley bounded on the north-east side by a high mountain range covered with brushwood dotted here and there with silver fir. A stream flows down the valley on its way to join the stream in the valley we had just left. The road, which follows the left bank of the branch stream, may be compared to the bottom of a wide mountain torrent full of boulders and not always dry.

The mountains on the south-west side of the valley, which was without a trace of cultivation, was covered almost entirely by juniper bushes, the branches of which are burned as incense by the Tibetans, for we have now practically entered the country inhabited by that race.

Shrubs and wild flowers lined the road frequently bounded with turf, from which peeped beautiful red and yellow flowers. Spiræa was in full white bloom, edelweiss was common, and here and there currant and gooseberry bushes and rhododendrons were visible among the brush-wood. Ripe strawberries of goodly size, as often as not nestling by the side of a boulder in the broad roadway, were abundant. The prickly oak, looking like holly, was frequently growing side by side with juniper and the blue-bell and foxglove. We breakfasted in the open 20 *li* from Cho-to, and immediately afterwards passed a caravan of yak breaking camp, and guarded by the usual Tibetan dog, which bayed at us as we passed. The loads of the yak consisted of yak-skins or hides. While we were breakfasting another caravan of yak, dzo, and ponies, bound for one of the large lamaseries in Tibet, caught us up. It was carrying tea and rice. The Tibetan lamaseries have lama agents resident in Ta-chien-lu, who make the necessary purchases for their use and a surplus for disposal in Tibet.

The Tibetan drivers of all these caravans are armed with swords, worn horizontally passed through their girdles in front, and most of them carry matchlocks with folding-up forked wooden rests lying along the underside of the barrel, and projecting beyond the muzzle. Unlike the passes we have already crossed, the road led to the Cho-to La by a gradual ascent along the left bank of the stream, which we ultimately crossed by a frail wooden bridge. We then kept to the right bank for a short time, and skirted a small basin, after which a steeper ascent led to the summit of the pass at a height of 13,923 feet above the level of the sea.

On the way up I saw a number of skeletons of yak which had perished while carrying out the baggage of the late Imperial Resident for Tibet, and a caravan of 50 yak with hides and wool descended as we neared the summit. The animals had to make room for us on the rough stone roadway. A few minutes later I rode on to the summit of the pass which was buried in clouds. An immense obo or cairn of stones surmounted by poles with fluttering flags stands by the roadside on the summit, and one of the soldiers of my escort dismounted and added his stone to the pile. The road, after crossing the pass, descends westwards into a valley bounded by rounded hills grass covered, for the most part, and treeless; but the lower slopes on the south side were abundantly clad with dwarf rhododendrons. Just under the pass, and at the foot of the southern mountain slope, a black tent was pitched, and a flock of sheep was grazing around it.

The northern road to Tibet and a road to Yünnan joining the Cho-to road to that province leave the Batang road at this point. On descending I espied in the bottom of the valley a bright red patch, which I took to be a plot of buckwheat in flower; but, on riding down to and passing through it, I found it to be an island of red blossoms, springing out of the beautiful green turf with which the valley is carpeted. We held on down the valley by the right bank of a stream which issued from a valley on the south side below the pass. The bed of the valley was carpeted with wild flowers in full bloom, from red, blue, and mauve tints to the yellow of the humble dandelion, which had been especially prominent during the day. Here was a botanist's paradise.

Herds of yak, ponies, and goats were browsing on the fine turf, and our ponies hurried down the valley, nibbling as they went. The endurance of the Tibetan pony is really wonderful. He will toil up the roughest stone road without a slip, as sure-footed as a cat, and will be as fresh at the end of a day's journey as at the start. He is not specially fed, but is turned loose at every stoppage during the day to graze with, if he is a pack animal, his load still on his back. After the day's work is over he is turned loose for the evening, and is then rounded up and hobbled during the night. He has thus to provide himself until the first stoppage next day, and it is not surprising that he takes every opportunity of nibbling as he goes. It is amusing to see the pack animals rushing along to have a few mouthfuls before they are caught by the drivers behind.

First one Tibetan house and then another appeared in the valley; but, fording the stream at the stone-built flat-roofed house known as Hsin-tien-tzǔ, we passed on to Ti-ju, or Ti-zu, 10 *li* beyond. To reach this we had to reford the stream, for Ti-zu lies just round the bend of the eastern end of the valley, which is hemmed in by a range of green treeless hills running north and south. There was a patch or two of nearly ripe barley round the two houses making up the hamlet of Ti-zu, which is one of the courier stations established all along the road to Tibet. At this station there are three families, one of which, in return for superintending the courier service of the station, holds sufficient land to produce 40 bags of barely each weighing 60 catties, while each of the others draws 5 taels a month from the Government for the up-keep of two horses as relays for carrying despatches to the next station.

On leaving Ti-zu we passed through what might have been an English lane hedged with wild gooseberry bushes, and soon crossing the stream, joined by another from the north, by a bridge turned west up another valley past hamlets of Tibetan houses looking in the distance like fortified castles. We arrived at An-niang-pa at 4.30 p.m., and took up our quarters at the headman's house, the largest in the hamlet, where we were welcomed by the master with out-stretched palms and tongue—the Tibetan salutation.

27th August
The road from the western descent of the Cho-to Pass to An-niang-pa is remarkably good, for the simple reason

that it is not a made road, and unpaved. So it is with the road from An-niang-pa to Tung-ngolo, a distance of 60 *li*. Leaving An-niang-pa at 6 a.m., we continued our course westward down the same valley and anon south-west, when the valley turns in that direction. The mountains bounding the valley became lower, and, although showing traces of having been formerly terraced and cultivated, were now grass-covered. The slopes were almost treeless, but, looking up smaller branch valleys, firs could be occasionally seen on other mountain slopes. A few Tibetan hamlets and farmhouses lay in the valley, and there were cultivated patches of yellow barley, greener wheat, and peas. A small white-faced lamasery lay higher up on the north side at the entrance to an opening in the mountains.

On leaving An-niang-pa the whole of our transport animals were changed, but, as the animal reserved for me had a sore back, I declined to take it, and was then supplied with a mare with a well-grown mule foal. We had gone only as far as Wa-chieh, a distance of 30 *li*, when the transport animals were again changed, and I had here to decline two yak which they tried to foist upon us as baggage-carriers. An attempt was also made to get back the mare I was riding, another pony with a sore back being offered and declined. On arrival at the hamlet of Ying-kuan-chai, over-looked by a ruined Tibetan fort, which we reached by a wooden bridge spanning the stream and by following the latter's right bank to the end of the valley, I held a meeting of all the drivers, and informed them that the Commissary at Ta-chien-lu had distinctly stated to me that the animals supplied to me at Ta-chien-lu would take me right through to Ho-k'ou, a five days' march, and that I would have no trouble with change of transport as far as that place. At this they were very much surprised, and I fear the Commissary is as ignorant of the transport service as I then was. I insisted that I should be at once supplied with a decent riding horse, and that no further change should be made until Ho-k'ou was reached. The promise was made; but I am under the impression that the original contractors to whom I personally paid the money at Ta-chien-lu wished to sub-let the remaining part of their contract at a cheaper rate, or that there is some arrangement among the villagers along the route to have a share in all contracts. As I had to speak through an interpreter—for these people know Tibetan only—I completely failed to get at the exact facts of the case.

We crossed to the right bank of the stream over a wooden bridge, and followed it to Ying-kuan-chai, which lies on the right bank of the stream, with another stream coming from a valley to the north. At this point the combined waters go south, down a valley, to join the Ya-lung. A road also goes south along its bank. Turning up the valley to the north, we marched up it, keeping some little distance from the left bank of the stream, which is joined by several tributaries entering it from the west. Several valleys open out from this valley, both on the east and west sides; and the main valley, which is of considerable width, is evidently liable to be flooded, for there were many standing pools sometimes submerging the roadway, and it was for the most part covered with coarse grass, in many places thickly dotted with edelweiss and here and there red and yellow flowers. At one place there was a flock of about 300 sheep, tended by Tibetan shepherds. At the north end the valley opens out into a number of smaller valleys, and the road, crossing the stream by a wooden bridge, passes over some rising ground and turns north-west and west, descending through many wild cherry trees into the wretched Tibetan hamlet of Tung-ngolo, where we arrived at noon and put up for the day. This short stage of 60 *li* is made in anticipation of the crossing of the Ka Ji La Pass to-morrow.

As we left the northern trade route to Tibet on crossing the Cho-to Pass yesterday we have seen nothing in the way of trade during the day. We are now on the official road to Tibet, and little more than local trade may be expected.

Many obo were seen during the day—round, oblong, and some of them like long stone dikes—heaped with stones and slabs engraved with Tibetan characters. Most of the obo were surmounted with pinnacles of white quartz, and some of them were built of alternate layers of stone and turf. Not a few of the Tibetan houses had their out-side walls adorned with representations of the heads of animals picked out in small white stones. There were several Ch'örtens, one in good repair, and round them were heaped clay figures moulded by the lamas. Those figures are made by pushing wet clay into brass moulds and eject-ing them while still in a soft state.

Gooseberry bushes and, as I have said, wild cherry trees were commonly seen during the day. The gooseberries on the bushes were small and unfit to eat. The slopes of the hills round Tung-ngolo were well clad with fir and poplar.

28th August

We were off from Tung-ngolo at 6 a.m., skirting the south side of the narrow valley into which we had descended at noon on the previous day. A couple of Tibetan houses lay in the valley, the smoke of juniper bushes was rising from their roofs, and the monotonous drone from a shell was borne to us on the still air. It was the hour of morning worship. At intervals were ruined buildings, and there can be no doubt that the country along the high road is being depopulated. The transport service which these hamlets and farmhouses have to ren-der to passing officials and others, on very inadequate terms, appears to be the cause of abandonment. At the same time the people appear to have insufficient land under cultivation to supply them with food, nor do they sufficiently utilize the farm manure to fertilize their fields. In some of the Tibetan houses in which I have lived I have seen the accumulations of years in the basement, which is the byre and stable, the living rooms being reached by a ladder or staircase from below. But the manure, if not applied to the land, has another use. It is made up into thin circular cakes, plastered on the stone walls of the houses, and when sufficiently dry is consumed as fuel. This takes place even where firewood is available; for at Tung-ngolo, where the houses were daubed with manure rolls or argols, almost every house had its pile of firewood stacked in lengths between upright poles on the opposite side of the street.

On leaving Tung-ngolo the road runs between hedges of gooseberry bushes and wild cherry trees, and at the west end of the valley turns south-west up a branch valley, whose bounding hills, clad with silver fir, wild cherry, and dwarf prickly oak, leave no room for cultivation. The branches of the trees, especially the firs, had long streamers, often a yard long, drooping from them. On O-mei Shan the trunks of the same fir were covered with moss, in which the seeds of other plants and trees had germinated and taken root; but here the moss, known as "Fairies' Scarf" (*Usnea barbata*), merely hung in masses like light-green seaweed from the branches, presenting a somewhat weird appearance. We forded the Tung-ngolo stream twice before reaching the solitary Tibetan house known as La-tza or Shan-kên, where we breakfasted. Leaving La-tza at 8.30 a.m., we ascended the steep face of a hill, soon catching sight of the Ka Ji La Pass in a mountain range ahead of us. It lay directly west, but we had to circumvent several bends over a good road lined with rowans in full fruit, red currants, silver firs, and prickly oak until, within a couple of hundred feet from the top, the road began to zigzag. To the north the mountain slopes were dark with timber, but their rounded summits, on which yak could be made out, were covered with grass only.

The hardy Tibetan pony which I rode landed me on the top of the pass (13,958 feet) at 9.45 a.m. On the left was a large obo, from the top of which prayer-flags were flying from poles, and each of my escort threw a stone, gathered from the ground while on horseback, on the pile, amid shouts of "Hla solo, solo!" Looking back, our eyes fell upon the deep, well-wooded valley we had just threaded and ranges of mountains behind capped with clouds. To the west lay the second pass, with its obo and prayer flags a mile away. Between the passes is a small shallow valley, dotted with round, undulating, rocky hills. Descending a few feet, we forded a streamlet going south, and immediately afterwards a rill which joined it from the west. This rill we recrossed, flowing north, before reaching the top of the second pass, which has a much easier gradient than the first.

Looking westward from the second summit (14,279 feet), we peer down into a deep, densely wooded, narrow valley bounded by high mountains, whose tops were grass-covered and dotted here and there with dwarf prickly oak. Further west were high mountain ranges, but no snow was visible anywhere. On the rounded hills between the summits were patches of scrub rhododendrons. On crossing the first we espied on their way to the second pass several yak caravans, and they crossed the latter just ahead of us. There is a spring of water just under and to the east of the second pass and several to the north of it on the way down. Crossing the pass the road runs northward by an easy gradient for a short distance and then west; but as we descend with the valley it becomes steeper, full of zigzags, and then narrow.

A stream flows down the valley, and we descend to it with the yak caravans, laden with brick tea bound for Ho-k'ou or Nia-chŭ-ka on the Ya-lung River. There were about 60 animals in all, and each yak carried six packages, three on each side of the wooden saddle, to which they were strapped with hide thongs, or a total of 128 lb. Some had finer teas sewed in hides. These hide packages were shorter, each ordinary package being divided into two, and six half-packages sewed into one hide cover. Of the latter each yak carried two hide packages. The yak is a somewhat stupid animal, and when a caravan comes to a narrow part of the road the animals crowd and crush together in inex-tricable confusion, with the result that the bamboo packages are frequently crushed, broken, and thrown from the saddle. Descending from the second pass I saw such an accident, and two hide packages of the finer tea rolled down into the deep valley. The driver went after them, and, instead of dragging them up to the roadway, threw them deeper down into the valley, to be picked up later when the animals descended. The yak are driven in a herd without connecting ropes, and each animal is controlled when in camp by a wooden ring strung through its nos-trils. A piece of rope is attached to the ring. It is not actually a ring: the two ends of a wooden rod are crossed and tied together after the rod has been passed through the nostrils. On the road the yak is controlled by shouting and whistling and by stones thrown by the driver.

On striking the right bank of the stream we descended with it to Wo-lung-shih, 70 *li* from Tung-ngolo, passing through fine avenues of silver firs, many of them rising straight up to a height of about 100 feet and laden with "Fairies' Scarf", wild cherry, and prickly oak, now attain-ing a height of about 20 feet. I measured one of the silver firs, and at 5 feet from the ground it had a girth of 10 feet. As we approached Wo-lung-shih, gooseberry bushes reappeared and a few patches of barley and wheat, and an arched grave, covered with stones, having a flag-staff and long flag attached, told us that we were nearing human habitation, for we had not seen a house since breakfasting at La-tza. Wo-lung-shih is a Tibetan-built hamlet of ten families, 2,629 feet below the second Ka Ji La Pass, itself about 500 feet under the highest point of the range immediately to the south of it. Tomorrow our road goes with the stream to the Ya-lung.

29th August

A thunder- and rainstorm broke over Wo-lung-shih a few minutes after our arrival there, and the rain continued overnight; but when we proceeded down the valley at 6 a.m. on the 29th of August the weather had cleared. The mountain tops were, however, capped with clouds. Our course lay west along the north side of the valley. There were many ruined Tibetan houses; but the mystery is how the inhabitants of these hamlets could have existed, for the arable bottom land was exceedingly limited, and the mountain sides were covered with forests of fine silver firs, and near the roadway grew prickly oak, wild roses, and a new tree—the maple. A Scotch fir was noticeable here and there, and I noticed that many of the rails of the fences surrounding the plots of wheat, barley, and oats were young birches. The method of fencing is primitive: a forked branch of a tree was driven into the ground and the end of a young birch placed thereon, the other end resting on a similar fork. In other cases two sets of holes were cut out of stout pieces of wood embedded in the ground and the ends of the rails placed therein.

The maples, with gnarled moss-grown trunks, became more prominent as we marched westwards, and continued noticeable during the day. Some were fruit-bearing, and none were more than 40 feet high, but their gnarled and stumpy appearance leads me to think that they had been lopped for fuel. Some of the prickly oaks, too, which were shrubs on the mountain sides, were fair-sized trees in the valley. An hour or more after starting we crossed to the left bank of the stream by a one-arched wooden bridge of somewhat peculiar construction. Two solid stone piers are built, one on each side of the stream, and barked trees are built into the piers with their exposed ends projecting upwards to a level with the tops of the piers. On these projecting ends timbers are laid lengthwise, and there is a rail on each side connected above and below the floor by stout cross-timbers, so that at every few feet a cross-timber on the floor of the bridge has to be stepped over.

My servant considered the two houses constituting the hamlet of Ja-lēng-ka too dirty to spread breakfast in, and when we came up we found the table laid out *al fresco* by the side of a small stone building containing a prayer cylinder, being driven by a tiny rill. The axle of the cylinder passed through the centre of a small horizontal water-wheel, and the inhabitants of the neighbouring large Tibetan house, grimy and dirty, were by this means always at worship night and day. It was a farmhouse; the hay had been cut, and pieces of wood were placed upright against the ricks. A plot of barley was almost ripe for harvest, but another of wheat was still green. Here I noticed a wild pepper tree, and bunches of red fruit growing on what from its foliage and general appearance was a species of hawthorn. The Chinese with me called it Yeh-p'u-t'ao ("wild grape").

As we marched down the valley which widened out, it became better cultivated, and a splendid Tibetan house in the centre of the valley soon came into view. It was large and three-storeyed, with a smaller two-storeyed building— private chapel—on the top. It had two rows of small windows all round the two upper storeys. It turned out to be the residence of a native chief, and my interpreter, who had passed a night there a year or two ago, greeted the inmates from the roadway. As we descended the valley the temperature became milder, and maize began to put in an appearance with every prospect of a good crop. Silver gave place to Scotch fir on the mountain slopes, and the birch became abundant nearer the valley. There was considerable cultivation on approaching the hamlet of Pa-ko-lou, so called from an octagonal stone tower at the western end of the hamlet. It is 45 *li* from Wo-lung-shih.

A short distance beyond Pa-ko-lou the valley closes in, leaving room for the stream only, and the road runs up and down a forest-clad mountain side, until there is no room for it on the left bank, when it crosses to the right by a wooden bridge such as I have just described. Before crossing we had our mid-day meal on a green piece of turf by the left bank. Our Tibetan caravan drivers snatched a hasty meal of tsamba at the same time, and instead of feeding themselves with their fingers in the usual way licked it from their cups. The road is very bad before reaching the bridge. It had evidently been washed away by the rushing torrent aided by land slips, and recently repaired by laying down branches of trees covered with stones and mud. This we experienced several times during the day.

Beyond the bridge another stream of about the same size joins it from a northern valley, and the united waters rush westwards down a narrow gorge between steep, rocky mountain sides clad with Scotch fir and prickly oak. In many places the roadway is cut from the solid rock, and is frequently very precipitous. It crosses from one side of the stream to the other four times, and as Ho-k'ou on its left bank, and at its junction with the Ya-lung, is neared it passes finally from the right to the left bank by a wooden bridge of two arches, a central pier being built on a rock in mid-stream.

The latter part of the day's journey was very tedious, and was made still more trying by rain. Range after range of mountains slope into the valley, and the road winds round the foot of each range in its westward course. There is scarcely a trace of life in this narrow gorge, which is a magnificent picture of nature run riot. In addition to the crops already mentioned, I noticed a patch of buckwheat and another of hemp.

30th August

Ho-k'ou (9,010 feet), or Nia-chǔ-ka, as it is called after the Ya-lung or Nia-chǔ, is a hamlet of 20 odd houses wedged in on a small terrace between the stream we have followed to its mouth, and a range to the south which drops down to the left bank of the Ya-lung. On the right bank of the stream rises a high, bare, rocky bluff, whose highest point is surmounted by an obo with prayer flags, and there is another obo lower down as the bluff dips to the Ya-lung. Beyond a patch or two of garden devoted to maize, cabbages, melons, and turnips, there is no room for cultivation. The hamlet is filthy outside and inside, and although the room I occupied in the Tibetan inn was clean looking, I suffered severely overnight from insect pests.

After breakfast I mounted to the roof of the inn, and had a good view of the Ya-lung flowing south-west past Ho-k'ou, and then turning south between high steep mountain ranges. The face of the range opposite Ho-k'ou was clad with prickly oak almost to its summit. The river, which is cooped up to the north by mountains, opens out opposite Ho-k'ou to a breadth of about 400 yards. There is a rapid just above the point where it opens out, and another on the right bank opposite the hamlet caused by projecting rocks. There is a gully on the west bank above the rapid, whence a stream joins the Ya-lung, and up this gully lies the road to Litang, Batang, and Tibet. A road crossing the stream goes north along the right bank of the Ya-lung to the State of Chantui, the border of which can be reached in two days, and its capital in 12. Another road leaves Ho-k'ou, and following the left bank of the Ya-lung, enters the Chien-ch'ang valley at the district city of Mien-ning Hsien. There is very little trade along these two roads.

The whole force of the small military official of Ho-k'ou, composed of eight men, met us on approaching the hamlet, and I was informed that all arrangements for change of transport had been made, and that I would be able to start westwards without the delay of even a day. All that the official required was the number of animals, and they would be at once supplied at the Tibetan village, built on rising ground on the right bank of the river opposite Ho-k'ou. The charge was 2 rupees per animal for two days, when transport had again to be changed. This was satisfactory, and the military official, in addition to his other kindnesses, insisted on sending half his Chinese force, and wished to send 20 Tibetan soldiers for our protection within his jurisdiction, but I hinted that half the latter would suffice.

Goods and passengers are ferried across the Ya-lung by boat and by hide coracles. There are three of the former in use, each manned by ten men, six working on two heavy spar oars at the bows and four on two stern sweeps. The people of Ho-k'ou depend upon the ferry for their livelihood, and each family owns a coracle. The best tea is ferried across by boat, the coarser by coracle. Passing down to the ferry at 8.30 a.m., I noticed quite a number of tea packages stored in a building close to the military official's residence, and was told that the tea accumulates there until a caravan is ready to start westward, when it is ferried across. On reaching the ferry boat, I found the military official awaiting to say good-bye, and, this ceremony over, the whole of my party embarked and the boat was headed up-stream to the foot of the rapid already mentioned, swung across the river, and brought up alongside the right bank below Ho-k'ou. Our baggage had all been ferried across ahead of us, and was piled on the river bank. It had now to be carried to the Tibetan village, where our animals were waiting. I walked up and paid the 38 rupees to the owners of the 19 animals; the baggage was carried up, and at 11 a.m. we resumed our journey westward.

The interval I spent in the house of the Tibetan chief, whose good lady brought presents of tea, milk, and eggs. The eggs I accepted and paid for in more than double their value, but, as she did not appear satisfied, I added as much again, with a resolve to accept no more presents. I should have stated that the military official at Ho-k'ou sent me on the previous evening a melon, three cucumbers, two cabbages, and a couple of turnips, for which, of course, I had also to pay. The chief's wife was got up for the occasion. She had a silver plate as big as a bread plate resting on the top and another attached to the back of her head. She also wore long ear-rings of silver inlaid with coral. Here also our Tibetan guard of ten men was waiting, five armed with matchlocks, with folding fork rests attached to the barrels, and five with spears. The guns were slung along the back with the rest extended, and the stock and flashpan encased in a hide bag, the hair inside. When all was ready we started up the valley to the north-west, keeping to the right bank of the stream which joins the Ya-lung. We soon crossed by bridge to the left bank, but had to re-cross it on entering a valley branching off to the south-west, and sending forth a stream as large as that we had just left, the two uniting below the bridge.

The rest of the day was spent in this valley, first on the left, and finally on the right bank, ascending it over what by the wildest stretch of the imagination may be called a road. Stone it was in many places, but so rough and terrible that I pitied to the heart the sturdy Tibetan pony that I rode. Its footing was marvellous, and it surprised me that horse and rider were not precipitated into the roaring dashing torrent—a series of veritable waterfalls—from the narrow, rough, stone pathway overhanging the stream. The attempt at a road, and a couple of simple wooden bridges were the only signs of human activity in this valley, which was practically a primeval forest. The steep mountain slopes were clad to their summits with silver firs, lighted with the light green of bunches of "Fairies' Scarf" drooping from their branches. The valley, at first running south-west and north-east, soon turned direct west, and I noticed that the silver fir was especially abundant on the northern slopes, while the southern slopes were for the most part given up to the prickly oak.

In the bottom of the narrow valley huge trees lay uprooted, forming in many places natural bridges across the torrent, and where the road had been blocked, pieces were cut out of the trunks to remove the obstructions. The maple was very common, and other trees unknown to me. Some of the silver firs were of enormous girth, and all straight as an arrow. It frequently happened that the torrent occupied the whole valley bottom, and wading over the uneven stones proved a severe task on our horses. For a long time there was nothing but forest gloom, but ultimately light showed ahead, and to the north the mountain slopes receded, leaving room for little patches of wheat, barley, and peas, with a single Tibetan hut. This was followed by a log hut, exactly like the log huts I have seen in Siberia, and later, by a wide cultivated valley and the hamlet of Ma-kai-chung (11,446 feet), which we reached amid rain at 3 p.m. Ahead the valley continues with ranges showing beyond.

We had a novel experience at Ma-kai-chung. Three hours after our arrival an earthquake★ of several seconds duration shook the house in which we were quartered. The timbers of the building creaked, and my writer, who was in the middle of a meal, came with scared face to ask what was the matter. Earthquakes are common in Ta-chien-lu and in the country to the west. There was no sign of any trade during the day, and scarcely a soul was met on the road. We have ascended over 2,000 feet in four hours, and tomorrow have to cross the Ra-ma-la Pass.

31st August
On leaving Ma-kai-chung the road—unpaved, and a decided improvement on yesterday's route—goes west up the valley, when cultivation soon ceases, and we are once again in nature's workshop. Densely wooded mountain slopes coop up the valley, and the silver firs and prickly oaks were festooned with "Fairies' Scarf", often a couple of yards in length. The oaks, especially on the northern slopes, form a dense forest without a sign of life. This valley is said to be the hunting ground of robbers, and our escort seemed anxious that the caravan should be kept together and move rapidly. Up we went till the forest ceased, giving place to grassy mountain summits and scrub juniper. We breakfasted on the grassy slope dotted with wild flowers just under the summit of Ra Ma La (14,948 feet), and at 9.45 a.m. reached its highest point over an open stony road, and, although the ascent was gradual, the altitude tried our horses severely, and many a stop had to be made to give them breathing space. I dismounted once

---

★ This earthquake played great havoc at Dawo, on the northern road from Ta-chien-lu to Tibet, and almost direct north of Ma-kai-chung. A large lamasery and a great part of the town were reduced to ruins, and a number of people were crushed to death.

and walked for some distance; but I found that I was soon affected as severely as my horse, and had to remount. My legs felt like lead, and I experienced considerable difficulty in controlling them. We looked back into the deep forest valley we had just left and at mountain ranges enveloped in clouds. On reaching the summit, escorts and drivers rushed to the three obo surmounted by poles and prayer-flags, and amid shouts of "Hla solo, solo!" added stones to the piles.

At the summit the road branches, one going south-west, keeping well up along the mountain side, the other descending into a hollow called La-ni-ba, where there is a post station, at which the soldiers had to change horses. The road zigzagged into the hollow, and the descent was so steep that we had to dismount for some distance. My chair took the upper road, which joins the lower road at the second summit of the Ra Ma La, known as Do-zé-la (15,041 feet), two-and-a-half miles to the west. In the hollow or valley rhododendrons and mountain ash were common, and in the bottom I came across what looked like rhubarb (*Rheum palmatum* L.) for the first time. The seed stems were about 3 feet in length, rising from leaves smaller and much narrower than the rhubarb cultivated in Europe. The plants were growing on a grassy slope. A stream goes south down the hollow with a valley to the north, where I noticed several black tents and herds of yak. The eastern slope of Do-zé-la is not so steep as that of Ra Ma La, and we rode on to it at 11.45 a.m. Here there are two obo, but our escort had already done their duty at Ra Ma La.

The descent on the west side is easy, and the fine turf tempted our horses to a feast and ourselves to a rest. As rain soon began to fall we hurried on by a very easy descent to the post station of Po-lang-kung. On the way, however, we were met at an untenanted guard-house by

the petty military official of Po-lang-kung and two soldiers, who, after greetings, hurried on ahead to receive us
at the station, which we reached at 12.45, and had a meal.
Here I enquired about trade, of which there is now no
sign, and the officer informed me that all the business on
this road is done by three caravans a year, which pass in
March, September, and December, and between times
there is little or no traffic along this road. Po-lang-kung is
simply the residence of this official, and nothing more. It
is a miserable place, but the owner was good enough to do
his best for us.

From the Do-zé-la we had an excellent view of the
country to the west—ranges of grass-covered mountains
seemingly on the same level as the pass on which we
stood. They were, of course, divided up by valleys; but the
scene gave us the impression of a grand plateau stretching
westward. There was a small road going northward from
the untenanted guard-house to the State of Chantui, only
a day's journey distant, so that here we were practically on
the borders of Tibet. In a forest of silver firs below the
summit of Do-zé-la we heard the call of the jungle fowl,
known as the "Ma Chi", and at a considerable distance
from the road a flock could be made out moving in the
grass at the foot of the firs. The bird is larger than a pheasant; it has a white breast, black back and wings, and a red
ring round the eyes. I hope to have a closer acquaintance
with it later. These and a vulture in the valley between Ra
Ma La and Do-zé-la were the only signs of wild animal
life seen during the day. The antelope is also found here,
and the proprietor of our last night's resting-place produced a skin with the spiral horns attached.

From Po-lang-kung we descended through a forest, part
of which had been destroyed by fire, and the bare white
branches of the silver firs rose ghost-like from the ground.
Soon a cultivated valley, well-watered and running north

and south, lay at our feet to the north-west, and we zigzagged into it down the mountain side through silver firs, prickly oaks, juniper, and hawthorn, till we reached the left bank of a good-sized stream going south. This valley divides up into a number of valleys to the north, and to the south it turns south-west, showing yellow patches of barley all along its terraced sides, for the bottom is grassland, being apparently little more than the bed of the stream. A large lamasery stands on a hill slope on the east side of the valley to the south of the high road. Our road lay northwards up the valley, crossing several eastern affluents of the stream till, nearing the northern end, it passes over a small wooden bridge to the hamlet of Hsi-ngolo. Here the only inn was so poor that we had no hesitation in arranging for quarters in a Tibetan house, and we spent the night on the roof among the barley.

Here we had to arrange a change of transport, and we had some difficulty in making the headman understand that the animals must be produced next morning at daylight. Hsi-ngolo is noted for the great number of transport animals always available in the valley, but it is also noted for the stubbornness of their owners, who try to extract from the traveller more than the tariff rate, under pretence of scarcity of animals. Another matter to be discussed was the number of stages to Litang; and I ultimately agreed to consider the 160 *li* three stages if, on accomplishing the first stage of 40 *li* on the morrow, I did not think it advisable to proceed further that day. If however, we reached the end of the first stage at an early hour, they would raise no objection to making 60 more *li*, and thus reduce the three to two stages. In the Hsi-ngolo valley the harvesting of barley had begun, and the grain was in several places stacked, grain downwards, with two sheaves laid on the top of each stack to keep the grain dry. On descending from Do-zé-la to Po-lang-kung we looked westward across the Hsi–ngolo valley to a sea of grass-covered mountain waves, divided by valleys whose bottom lands were well wooded.

1st September

We were astir early, and by considerable pressure we were able to effect a start at 6.30 a.m., in spite of new animals and new drivers. The headman had a curious system of allocating the loads. Each owner of an animal handed over his garter to the chief, and when the number of garters, which he carefully counted, was equal to the number of animals he placed a garter on each load, and the owner proceeded to pick up his garter and place on his animal the load it marked.

From Hsi–ngolo the road runs north–west and west up a forest-clad hillside to the grassy waves we had looked upon yesterday. Deep down to the south-west lay a valley yellow with ripe barley, where the reapers were already at work. The road lay through silver firs, wild cherry, and prickly oak, till higher up stately silver firs were dotted singly or in groups on beautiful turf, dotted with wild flowers in full bloom. As we rose, however, the trees disappeared, and we looked down into well-wooded valleys. Crossing a pass with an obo, we descended on the other side through stately firs to the solitary post station of Rih-kung-ta, lying on the left bank of a stream flowing south. Close to the stream were a couple of black tents surrounded by a zareba of dried branches, and their herds of yak were fording the stream to graze on the opposite bank as we descended. Higher up the stream, and along the left bank, a road was visible, and the Tibetan postmaster described it as a small road to Litang. He also said that gold is found in this stream, and of this we had corroboration during the day. We had been told by the military official at Po-lang-kung to keep a good look out for Ma Chi (jungle fowl) on this part of the road, but the only thing that crossed our path during the morning was a grey-coloured squirrel.

This stream joins the stream that flows down the Hsi-ngolo valley, and we skirted its left bank till it disappeared in a thickly wooded gorge. The road then crossed the stream by a wooden bridge and ran westward up a branch valley, down which came an affluent to the stream we had just left. This we also crossed by bridge, and proceeded up its right bank in the thickly wooded valley to the solitary Tibetan house called Tsa-ma-la-tung, which is reckoned the end of a stage; but, as we had accomplished this distance before 11 a.m., and the weather was fine, I resolved to push on and endeavour to make a second stage during the day. In this valley I first noticed the large-leaved rhubarb (*Rheum officinale* L.).

The road soon enters another branch valley, and we ascended it south-west along the right bank of a streamlet through forest, till the latter gave place to grass-covered hills on both sides, with occasional dwarf rhododendrons. Gold washers were at work on the left bank of this stream-let. Two men, a girl, and a boy were at work. They had constructed a small conduit at the side of the stream, and at the outlet pieces of turf were placed to retain the parti-cles of gold washed from the shingle they were shovelling into the conduit. It was impossible to get any information from these Tibetans in regard to their work. They were very much afraid at our approach, and the girl and boy actually ran away, but, seeing that we had no evil inten-tions, soon returned. The road gradually ascended up the grassy valley, and we reached the summit of the Dé-rih-ka La Pass (14,137 feet) a little after noon, and spread our mid-day meal on the grass-covered mountain side ablaze with mountain flowers. We then descended into a wide, marshy valley to the right, and marched up it several miles to the road leading up to the Wong-gi La, or Chien-pa-ting Pass (14,560 feet).

At the head of the valley, and near the foot of the pass, was a solitary Tibetan house, called Luan-shih-ch'iao, and a number of black tents, with yak spread all over the hillsides and along the high road. The lower part of the ascent was fairly stiff climbing, and at one time we thought we had gained the summit only to see an obo a long way higher up. To add to our weariness, we were caught in a downpour of rain and thoroughly drenched. We passed the summit and the second obo at 3.15 p.m., to find my escort dismounted on the other side and blazing away at four robbers ("Chia Pa"—Tibetan for robbers) moving up the mountain side on our right. This pass is noted for the presence of highway robbers, and the escort had no hesitation in declaring the four men to be part of a band. The men were far beyond range of a Chinese muzzle-loader, and they moved slowly up the mountain side without taking any notice of the firing, and disappeared in a hollow.

From the summit of the pass there is a steep descent into a narrow valley leading to the hamlet of Ho-chŭ-ka on the left bank of the Ho-chŭ River. In this valley, which, owing to our long march, seemed endless, rhubarb was especially plentiful along both banks of a stream going south-west to join the Ho-chŭ River. The road—a marsh full of stones—was exceedingly bad going, and my followers were all grumbling at the long march. Owing to mountain sickness several of my bearers had fallen out, and during the day I did not see my chair till after we had crossed the Wong-gi La, where, owing to the presence of robbers, I considered it advisable to wait until all my men had turned up. All but two appeared, but we could not wait longer.

On approaching Ho-chŭ-ka we met three mounted Tibetans armed with guns and swords. My escort called a halt, and although the men dismounted when my chair passed, they were declared to be robbers without a doubt, for, in reply to the escort, they simply said they were going up the pass, and declined to give any further information regarding themselves or their movements. The military official at Ho-chǔ-ka, which we reached at 6 p.m., was good enough to ask us to share his miserable residence for the night. The whole hamlet (13,096 feet) consisted of five or six houses at the mouth of the valley, barred by the Ho-chǔ River and a mountain range rising from its right bank. The yamen was in a very tumble-down condition, and the official was good enough to remove a rooster which had already perched for the night on a pole over my bed-place. The four soldiers who had escorted us from Po-lang-kung came in the evening for the usual gratuity, and stated that they intended to start back at once and travel by night. They said they were afraid to travel by day on account of robbers, and would escape observation in the dark. Night travel is also common among merchants and others, showing that the country is in a very unsafe condition. Indeed, my caravan has within the last few days been joined by others, including a Tibetan woman and child going to Batang, they being afraid to go in small parties.

On our arrival the Ho-chǔ-ka official sent one of his soldiers a-fishing, and he soon returned from the Ho-chǔ with three fish weighing about $\frac{3}{4}$ lb each. These he presented to me, and they proved of excellent flavour. They were caught with a couple of sticks lashed together, a piece of twine, and an unbarbed hook with worm bait.

2nd September

We forded the stream whose left bank we had followed yesterday to Ho-chǔ-ka, and crossing the Ho-chǔ by a two-arched wooden bridge with stout stone piers built up of loose stones surrounded by stakes, marched north-west and west up its right bank between grassy hills to the solitary Tibetan house known as Yao-cha-tzŭ, where we left the river and began the ascent of the last pass which separated us from the plain of Litang. Rhubarb, whose roots are dug up in October, was very plentiful in the valley. There were a couple of black tents pitched on the right bank under Yao-cha-tzŭ, and gold washers were at work, men and women, clearing away surface shingle preparatory to a search for the precious metal in the lower strata. One of the women was gaily ornamented with a head-dress on which round and oval plates of silver were fixed, and many strings of coloured beads, principally white and red, hung down her back. Her hair, with the exception of a front lock reaching to the point of her nose, was made up into a series of small plaits at the sides and back of her head. I wished to examine the head-dress, especially the beads, but she was suspicious of my intentions and declined to part with it even for a moment. Other women were similarly decorated, but not so profusely. Questions as to the output and value of the gold elicited the statement that 15 men could produce one Chinese ounce ($1\frac{1}{3}$ oz English) in a month, which could be sold at Litang for 90 Chinese rupees.

A gradual ascent leads to the summit of the pass (14,165 feet) Hsieh Gi La; but it was not till we had skirted the brow of a hill with a deep valley on our left that we looked down into the plain of Litang, bounded on the south by magnificent ranges of mountains topped by three stately cones. Not a patch of snow was visible on these mountain tops. On reaching the plain, grass-covered and uncultivated, in some places sandy and with no depth of soil, we proceeded west along its northern side bounded by high grass-clad mountain slopes which send down several spurs into the plain. These we had to surmount, and at last came in sight of a large Tibetan house, the residence of the native chief, and of a Tibetan hamlet; but Litang itself, which lies in a fold of the mountains in the north-west of the plain, is not visible till, rounding a corner, the large lamasery of Litang is seen high up in the fold, with the town of one street lying on the ridge forming the other side of the fold.

The lamasery of Litang is a magnificent building, or collection of buildings, lying on a hill slope facing south. It is adorned with two separate roofs and a number of pinnacles covered with gold-leaf. It has a resident population of some 2,700 to 2,800 monks; but twice a year that number swells to some 3,000 when the smaller monasteries throughout the district send in their representatives. I was informed by the Commissary that the total population of the town, including the lamasery, numbered about 5,000; but, as there is only one street with some 145 Chinese and 235 Tibetan families outside the monastery, I am inclined to think that 4,000 would be a nearer approximation to the actual resident population. This lamasery is noted for its arrogance and defiance of all Chinese authority; but, as the result of a dispute, the heads of the abbot and his brother fell last year, and a more peaceful state of things now prevails.

The plain of Litang, some 10 miles long and several miles wide, yields, owing to its altitude (13,234 feet), nothing but grass and wild flowers. Grain will not ripen, and the food supply of the population of the town has to be brought from the east and from Batang in the west. This trade in food-stuffs is entirely in the hands of the lamasery, which will sell only when it pleases and at its own price. The chief industry of the town is the manufacture of silver jewellery for the Tibetan market. The plain is exceedingly rich in gold, especially along the banks of the Li-chŭ, but the lamas prohibit its exploitation. Such was the statement made to me by a gold merchant in the town.

The Litang State or district, with its five native chiefs, two of whom reside in a Tibetan hamlet on the plain just below the town, is bounded on the north and south by Tibet (Chantui) and the Province of Yünnan (Chung-tien T'ing) and on the east and west by the States of Chala (Ya-lung River) and Batang (San-pa) respectively. It is a three days' journey from Litang to the frontier of Chantui, and seven days to the capital of the State. The products of the district are gold-dust, musk, deer horns in the velvet, old deer horns, Ch'ung Ts'ao (*Cordiceps sinensis*), Pei-mu (*Coelogyne henryi* Rolfe), sheep's wool, sheep-skins, and yak-hides. The amount of gold-dust, some of which comes from Chantui, annually brought to the town of Litang for sale is about 3,000 oz, and is worth from 82.5 rupees to 85 rupees an ounce, or $1\frac{1}{3}$ oz avoirdupois, according to quality. It is brought by Chinese agents from Ta-chien-lu and sent eastward. It is estimated that 60,000 pods of musk, worth from 20 to 50 rupees each, according to size and quality, are sent annually from the district through Litang to Ta-chien-lu, where they are trimmed and prepared for the Chinese and foreign market.

Deer horns in the velvet of the value of 5,000 taels also find their way annually to the same place. These are a popular Chinese medicine, and are valued at Litang at from 2 to 20 rupees a catty. Rupees, worth 3 mace 2 candareen to 3 mace 8 candareen each, are the only currency of the country west of Ta-chien-lu. For trade convenience the coins are cut up into halves and quarters; but even quarters are too large for small retail purchases, and the introduction of a bronze coinage into this part of the country seems desirable. Most of the Indian rupees were of the reign of the late Queen Victoria, those with the crown being preferred, but I was able to pick out several of William IV. Old deer horns, worth a rupee per catty or catty and a half, are exported to Ta-chien-lu to the amount of from 6,000 to 7,200 catties of an estimated value of about 2,000 taels. They are used in the manufacture of medicinal glue.

That extraordinary combination of animal and vegetable known as Ch'ung Ts'ao (*Cordiceps sinensis*), which is held in high esteem as a medicine throughout the Chinese Empire, is found in considerable quantity in the Litang district. The dried caterpillars, each with its adhering parasitic plant, appear in commerce made up into small bundles, weighing each about a quarter of an English ounce, bound with red thread. It is worth at Litang 5 to 6 rupees per catty, and the annual export to Ta-chien-lu amounts to about 2,400 catties of the value of some 4,000 taels.

Pei-mu, the small white bulbs of *Coelogyne henryi* Rolfe, about the size of coffee-beans but more rounded, are found in the forests in the Litang district. They are used as a medicine, as well as being a vegetable delicacy. They are also the favourite food of the Ma Chi, the jungle fowl already referred to. There are two qualities, called respectively Ch'ing Pei-mu, worth 3.5 rupees, and Chih Mu, valued at 1.5 rupees a catty; but I think the latter is yielded by a different plant (? *Anemorrhena asphodeloides* Bunge). The annual output of the former is given as 13,200 catties, worth over 10,000 taels, and of the latter, 2,400 catties. They are sent to Ta-chien-lu for export.

A rupee will purchase 7 to 8 catties of sheep's wool at Litang, but the total annual export to Ta-chien-lu does not exceed 72,000 catties, worth something over 3,000 taels. Sheep-skins, the best and largest of which can be had for 1 rupee, while that sum will purchase two or three of small size, are mostly consumed in the district for clothing.

About 3,000 yak-hides find their way annually to Ta-chien-lu, and are there utilized for packing the finer teas for the Tibetan market. At Litang they are valued at 2 rupees to 3 rupees each. Ten of them go to a load, which weighs from 130 to 140 catties.

4th September

It rained heavily overnight at Litang, and our fresh transport animals not turning up till late, we did not get away till 7.45 a.m. The Commissary, in whose yamen we lived, prepared quite a display in our honour. I left, preceded by a number of runners and a red umbrella, but I dissuaded him from accompanying me out of the town. A tent had been erected by the roadside near the native chief's residence, whither he had proposed to accompany me and say good-bye, and chairs with the usual red trappings were placed therein for the formal ceremony; but, as I had vetoed the formality to avoid delay, the official's servant awaited with his card to say good-bye. The military official also paid me the same compliment soon after I left the town. We passed close to the native chief's house in a south-westerly direction, crossing several spurs dropping into the plain from the northern bounding hills. Tents, black and white, were dotted over the plain, and herds of yak and ponies and flocks of sheep were grazing on the marshy grass.

At a distance of 25 *li* from Litang, on rising ground to the north of the plain, there is a lamasery, and just beyond, in a rocky gully in a spur, are hot springs, over which houses have been erected and baths built. There is also a small lamasery beside the bath-houses for the accommodation of lamas. The water had a temperature of 112° Fahrenheit in the bath and 119° Fahrenheit where it issued from the rock. On the opposite side of the plain and at the foot of the mountains steam could be seen rising from the ground. From the hot springs we proceeded south-west over the plain to the Li-chŭ River, about 50 yards wide, which we crossed by a bridge of four arches consisting of planks laid on loose stone piers cased with timber. The river, of a yellow muddy colour, rushes very swiftly eastward. Stones were heaped on the planking, which is frequently washed away when the river is in flood.

Across the bridge we ascended about 50 feet to a Tibetan post station—a single hut with a small black tent in front of it. We preferred the tent to the hut, although it was thick with the smoke of argols and dwarf rhododendrons. Calling in our interpreter who is half-Chinese, half-Tibetan (Tao Man pu Han), we asked him to blow the Tibetan bellows, which he did with such vigour that the open fire in the middle of the floor was soon red, and the smoke escaped through the hole in the roof of the tent. A Tibetan bellows consists of the neck half of a sheep-skin with a metal spout fitted into the neck. Seizing the two sides of the open half of the skin (wool outside) the performer opens and shuts it with both hands so dexterously that the air is driven through the spout with great effect.

Here we had breakfast, to the great edification of two Tibetan ladies—the inmates of the hut. They were well-built lusty women, with the Litang forelock; but one of them had the upper part of her face blackened with soot or other oily substance to detract from her charms. In her case the disfigurement was quite unnecessary. This custom has, I understand, been decreed by the abbots of certain lamaseries, so that the clergy may not be enticed from their devotions by the charms of the world. As, however, Tibetan women consider it an honour to consort with lamas, it is to be feared that the abbots' decrees are not very effective.

From the post station, called Ta-ch'iao after the bridge, we ascended south-west up a valley down which flows a streamlet to the Li-chŭ. Soon, however, the valley became so stony and full of boulders that we took to the brow of a hill to the left, and rode over it through patches of dwarf rhododendrons and juniper, striking the valley higher up, still full of boulders and stones, and resembling the bed of a glacier. There is a small rocky basin at the top of the valley, and crossing the rim the road descends into another valley with a fair-sized stream flowing north-east. We followed the right bank of the stream till the wide valley is split up into two by a rocky range, and, fording the stream flowing down the valley to our left, marched up the right valley between high rocky mountain sides, dropping at a distance of 30 *li* from the Li-chŭ into the Chinese post station of T'ou-t'ang, or Jiom-bu-t'ang (14,555 feet), with its four houses and two Tibetan and two Chinese families.

Litang has the reputation of being very rainy, and when it rains in the plain it snows on the mountains to the south and north-west. When we left Litang in the morning the slopes of the high mountain peaks were white with snow.

Our escort consisted of nine Tibetan and eight Chinese cavalry, in addition to two mounted soldiers from Ta-chien-lu. Our Tibetans were armed with their fork-rest matchlocks and swords jewelled with silver, and ornamented with turquoise and coral. Arms are not confined to the soldiery. As a rule, every Tibetan trader, caravan driver, or traveller has a matchlock slung on his back, with the rest lying along and under the barrel, and extending a few inches beyond the muzzle. He also carries a sword passed through the front of his girdle, the hilt and point of the jewelled scabbard projecting on either side of his body. The Tibetan takes great pride in his gun and sword. They are heirlooms, and each individual owner does his best to add to their ornamentation. The tribesmen of the Mao Chou district, which lies to the north-west of Chengtu, are famous for their skill in gun-making, and the gun-smiths come to Ta-chien-lu to ply their trade. From the same district also come stonemasons and house-builders.

5th September

We left T'ou-t'ang at 6 a.m., proceeding up the valley in which the post station lies. Fording the stream, we zigzagged up a mountain side strewn with boulders, over a most difficult country. As we advanced the country became still more rocky, till we were surrounded on all sides by bare, rocky, loose, granite cones and basins of evident volcanic origin. There was not a speck of vegetation on these rocky heights, but the granite-strewn basins were covered with marshy grass. We had breakfast on a flat granite boulder, just above a lake, at the foot of a bare mass of rocks. A gradual ascent led to the summit of the Huang-t'u-kang or Nga-ra-ka Pass (15,429 feet), with the usual obo and prayer-flags. Beyond was a small lake on our left, which drained into a stream and down the valley with us, the pass forming the watershed.

The descent on the other side was simply execrable, and my personal servant was thrown from his horse against a boulder and so badly stunned that he had to be packed in my empty chair and carried to the end of the stage, which, owing to the accident, I made a short one. The day was bitterly cold, and did not add to the enjoyment of the march. Sleet fell as we crossed the pass. As we descended from the pass, a fine range of mountains, clad with snow, running north and south, loomed high above lower ranges to the west. We had crossed the pass at 8.20 a.m., and at noon we left the forbidding rocky country, turning west down into a deep hollow and fording a rapid stream flowing north. The road then led us over a grassy ridge, and west into a deep valley, on whose lower slopes we once more came upon the silver fir, birch, juniper, prickly oak, dwarf rhododendron, and gooseberry. From west we turned down north into the hamlet of La-êrh-t'ang, having made only 70 *li* instead of 95 *li*. We had wretched accommodation in a low mud hut, but I was afraid to carry my servant further that night. The only trade we saw during the day was a few yak laden with tea, and, curiously enough, one yak had a load of wool, which seemed like carrying coals to Newcastle.

6th September
My servant was very ill overnight and required special attention with the result that it was rather a gloomy procession which left La-êrh-t'ang at 7.30 a.m. He was carried on a stretcher in my chair, for I could not leave him behind in the miserable hut in which we had spent the night. The nearest Tibetan village was still 25 *li* distant. Proceeding north we soon turned west, fording and refording six times a brook flowing down the valley through silver firs, birches, goodly-sized rhododendrons, prickly oak, currant and gooseberry bushes. At the lower end of the valley the stream is joined by another of about the same size from the north-east, and the united waters flow south-west, in the direction in which our valley of the morning turns. We had again come within the area of cultivation.

Barley and turnips were growing round the village of La-ma-ya (12,476 feet), which we reached over a wooden bridge spanning the stream at 9.30 a.m. Here we put up in a good Tibetan house, and I made arrangements to leave my servant behind in charge of one of my chair-bearers, until my return from Batang. We spent the rest of the day and night at La-ma-ya and watched the life of the village. At 6 p.m. the cattle (yak), horses, sheep, and goats—the property of the whole village—were driven from the grassy hills into the village by a couple of shepherds, and, as they approached, the youngsters— mostly girls—turned out and took possession of their flocks and herds, carefully examining them the while, especially the eyes and neck, to see whether they had suffered any damage during the day. I watched the whole process from the roof of my Tibetan house. In the country districts west of Ta-chien-lu splinters of fir are the usual illuminant, and here I also found dried birch bark and the root of a plant called in Tibetan Sa Tung Chu, sticky like India rubber and smelling like gutta-percha when burning, used for the same purpose.

7th September

We left La-ma-ya at 6 a.m., having previously seen each family turn out its flocks and herds to the hills in charge of shepherds. There is a road leading south-west down the valley to Yünnan, but we struck west and north-west up a narrow valley to the summit of the pass called Yeh La Ka, whence there is a steep descent into a basin, down which flows a stream made up of brooks rushing out of numerous valleys in the mountains in the opposite side of the basin. At its north-east end the basin is stony, followed by marshy ground extending to the south-west. The road crosses the stream by a wooden bridge, and on the right bank we had breakfast on a boulder of lava. A hundred yards above the bridge, and on the right bank, there is a hot spring of no great size. From the bridge we struck south-west and west across the basin, which is entirely uncultivated, past numbers of fine large oblong obo, composed of slate, engraved with Tibetan characters. The road then ascends and crosses the Mang-ga La Pass, descending into a basin of grassy rounded hills, ending in a fine plateau, from which we obtained a magnificent view of a snowy range to the west.

A steep descent south-west leads into a narrow valley lying, north-west and south-east, with a goodly stream flowing in the latter direction. The Tibetan hamlet of about a dozen houses called Lei-kan-do (12,048 feet) lies on the left bank of the stream, where the road strikes the bottom of the valley, but we passed north-west up the left bank. At Lei-kan-do and below it, cultivation of barley and turnips was general, but, as we ascended, it ceased entirely, and gave way to a grassy bottom with bounding mountains, clad on the one side with silver fir and birch, and on the other with yew. The wild cherry, gooseberry, and currant also put in an appearance. Higher up the silver fir gave way to rhododendron, and on the summits the latter was replaced by grass.

As we neared the end of the valley, a magnificent view burst upon us. The valley opens out as the hamlet of Erh-lang-wan or Nenda (12,767 feet) is approached, and behind it, and towering some 7,000 feet above it, is Mount Nenda or Gé Ni, clothed a third of its height from the summit with a thick garment of perpetual snow. Below the snow-field the mountain was bare but green, while the valleys in the lower slopes were dark with trees. The south-east of the Nenda valley is bounded by high precipitous cliffs, such as are seen on the banks of the Upper Yang-tsze. To the north of Mount Nenda several snowy peaks showed themselves through a gap dividing Mount Nenda from the range which runs north and south. Obo were very plentiful in the Nenda valley.

Of trade there was not a sign during the day, but I learn that the trade between Litang and Batang is conducted by a small road which, leaving Litang, passes through Mai-ya-kou, a continuation of the Litang plain, and joins the high road at Ta-so, where we shall stay the day after tomorrow. So far as I can learn, brigandage and lack of good pasture, principally the former, has driven trade to leave the main road and seek a safer and better channel.

8th September

The steep cliffs which bound the Nenda valley on the south-east mark the entrance to another valley, along which lies the high road to the west, and down which flows the main branch of yesterday's stream. Proceeding south-west from Nenda, the road crosses a streamlet by a bridge and runs up the brow of a hill to the cliff valley, which opens out and presents some magnificent scenery. In the bottom flows the stream, and higher up, on the left bank, through a forest of silver fir and yew, runs the high road south-west. Between the right bank of the stream and the high fir-clad hills bounding the valley, fine grassy glades and plateaux slope down to the stream, presenting what would be incomparable sites for building purposes in any country but this, where there is no sign of life—not a house, not a human being, not an animal—to break the peaceful scene.

After a couple of hours in this beautiful country the valley turns direct east and west, and we followed it in the latter direction during the rest of the day along the left bank of the stream, now up above, and again down to its bed, and here and there wading where it had encroached on the roadway. The two Tibetan dogs accompanying our caravan had occasionally to swim at these places. The slopes of the mountains bounding the valley in the south were thickly clad with silver fir and birch, while the northern slopes were less wooded with yews and opened out in one or two places, through which we obtained excellent views of the snow-fields on Mount Nenda. There were numerous obo built up in the valley—layers of stone and turf surmounted by roofs of slate with Tibetan inscriptions—each surmounted by a carved wooden pole. We breakfasted beside one of these obo, and on the right bank of the stream opposite lay the remains of a Tibetan village, entirely deserted.

A little higher up we came suddenly upon a large caravan in the act of striking camp. It was encamped on the grassy left bank of the stream. There were over a hundred ponies and mules. They had just been brought in from grazing, and their pack-saddles were being adjusted. The loads were piled, and consisted of goat- and sheep-skins and Tibetan undyed cloth (Mu-tzŭ). In answer to our enquiries, we learned that it was bound for Litang from Batang. At a distance of 30 *li* from Nenda a wooden bridge called the Yünnan-ch'iao crosses the stream, and over it a small road leads to the Province of Yünnan.

As the head of the valley is neared, a stream enters the valley from the north, and silver firs give way to dwarf rhododendrons and ultimately to grass. This is very marked on the south bank. The road crosses the tributary by a wooden bridge, and keeps to the left bank of the main stream until the whole valley opens out, when it crosses the stream and runs north-west to the post station of San-pa or Ra Ti (13,286 feet), lying just beyond a hollow with a streamlet flowing southwards into the valley. Looking north-west from San-pa a good view is had of Nenda with the snow-fields creeping down its south-eastern flanks, and to the north and north-west other peaks are seen laden with snow.

San-pa is a miserable, dirty post station with five fami-lies, and we are occupying the best house, my room having no other light than that supplied by a hole in the roof, which also answers the purpose of a chimney. It is log-built, with flat roof, and is guiltless of windows. It is, I am told, the house and the very room in which a fellow-countryman died of fever six years ago when travelling westward bearing the torch of Christianity. His grave, covered with stones, is one of several stone-clad mounds making up the post station's cemetery on the left bank of the stream, a couple of hundred yards below the station itself. The Tibetans of the hamlet led us to the cemetery and pointed out his grave.

9th September

From San-pa, which we left at 5.45 a.m., the road runs west up the brow of a mountain, for the valley to the north-west is blocked by a cross-range, and turns north, becoming a deep gully, down which flows the stream into the San-pa valley. The cross-range is dark green in its lower slopes with silver fir. From the mountain brow the road leads up a stony valley, grass-green on both sides, and the bottom covered here and there with dwarf rhododendron and juniper. As we ascended we entered the clouds, and deep valleys on either side loomed through the gloom. After a two hours' ascent we arrived at the summit of the Rung-sé La or San-pa Shan Pass (15,437 feet). The ascent is gradual until within a few hundred feet of the summit, which has to be reached by a series of zigzags. The shouts of "Hla solo!" by our escort greeted the large obo and the large prayer-flags on the summit.

The descent on the opposite side is very steep, and we all dismounted. The road, of loose stones and shingle, leads down into a narrow valley, and zigzags north-west down a mountain side through a magnificent forest of silver firs, ultimately landing in the bottom of a narrow valley running north and south. Many of the firs measured from 12 feet to 20 feet in circumference at the base and must have been over 100 feet in height. By the roadside grew the tree-rhododendron, mountain ash, gooseberry and currant bushes, and under the firs stretched beautiful turf from which peeped wild strawberries. Facing us as we descended, rose from the west side of the valley a range of precipitous bare rock some 2,000 feet high, clad with silver firs in dense masses wherever they could find a foothold, the barren peaks rising high above the dark greenery of the trees.

Before reaching the bottom of the valley we came upon a fine circular clearing, so evidently intended for a halt that our whole caravan at once settled down to breakfast, and four different messes were soon at work lighting fires and preparing their respective meals. While preparations were proceeding, a small military official, with half-a-dozen Chinese soldiers, suddenly appeared from the forest below, and, having presented his card, informed me that he had been sent from Batang to meet and welcome me. He did not accompany us after breakfast, however, and I learned that he had business at San-pa, our last night's resting-place, to which he had proceeded. Descending through the forest to the valley through giant firs, many of which had fallen and obstructed the roadway and had to be cut in two to clear the way, we found a stream flowing south under the towering cliffs bounding the valley on the west side. The valley running north and south is from a quarter to half a mile wide in places, and opposite the western cliffs is bounded by a turf-clad mountain range bedecked with silver firs, and here and there surmounted by bare crags as on the west side. Low spurs drop here and there into the valley from the east side, and in several places the silver firs formed belts across the valley to the left bank of the stream, which is strengthened by mountain brooks from the east. The road runs northwards up this magnificent valley carpeted with beautiful green turf lit up with edelweiss and beautiful blue- and red-belled flowers.

In this, as in many other valleys through which we have recently passed, there is not a trace of cultivation. True it is that in the neighbourhood of the post stations there are a few enclosed fields containing hay which is cut for winter use, but these valleys are used for pastoral purposes only. On leaving the San-pa valley this morning there were scores of black tents dotted about, and yak and sheep were grazing in the valley and on the mountain side. Today's valley, called Sung-nung-kou, is no exception. Black tents are dotted round the few Tibetan houses forming the post station of Ta-so. To reach this place we followed the valley northwards, keeping to the left bank of the stream, which goes south to join the Chin-sha Chiang or Yang-tsze, until the road turns north-west across the stream over a three-arched wooden bridge to the foot of the bare rocky cliffs, at the base of which Ta-so lies. Before crossing the stream an excellent view was obtained, north-east up the valley, of a snow-clad mountain range.

A one-day's journey down the valley brings the traveller to Pomi, and four days more to Romi, where all kinds of cereals, except rice, are cultivated. I have already stated that a small trade road runs from Litang to Ta-so. It leaves Ta-so and enters a gully to the north-east and, passing to the north of Mount Nenda on to the Litang plain, is covered in three days, but there are no houses *en route*, and camping out is the rule. Ta-so is at a height of 12,992 feet above the level of the sea. Tomorrow's road enters between the rocky cliffs to the north-west of this Tibetan hamlet. One of the soldiers of the station has been informing me that deer occasionally visit the valley, and has just shown me the skin of a young lynx shot in the neighbourhood. We arrived at Ta-so at 1.15 p.m. We met two pilgrims in the Sung-nung-kou valley. They were returning from Lhassa, and had been two months on the way.

10th September

Rain fell overnight at Ta-so, and on the morning of the 10th September the summits of the mountains bounding the Sung-nung-kou valley were white with snow, while white fleecy clouds hung between the snow and the bottom of the valley. Entering between two rocky heights to the north-west, the road runs up a valley clad on both sides with silver firs, which, as we ascend, give place to junipers and ultimately to dwarf junipers as the tree line is passed. The valley is soon contracted by a mountain range, and the road keeps to the right along the left bank of the brook which emerges at Ta-so. Sleet and snow began to fall, and a pall of whiteness and gloom hung over the valley and the mountains bounding it. Up goes the road over ridge after ridge, till it passes a small lake lying at the base of bare, rugged, fantastically shaped, peaked heights, which seemed to bar future progress.

Through these, however, lies the road, which zigzags backwards and forwards over a face of small, loose, slippery stones, till the summit of the J'rah La Ka or Ta-so Shan Pass (16,486 feet) is reached. This is the highest and most difficult of all the passes between Ta-chien-lu and Batang, and many a shout of "Hla solo!" was raised as the large obo on the summit was reached at 9 a.m. The descent on the west side is very steep and slippery, and after sliding down about 800 feet we breakfasted in the tent of our Tibetan drivers, hastily erected to shelter us from the thickly falling snow. A few feet below us, on our left, there is a small lake.

After breakfast we again mounted our ponies, and descended north-west deep down into a valley, through a forest of silver fir, from which hung "Fairies' Scarf" in great profusion. Hour after hour the descent continued, over an execrable stone road, amid snow and sleet till, at 12.30 p.m., we made the post station of Pang-chai-mu or Pang-cha-mu, occupying a small piece of land in the south-east of the valley. It was pleasant, however, to look upon the small plots of yellow barley which lay round the five or six houses composing the post station. Pang-chai-mu is 12,875 feet above the level of the sea, so that in three-and-a-half hours we had descended 3,611 feet.

During the afternoon a despatch bearer arrived at the station with 40 or 50 letters and despatches from Lhassa, dated the 17th August. They were enclosed in a sheep-skin bag, and immediately reforwarded eastward by a messenger belonging to Pang-chai-mu.

Sleet and snow fell heavily after our arrival, and we spent the greater part of the night dodging the leaks in our miserable mud room, whose flat roof resembled a sieve. It was not a pleasant pastime, and when morning broke and immense snowflakes were silently spreading a white mantle on the ground, we were as loath as our followers to make a start, but another night in that room would have been unendurable.

11th September

There was no help for it. At 7 a.m. a start was at last effected, and our steep descent of yesterday was continued through the forest. The silver firs and prickly oaks, both laden with "Fairies' Scarf", were of great height and girth, the latter especially being larger than we had yet seen. Here and there immense silver firs had blocked the path, and had been severed by axe to clear the way. As we descended the firs became less dense, the snow turned to sleet, and by the time we had descended to the hamlet of Hsiao-pa-chung (Ma-chioh-hsi), 30 *li* from Pang-chai-mu, the sun was making great efforts to show his face. Below the region of the firs, raspberry bushes, laden with red, ripe fruit, frequently lined the path. A few cultivated patches surrounded Hsiao-pa-chung, and buckwheat put in an appearance.

On the way down we had heard the deep roaring of a brook as it tumbled down the deep valley on our left. This was joined by a similar stream issuing from a forest-clad valley to the north-east. The latter we crossed by a wooden bridge. The combined streams enter a narrow defile running north-west and south-east. Steep rocky mountains bound the defile, which frequently has room only for the mad rushing stream flowing north-west; and the road which, except for a few hundred yards, follows the right bank, is carved from the mountain side and in some places supported by rude wooden poles. The boulders scattered by the roadway and riven from the mountain side, and the narrowness of the path, which frequently overhangs the roaring stream below, do not add to one's feeling of security. In this defile the stream is bridged in two places, and we crossed from the right to the left bank for a few minutes, where the right bank proved too precipitous and rocky to carve a footpath. In this defile I was met by soldiers, under a petty officer, from Batang, who fired several volleys in my honour. The defile at last turns north and the road follows it, passing through an archway surmounted by a red Ch'örten. Another red Ch'örten stands by the roadside some distance beyond. Here two native chiefs, with a goodly following of Tibetans, met me. These were succeeded by the elders of Batang, and at the entrance to the town the Commissary and Captain welcomed me with tea and fruit. They informed me that they had prepared a house for myself and followers.

An elbow from the west side of the valley blocks the view of the Batang plain, and it is not until this is rounded that one looks down on green fields sloping to the left bank of the Batang River flowing westward at the base of a range of mountains showing a small glint of cultivation not far under the summit. The first house that meets the eye is a white lamasery of no great size; but, rounding the corner of the elbow, we enter, a few yards beyond, the brown-mud- and stone-built town of Batang, which lies on the right bank of the stream we had followed down the valley from Hsiao-pa-chung. Batang consists of about 400 Tibetan houses, with 500 families, only 70 to 80 of which are Chinese. The population, not including the occupants of the fine lamasery (itself nearly as large as the town, and situated on the left bank of the river above its junction with the stream on which Batang lies), amounts to about 2,000. The industries of the town are the manufacture of black leather and a kind of very inferior tasteless beer from barley.

The plain of Batang, which runs east and west, is some 2½ miles in length, with a breadth of from three-quarters of a mile to a mile. In the high mountains surrounding it there are three openings—the valley of the Hsiao-pa-chung River to the south-east by which we entered, and two valleys to the north-east and south-west by which the Batang River obtains ingress and egress. Three roads lead along these valleys—to Litang, to the State of Dergé, whose frontier is a couple of days' march distant, and to Tibet and Yünnan respectively.

The plain slopes gently from the town on the south side to the left bank of the Batang River, which flows along the base of the mountains bounding it on the north. It lies at an altitude of 9,184 feet above the level of the sea, and the climate is sufficiently temperate, owing to its sheltered position, to allow of two crops being harvested during the year. Wheat and barley are the two great summer crops, followed by the two buckwheats and millet. The autumn crops were in the ground at the time of my visit; sweet buckwheat (*Polygonum fagopyrum* L.) was casting its red blossoms, while bitter buckwheat (*P. tataricum* L.) was just opening its small white flowers. The latter is the taller plant of the two, and I was assured that it yields 50 per cent more in grain. I also noticed a patch or two of tobacco. The neighbourhood of the town is fairly well wooded with walnut, peach, and some mulberry trees. There was a vine in a garden at the back of the house in which I lived, and melons were in flower and fruit.

The town itself, which was completely destroyed by an earthquake in 1871, lies as I have said, on the right bank of the smaller stream. I wandered about its cobble-paved streets in the hope of collecting some information regarding its trade, visiting what the people were pleased to call shops. There were some half-a-dozen of them, but, so far as I could see, they contained nothing but the most trifling native goods, and I was assured that the total trade of the place was only about one-tenth of the trade of Litang.

In the course of my rambles I asked one of my escort where I could buy some honey. He replied that I might possibly be able to procure it at the lamasery. It is the same old story. As at Litang, the trade is almost entirely in the hands of the lamas, who are able to dictate their terms to the lay population. The lamaseries are gigantic trade concerns, and their practical monopoly accounts to a great extent for their wealth; but they have other sources of income. The personal belongings of every Tibetan layman fall, at his death, to the lamasery. A Tibetan in financial difficulties goes to the lamasery, which is only too willing to lend at exorbitant interest. Failure to pay interest and repay the loan lands the debtor and his land in the hands of his creditor, and whole families become what is called "Lama ssŭ poh hsing"—lamasery people—in other words, slaves. Half the land in the Batang plain (I was told officially one-third) has in this way come into the hands of the lamasery, and strengthened its hold of the grain trade.

The people of Batang are sombre and dull-looking compared with the Tibetans of Ta-chien-lu or even Litang. They are undoubtedly poorer, and certainly lack good looks. Nor do they affect ornamentation to any great extent to make up for the beauty which they lack. True, the fair sex wear silver ear-rings, rings, and bracelets; but, although I watched from the window of my room on two separate mornings women and girls carrying the day's water supply from the small river, I failed to see one that could in any way approach in looks the girls who carry firewood into Ta-chien-lu. The woman of Batang wears her hair parted in the middle and made up into a number of small plaits, which are caught behind in a long queue bound in three places with red cord, and finished off near her heels with a number of coloured silk tassels. She is not gay, and she is not attractive, and yet Batang is reputed to be the most immoral place west of Ta-chien-lu, which has nothing to boast of in this respect.

The Batang lamasery, which stands in the west of the plain near the left bank of the Batang River just above its junction with the small river, is a very large and imposing group of buildings surrounded by a high white wall encircled by a row of cypress and willow trees, It has two golden roofs and numerous pinnacles, like the monastery at Litang. It accommodates lamas or priests, variously estimated to number from 1,300 to 1,700, but it must not be supposed that this number is always resident, for lamas have the privilege of coming and going and apparently living as they please. I was here the spectator of a performance somewhat similar to that given at Ta-chien-lu. The scene was the grassy right bank of the Batang River below its junction with the small river, to reach which the former had to be crossed by a wooden bridge near the lamasery. Here tents were pitched in the form of a square, with an audience of lamas on two sides, while the other two sides were given up to the lama performers and the spectators from the town respectively. Round the square were smaller tents pitched by the well-to-do, and kitchens were hard at work cooking for their inmates. We strolled through the different booths, and created no little excitement.

An attempt is being made by the Chinese Government to reclaim and bring under cultivation all the waste land in the Batang plain and neighbourhood. Operations began in spring of the present year on the right bank of the Batang River in the east of the plain at the foot of the northern mountains, as well as on the left bank of the small river before it enters the plain. Some 200 Tibetans and Chinese are engaged in the work, and some 200 *mou* have been cleared, while 70 to 80 *mou* are already under crop, principally buckwheat. Houses have been built for the labourers, and these with the cleared land will be leased to intending farmers. A conduit for conveying water from the higher reaches of the small river to the cleared land on the latter's left bank was in course of being built. The scheme is at present in the hands of the Commissary, who is looking about for more land to conquer. Needless to say, it is not regarded with a favourable eye by the lamasery, which sees its percentage of land and crops being lessened and its profits likely to be curtailed.

The district of Batang is bounded on the north by Dergé, on the east by Chala, on the south by Romi, and on the west by Tibet. Dergé, Chala, and Romi are ruled by native chiefs under Chinese jurisdiction.

13th September

Having come as far west as Batang, it seemed to me desirable to continue my journey to the Tibetan frontier, only three-and-a-half days' distant. Although the local authorities promised me every assistance in procuring transport, no sooner had the animals arrived and been paid for, on the morning of the 13th September, than three of the four drivers promptly left with the money and did not return, and my own chair-bearers came at the last moment and declared that an employé of the yamen to whom they had given money to buy flour for them had been unable to procure any. There was a conspiracy somewhere, but with the assistance of the one driver, my interpreter, and a begging Tibetan, I was able to get the loads strapped on the pack animals and we started at 10 a.m. I had been told that the Commissary and Captain intended to accompany us, but they had not put in an appearance when we started. Four Tibetan soldiers, sent by the native chiefs, and a couple of Chinese soldiers escorted us, and I was preceded for some distance by a few boys, yamen runners, and a red umbrella sent by the Commissary.

Crossing the bridge over the small river on whose right bank Batang lies, we marched south-west down the valley. The small river joins the Batang River below the lamasery, and we followed the left bank of the combined waters down the valley, passing several Tibetan houses with their cultivated patches of buckwheat. The bounding hills were clad with grass and brushwood, principally dwarf rhododendrons, but in the neighbourhood of the farmhouses were peach, walnut, willow, and other trees. The peaches, which were almost ripe, were very small and flavourless. Here we met a caravan, mostly of donkeys, laden with bags of salt. The salt wells lie four days' journey to the south, and the place where the salt is produced is called Yen Ching, i.e., salt wells. Yen Ching, Yerkalo, or Ya-k'a-lo, lies on the left bank of the Mekong. There are brine wells on both banks of the river, and the salt is the product of sun evaporation.

During the morning, owing to the scarcity of drivers, we were considerably delayed by stampeding among our pack animals. The mule with the provision boxes and an adjustable table on the top, packed in oil-cloth, determined to return to Batang, and was chased for at least an

hour through the brushwood by the escort, resulting in
the destruction of the oil-cloth and the scattering of the
pieces of the table. These had to be collected, and the
mendicant Tibetan solved the difficulty of their carriage
by putting the smaller pieces in the capacious folds of his
gown and the round top of the table up his back. In this
guise he led the provision mule the rest of the day.

A mountain, capped with snow, loomed ahead to the
south-west, and snow-peaks appeared wherever there was
an opening in the valley from which the distant mountains
could be seen. When the Batang River took a westerly
course, leaving no room on its left bank for the road, the
latter zigzagged up a steep hillside—the Ch'a-shu Shan—
whose summit is adorned with an obo and prayer-flags.
Beyond the pass the road, now broad and good, slopes
gently down into a deep valley, and soon a patch of yellow
muddy water was seen at the base of mountains to the
west. At last we had reached the Chin-sha Chiang (the
Yang-tsze). Deep down on our right the Batang River had
ceased to hurry, and its green waters were peacefully glid-
ing to the Great River.

The Yang-tsze, even here a noble river from 400 to 500
yards wide, and narrowing in places to less than 300 yards,
was issuing from a tortuous mountain defile to the north
and flowing southwards. It lay 1,000 feet or more below
us, and had the same muddy colour as in its lower reaches.
The road running along its left bank descends gradually to
its bed till, at the hamlet of Niu-ku, our ponies were wading in the edge of the river. Looking back at its confluence
with the Batang River, we noticed a sharp line of demar-
cation between the latter's clear and the Great River's
muddy water. The mountains bounding the Yang-tsze are
treeless and are scantily clad with grass and undergrowth.

At Niu-ku, where the Yang-tsze contracts to about 250
yards, there were two wooden ferry-boats, and a road

zigzagging up the opposite bank leads to Ch'amdo in Tibet. This is the small road which passes through the town of Hsi-sung-kung, 30 *li* distant, and through the State of San Ai, in which is the Chala lamasery with 200 lamas, whose abbot is paid 400 taels a year by the Commissary of Batang to keep that part of the country quiet. This sum is paid from the salt revenue of Batang. The distance from Batang to Ch'amdo by this small road is 12 days against 17 by the main road. San Ai is the country of the red lamas (Hung Chiao). A mile south of Niu-ku, and on the same bank of the river, are three houses and a small lamasery with two red Ch'örtens overlooking the Yang-tsze. The hamlet, called Shui-mo-kou, distant 40 *li* from Batang, lies at the mouth of a narrow valley down which flows a brook to join the Great River. Looking up the valley, a snow-capped peak appeared in the far distance.

We found excellent quarters in a Tibetan house in the hamlet, which we reached at 2.30 p.m. Had we gone further it would have been impossible to find accommodation before dark, and, as comfort of any kind is exceptional in this remote region, we had no hesitation in making up our minds to remain for the night. A few minutes after our arrival the Commissary and Captain of Batang turned up with a following of 13 or 14 men, and expressed their intention of accompanying us to the frontier to see that all was safe. I am aware that information has reached these officials that the British have entered Lhassa, but the date of entry I have not yet ascertained. A memorial to the throne by the Imperial Resident for Tibet arrived at Batang yesterday.

14th September

Starting from Shui-mo-kou at 6 a.m., we followed southwards the road which runs along the left bank of the river

as far as Chu-pa-lung. The road is fairly easy, with occasional sharp and rocky corners, where ridges come down
to the river. Chu-pa-lung (8,430 feet) is the regular ferry
station at low water, but about a mile south of it, and on
the opposite bank, the River of Golden Sand is joined by
a tributary issuing from a valley, and fording of it by pack
animals is a difficulty at high-water season. The result is
that the ferry is lower down. Just below the junction
there is a shingle island, partly clad with grass and brushwood, in mid-river. Chu-pa-lung was surrounded by
willow and walnut trees and an occasional persimmon,
and to show its mildness of climate, I may mention that
the garden of the house in which we breakfasted was full
of cabbages, melons, onions, carrots, capsicums, and
tobacco in full leaf. There is a village on the right bank
opposite Chu-pa-lung, and under the latter there was a
large shingle bank.

When we left Shui-mo-kou I observed a couple of
hide-boats alongside the left bank, and soon afterwards
they passed us, carried by the current and propelled by a
single paddle. Those hide-boats, with hair outside, are
made by lashing four pieces of wood together in the shape
of an oblong, the two side-pieces being longer than bow
and stern. To these stout twigs are attached and bent round
to form the bottom of the boat of a depth of some $2\frac{1}{2}$ feet,
and the bottom and sides are covered with raw-hide. They
are exceedingly light, and are transported from water to
land and land to water, each by one man, the boat, being
turned upside down with the bottom resting on the individual's head. There was a long wooden ferry-boat at
Chu-pa-lung, but it was leaking and not in use. It was
divided up into several compartments and measured 9 feet
by 60 feet.

Proceeding down the left bank through dense brushwood, we struck the high-water ferry, after traversing

about 3 miles. The ferry-boat (there was only one) was nearing the opposite bank when we arrived, and there was a large caravan waiting opposite. This caravan, as we discovered on crossing, was made up of about 150 animals, and was in the act of carrying brick tea from Litang to the Chaya lamasery, four days distant from Chiangka (Gartok), which in turn is six stages from Batang. Three trips of the ferry-boat, which was manned by six men—three and two respectively on two long oars near the bows and one on a spar helm—were required to carry our caravan across, including the two Chinese officials and their retinue. The passage occupied five minutes, and the boat was carried down river about 500 yards. On reaching the right bank I noticed tea stacked on the left bank some distance below the ferry, and guarded by Tibetan watch-dogs. It belonged to the caravan whose pack animals and part of the tea had already crossed, but their work was interrupted by our arrival. The caravan drivers stated that they had been two days at the ferry, and did not expect to complete the passage that day. The road along the left bank does not cease at the ferry, it continues south to Romi, a four days' journey from Batang.

Our road now lay along the right bank of the river, through thick scrub and brushwood, in which grass and other wreckage had been caught during floods. About a mile below the ferry the river, which from the time we struck it after the passage of the Ch'a-shu Shan, had been placid with a strong, but not rapid, current, is blocked by two long parallel ridges of rock and loose stone, turning its course from south to south-east, and converting it into a mad, dashing torrent, which has swept away a great part of its mountainous east bank, leaving a bare, steep precipice. Beyond, it contracts to a little over 100 yards in breadth, and becomes a roaring mass of white billows, baffling any thought of possible navigation.

The road further south was somewhat dangerous, pass-ing under a precipitous earth and boulder bank showing signs of frequent collapse. At last the valley is blocked by rising ground, on which the hamlet of Kung La, or Go Ra, with some cultivated patches of barley and buck-wheat, is perched, and the river, again placid, turns south-east to avoid a mountain side, and resumes its southerly course in a valley a few hundred yards beyond. Tibetan farmhouses with cultivated patches were fre-quently seen along the river, especially on the right bank. At these spots trees, especially walnut, were in evidence, contrasting with the general grass and scrub covering the mountain sides bounding the river itself.

We reached Kung La or Go Ra at 4.20 p.m. only to find that it was not the end of the stage, and that we had still 20 *li* to accomplish. On rounding Kung La the road, after several windings, runs up a steep mountain side and ascends a valley, down which flows a streamlet to join the Chin-sha Chiang. Below us lay patches of yellow barley, buckwheat in bloom, and green millet. The road runs south-west up the valley, crossing and re-crossing the stream, and it was 6 p.m. and all but dark before we reached the hamlet of Ta-ko-ting. This valley is full of obo, consisting of oblong platforms of stones, with pyra-mids of marble slabs cut with Tibetan characters piled round carved wooden poles. Some of the slabs contained the whole prayer *Om Mani Padmé Hum*, but the majority had only a single syllable of the prayer, and in nearly every case the letters were coloured.

My chair did not turn up until two hours after we had ridden into Ta-ko-ting, and I had to send out several of my escort to bring the bearers in, for they were utterly demor-alized, having assured me at Kung La that they had had nothing to eat since morning; that two of their number, who had been left behind at Batang to bring up a supply of flour, had not arrived; and that they were completely exhausted. Rice is unprocurable, and they do not take kindly to the tsamba, which is practically the food of the Tibetans among whom we are travelling.

15th September

On leaving Ta-ko-ting the road enters a narrow defile ascending through a forest of silver fir, prickly oak, wild cherry, peach, and other trees, and crossing and re-crossing the descending brook at least a score of times until after a couple of hours' climb the summit of the K'ung-tzŭ-ka Pass is attained. Many a noble specimen of fir lay across the defile and formed a natural bridge across the brook. From the summit an excellent view is obtained of the valley of the Yang-tsze we had been threading the two previous days.

A quarter of an hour's easy descent from the summit through a grassy basin brought us to the hamlet of K'ung-tzŭ-ting (11,964 feet) with its score of Tibetan houses. To the south-west lies a deep valley bounded by high mountains clad with fir and oak, a range of snow-clad mountains running parallel to the valley on the south-east side behind the bounding range. Round K'ung-tzŭ-ting, and creeping down into the valley, were many cultivated patches of barley, wheat, turnips, and peas, while raspberry and gooseberry bushes hedged the roadside. Cultivation ceased at a deep valley to the south-east which a stream, flowing down the main valley, enters, to disappear in the direction of the snow-clad range. Forest now takes the place of cultivation, and the valley is narrowed by a spur jutting into it from the south-east.

Forest is again succeeded by cultivation and grassland, on which herds of cattle, horses, donkeys, goats, and pigs were feeding, and in the neighbourhood of Chung-mang-li a pretty well-wooded valley creeps up between the mountains to the south-cast and is overlooked by the snowy range behind. In the main valley are lines of obo marking the roadway, and every homestead in the valley seemed to have, in addition, a private obo of its own. In this valley, as well as in the Yang-tsze valley, the women, old and young, were very badly afflicted with goitre. South-west of the grassland cultivation became more general, till it ceased at the hamlet of Pang-mu-t'ang (12,161 feet), lying near the foot of a range of grass-clad hills on the west side of the valley.

Pang-mu-t'ang, Shang-mang-li, or Trang-ba-la-tza, as it is also called, is the meeting point of two roads, one going south by way of A-tun-tzŭ to Yünnan, and the other west to Lhassa. The frontier of Ssuchuan and Tibet along the Lhassa road is distant about 4 miles from Pang-mu-t'ang, and I resolved to visit the frontier, which is stated in Chinese books to be marked by a boundary stone erected in 1727. Rumours had reached me all along the road, after leaving Ta-chien-lu, that the Tibetans had heard of my approach at the head of an army and were prepared to resist an invasion of Tibet from the east. My caravan had arrived within 4 miles of the frontier; the wildest rumours were now afloat, and the Chinese officials who accompa-nied me from Batang were manifestly disconcerted. The Tibetan elders of Pang-mu-t'ang had ridden as far east as K'ung-tzŭ-ting to announce that Tibetan scouts were waiting in the village to carry the news of my arrival to the Tibetan chief guarding the frontier. I had informed the Chinese authorities that I had no intention of entering Tibet; that my journey, as they could see from the number of my followers, was a peaceful one; and that I merely wished to visit and personally see at this point the frontier of Ssuchuan and Tibet. We arrived at Pang-mu-t'ang at 1.30 p.m. of the 15th September, and, as the Chinese authorities wished for time to arrange matters, I resolved to defer my visit to the frontier until next morning, and informed them that I would start early. Rumours brought to me during the afternoon and evening were so conflicting that I made up my mind to disregard them entirely.

16th September

The coming and going of armed cavalry along the Tibetan road during the afternoon of the 15th September showed that negotiations regarding my visit to the frontier were proceeding between the Chinese and Tibetan authorities and next morning I was informed that the matter had been satisfactorily arranged, but, as the Chinese officials told me later, they were not altogether easy in their minds as to the reception I might receive from the Tibetan soldiery. The Commissary expressed the wish that I would allow them to have a good start, and at 6 a.m. the Commissary and Captain, preceded by a few unarmed Tibetan (Ssuchuan) cavalry, set out. I followed a little later with Mr James Moyes—of the China Inland Mission, who was good enough to accompany me from Ta-chien-lu to the frontier and back, and whose knowledge of Tibetan was of great value—my writer, interpreter, and the Chinese and Tibetan soldiers who had escorted me from Batang. The escort numbered 15 Tibetans and eight Chinese. We were all mounted and unarmed.

Proceeding westward we zigzagged up the face of the hill which lies behind Pang-mu-t'ang, and then skirted a continuation of yesterday's valley, wherein were signs of former cultivation. Entering an open valley running south-west, we saw coming towards us what at first appeared to be a merchant caravan, but which on its nearer approach turned out to be part of the entourage of a lama of high rank. The pack animals were laden with personal baggage, and enquiry of the drivers and others led to the statement that the owner was the Lama of Hsi-ning or Amdo, on his way out from Ch'amdo. I afterwards learned that he had passed through Batang, *en route* to Lhassa, in May, but that, owing to the troubles in Tibet, he had proceeded only as far as Ch'amdo, and was now on his way out. Lamas of inferior rank, with tall, gilt, pagoda-shaped hats, were in charge of the advance guard of the caravan.

As we were ascending some low hills beyond the second valley we met the lama himself, travelling in a green sedan chair borne by four Chinese bearers, with relief bearers, and escorted by a retinue of from 30 to 40 mounted men, Tibetan and Chinese, some of the latter with buttons on their official hats. The sedan chair was closed, and only the vague outline of a human face could be seen through the glass window in front. There was a running fire of questions as to our respective destinations, and one grey-bearded old man asked whether we were going into Tibet. When I answered that we were proceeding only as far as the frontier, he said, "You have not far to go", and such proved to be the case, for we soon turned north-west up a steep hillside—the Ning-ching Shan— the ridge of which forms the boundary line at this point of Ssuchuan and Tibet.

Under the brow I was met by the Chinese authorities, who again begged me not to cross the boundary line, which lay a few yards above us. Having been reassured that I had not the slightest intention of setting a foot in Tibet, they begged me to wait a few minutes, until they made the necessary disposition of troops along the boundary line, which was guarded on the Tibetan side by armed soldiers. In a few minutes I was invited to ascend the brow of the hill, where I found the Tibetan soldiers arranged in a line running north-east and south-west. In front of the Tibetan soldiers another line of Ssuchuan Tibetan soldiers, equal in number to the latter, was drawn up. The Tibetan soldiers, who were armed with matchlocks and swords, were under the command of a chief, and a lama with a gilt pagoda hat stood by his side. There was perfect silence as, escorted by the Chinese authorities, I went up to the boundary stone which marks the frontier of the two countries, but I could see a fixed determination on the faces of the troops to resist any attempt on my part to cross into Tibet. The boundary stone, which stands some 30 yards to the north-east of an obo by the roadside, is a well-worn, four-sided pillar of sandstone, about 3 feet in height, each side measuring some 18 inches. There was no inscription on the stone, and when unthinkingly I made a movement to look for writing on the Tibetan side, the Chinese officials at once stepped in front of me and barred the road to Tibet.

Looking into Tibet the eye met a sea of grass-covered treeless hills, and from the valley at the foot of the Ning-ching Shan rose smoke from the camp fires of 400 Tibetan troops charged with the protection of the frontier. There was no time to make any prolonged inspection, for the Chinese authorities were anxious for me to leave as soon as possible. As I had attained one of the objects of my journey—a visit to the eastern frontier of Tibet—I had no wish to remain longer, and mounting our horses, we rode down the Chinese slopes of the Ning-ching Shan. No sooner had we descended, than first a mounted scout, and then a swarm of Tibetans on foot, rushed to a hill-top commanding a view of our road back to Pang-mu-t'ang, and I am under the impression that they were satisfied that they had successfully resisted a British invasion from the east.

Some official details of the occupation of Lhassa by the British reached the Commissary the first day west of Batang; that the British, 3,000 in number, reached Lhassa without fighting on the 3rd August; that the Dalai Lama fled to the district of Nagch'uka on the 26th July; and that the two lamaseries of Drébung and Sérá had supplied the invaders with 3,000 loads (6,000 sacks) of grain. The

Gadän lamasery, I was told, was still bitterly hostile, which is probably attributable to its greater distance from Lhassa. Whether the Tibetan troops on the frontier were aware of these details on the morning of my visit is doubtful. At any rate, no hostility, nothing more than a determination to prevent the passage of the frontier, was shown to me.

17th September to 5th October

The return journey from the frontier to Ta-chien-lu was accomplished in 20 days, including one day's rest at Batang and another at La-ma-ya, where I picked up my servant who was fortunately convalescent and able to proceed. The road was the same; but we varied the stages so as to avoid the places where we had spent uncomfortable nights—a plan which was not altogether successful—and to accelerate our progress through a country no longer new to us. Even in that short time, however, the aspect of the country had considerably changed. Winter was approaching; the leaves of trees and shrubs, especially the prickly oak and maple, had taken on their autumn tints, and in many places thickly carpeted the ground; most of the wild flowers had dropped their petals and were going to seed; and the harvesters were mowing, with reaping hook, their crops of barley, wheat, and oats.

In some places in the lower valleys only the stubble remained on the ground, and the golden sheaves were stacked on the roofs of the homesteads. Snow lay on one or two of the passes. Black tents were pitched in great numbers in the valleys where not a tent had previously been seen, and enormous herds of yak and horses were grazing in the bottom lands and large flocks of sheep dotted the mountain slopes. One valley we passed through reminded me forcibly of a cattle market, so densely was it packed with horses and yak. The colder weather had driven them from the uplands to the valleys, and when winter arrives they will follow the latter southwards.

The people of Tibet

As the country was no longer new to me, I had more time to devote to the people, their life and habits, and I propose now to say a few words on this subject.

West of Ta–chien-lu the country is to all intents and purposes Tibetan. There are here and there Chinese courier or post stations along the high road; but the soldiers stationed there, exceedingly few in number, take to themselves Tibetan wives, and are practically absorbed by the race around them. They learn Tibetan, and their children speak Tibetan better than Chinese. Even the Tibetan prayer-flags float over the roofs of their Tibetan houses. The people therefore—their houses, clothing, food, language, and religion—are Tibetan. Physically, the Tibetans are a much finer race than the Chinese. It is rare to meet an under-sized male. They are tall, lithe, and wiry, and, except among the lamas, who lead a more sedentary life, there is an absence of obesity. Their magnificent climate, outdoor life, and abundance of exercise make men of them. They carry gun and sword in defence of caravan, or when called upon to form an escort, and they shoot with wonderful precision, considering the weapon with which they are armed. The swords I have not seen in use except for collecting firewood in the forest. But if one admires the man, how much more the woman?

In a land where each family devotes one or even two of its sons to the priesthood, female infanticide is unheard of, and woman is a very valuable asset. She is the life, the mainspring of the Tibetan household. She milks the cattle before they are sent out to graze in the early morning and on their return in the evening. This done, she slings the empty wooden water butt, some $2\frac{1}{2}$ feet long by 18 inches or more in diameter, on her back and runs off to the nearest stream for the day's water supply. Filling the butt by means of a birch-bark baler, she balances it on her back, the bottom resting on an adjustable pad of cloth or fibre, and the upper part kept in position by a rope or raw-hide thong encircling butt and chest. This visit to the stream she repeats several times during the morning, storing the supply in a large round wooden vat. She makes the butter, an important article of food in a country whose altitude defies the growth of oil plants, and where the difficulties and cost of transport are prohibitive, in the wooden churn of our forefathers, without, however, that care and cleanliness which they bestowed upon it. She prepares the food, she weaves the cloth, and she attends to the many other duties of the household, besides engaging, when necessary, in the usual outdoor work of the farm. Where, too, there are no male members in a family, or when they are otherwise employed, she accompanies the transport animals as a driver and sees that they are properly cared for and taken back. She trudges along merrily with the other drivers, entering into the amusements and gossip of the road.

A Tibetan family

I stayed two days in a Tibetan house in the Litang district and watched the life of its inmates. They were a widow, exceptionally short for a Tibetan woman but exceedingly active, of under 50, two sons of 30 and 26, and two daughters of about 17 and 14. The elder son, who was or had been a priest (he still wore the dress of a lama), was married, and his wife and child of about four were members of the family. They were seven in all. The elder son was, owing to his profession, a loafer, and, so far as I could see, his duties consisted in keeping the keys of the store-room and family shrine, which he entered from time to time to dispose of tsamba to my followers, and perform the religious duties of the house. Our residence may, however, have had something to do with his confinement to the house, for he had a keen eye and longing for an empty water bottle, which, owing to breakages, I was unable to satisfy.

The younger son was not so much in evidence: he had some outdoor work to attend to; but the women and girls were always on the move and at work in the house or out of doors. They all wore the Litang forelock hanging down to the tip of the nose, another device for concealing their charms, and their hair was done up in numerous plaits which straggled down the back, but hidden, in the case of the widow and wife, by an elaborate head-dress. A cross band of black cloth was affixed to the top of the head, and central and side bands attached to it hung down the back, and the ends of these rear bands were joined together with strings of beads—red, white, and green. The cross band on the top of the head had two round silver ornaments attached to it, one on each side of the crown, and a larger heart-shaped silver ornament lay on the back of the head, fixed to the central band behind. These were set with coral in the centre and were the most conspicuous; but the rear bands were laden with smaller silver circular pieces about the size of a rupee. The girls wore a couple of small silver disks on the crown, and their head-dress was completed with the usual strings of coloured beads. Butter is their hair oil. They all had the usual silver ear-rings and brooches at the necks of their loose gowns, made of grey undyed woollen cloth woven on the premises.

There was a loom on the roof of the house, where one of the girls was occasionally to be seen weaving. It had four healds, worked by foot in the usual way. The shuttle was long and flat, and the woollen weft threads were driven home by both hands. The cloth was 12 English inches wide. It is frequently dyed red for wear by both sexes, and the dye used is *Rubia cordifolia* L. Their natural feet were encased in long cloth boots soled with soft hide.

I joined this family at one of their meals and took a minor part in its preparation. Husked barley is baked for a short time in a flat cooking-pot and then ground into flour in the usual stone mill worked by hand. The barley-meal, called tsamba, is collected and placed in a hide bag. A handful of brick tea is thrown into a large copper cooking-pot narrowing slightly at the neck. A little cold water is poured into the pot, and as soon as it comes to the boil more cold water is added. When this in turn boils, the contents are removed by copper ladle and passed through a conical strainer into a small churn, wherein some butter (in this case about $\frac{1}{2}$ lb) had been dropped; a little salt was also added. The duty assigned to me was to churn the tea and butter together, and, as the churn had no lid, I succeeded in splashing myself with the liquid compound at the first attempt. The dasher, however, must not be worked vertically, as I thought, but sideways, and I soon learned the art of mixing butter and tea.

The compound was then ladled out and passed through the strainer into a large copper teapot, whence it is poured into the usual wooden cups. We all sat on the floor—for a Tibetan house is practically devoid of furniture of any kind—holding the cups or bowls in our hands. Each sipped about a third of the buttered tea, and then took a handful of tsamba from the hide bag and placed it in the cup, kneading the whole into a dough with the fingers. There are no spoons, forks, or chop-sticks, and pieces of the warm dough are simply carried by hand to mouth. This is the ordinary Tibetan meal, the cups being replenished at will; but several times a month beef or mutton is partaken of in the early morning or in the evening, not with the tsamba meal. It is boiled without salt, divided up by knife, and eaten with salt by hand. It is occasionally eaten raw. So with vegetables, such as turnips: they are eaten uncooked, and a favourite tit-bit is the green husked grains of barley, which they toss into their mouths with remarkable dexterity.

The State of Dergé is justly famed for its copper work, especially teapots; but many of the copper cooking utensils used in this part of the country are made at Ning-yüan Fu in the Chien-ch'ang valley.

It is a pity that some of the water drawn every day for the Tibetan household is not used on the person. Dirt, like the writing on their prayer-flags, is considered a phylactery. We had many visitors during our stay in the Tibetan house, and I asked the men how often they washed their faces. Quite unabashed, they readily replied, "Four or five times a year". It was very amusing to watch the women washing their hands. Filling a large copper ladle with cold water, the lady of the house placed the handle between her teeth and tilted it over so that the water fell in driblets on her hands, which she rubbed together vigorously. No soap or other material was used. This was no isolated case; I saw the same performance in various parts of the country.

Every Tibetan male carries, suspended from his girdle, a small leather steel and tinder case usually handsomely mounted with silver. This is not for lighting his pipe, for smokers are the exception, but for igniting the match of his gun or kindling a fire in camp. Nearly all the men take snuff, and the snuff-mull, which is carried in the capacious breast of the gown, is handed round the company, as in our own land not so many years ago. The mull is made of yak horn, with a tiny outlet at the squared tip, and it requires considerable effort to make it part with its contents on the thumb-nail. Many of the mulls are beautifully mounted with silver. The snuff itself, however, is very inferior; it is manufactured by spreading tobacco leaves on a slab of stone and crushing them to powder with a large pebble.

Tibetan architecture

I have already indicated in a general way the nature of
Tibetan architecture; but it may not be out of place to give
a few details regarding a Tibetan house. The building is
square or oblong, with walls about 30 feet high and from
18 inches to 2 feet thick, built entirely of brown stone and
mud. There is more solidity than beauty about the struc-
ture. The stones, which are small and irregular in shape, are
squared or flat on one side only, and are fitted together
with mud so evenly as to suggest the use of a plumb-line.
About 15 feet from the earthen floor stout round beams
are let into the walls, and these are supported by heavy,
round wooden pillars resting on stone bases embedded in
the ground. When the beams are of insufficient length to
cross from wall to wall, the ends of two beams are placed
together and a hollowed-out block of wood fitted below
their point of contact, on each side of which it projects
several feet. The centre of this block rests, of course, on a
pillar forming, so to speak, its crown. I have counted as
many as 20 of these pillars in the lower storey, which is the
basement of the whole superstructure.

The basement, which is windowless, is invariably the
byre and stable combined, and in the lower part of each
pillar a hole is drilled, giving passage to a rope for tying up
the cattle overnight. Entrance is had to the basement by a
large oblong doorway fitted with a solid two-leaved door,
which is closed by a cross-bar fitting into holes in the side
walls. On the beams a thick layer of branches or long cut
pieces of wood are laid, and on these earth or mud is
spread and beaten hard. This is the ceiling of the basement
and the floor of the next storey, but an opening some 6
feet by 5 feet is left in it through which access to the second storey is gained. Against the centre of one of the sides
of this opening a broad-stepped ladder or, more generally,
a notched log of wood rests, and, to one unaccustomed to

the latter, the ascent, owing to the smoothness of the notches, is by no means easy.

The second storey, containing the living rooms, is similarly constructed, but here the walls have a number of small oblong openings, sometimes with lintels, which serve as windows. They have frames with one wooden bar down the centre, and in more pretentious houses two such bars may be seen. They have neither glass nor paper, but can be closed in cold weather by two-leaved shutters fitted inside on the sill. In the ceiling there is another large opening, leading by another notched log to the mud roof, as well as a number of small square holes, sometimes fitted with open-work wooden caps to keep out rain or snow. These admit light, but their use is to allow the smoke to escape from the rooms below, for a Tibetan house has no chimneys.

Running along one side of the roof, in country houses at any rate, there is another flat-roofed building open in front with wooden pillars. This is the granary, where sheaves and grain are protected from the inclemency of the weather. On the top of this again is built the small round or square furnace with conical roof, fitted usually with the narrow neck of an earthenware jar as a chimney. Here the juniper or other green branches are burned as incense in the early morning, and by its side are usually planted one or more poles with fluttering prayer-flags. Where there is no granary the furnace is built on the roof. Occasionally there is a parapet round the roof, but, as a general rule, the latter is on a level with the top of the wall.

With the exception of one or two tables about a foot high there is no furniture in a Tibetan house. The inmates sit and sleep on the floor, which, in the living rooms, is usually boarded. As a rule, there is only one large bedroom, where the inmates sleep huddled together under a mass of fur clothing. In warm weather they sleep on the roof, and

I have frequently seen children emerging half-naked from what I took to be clothing being aired. In the room set apart for the kitchen the cooking range consists of a plat-form of mud and stone, with circular openings for the pots, and large arched furnaces underneath for the fire-wood. Not a nail is used in the construction of the house.

Tibetan agriculture, flora and fauna
The country between Ta-chien-lu and the Tibetan frontier is a land of mountain, forest, valley, and river, rarely falling below an altitude of 10,000 feet above the sea. Grass and certain wild flowers seem to grow at any height; but, so far as my observation goes, the limit of cultivation of any kind is under 13,000 feet. In valleys between 12,000 and 13,000 feet certain cereals, such as barley, wheat, and oats, as well as small round turnips are grown; but immediately that height is exceeded grass covers the land. But even when working cultivable areas the Tibetan is a poor farmer. With his team of yak or couple of yak harnessed to his one-handled wooden plough, he does little more than scratch the surface of the ground, and he fails to warm and suffi-ciently enrich his fields with his abundant stable manure.

I took many opportunities of examining his standing grain, and while the ears were, on the whole, well devel-oped, and there was good length of straw, the crop was, as a rule, exceedingly thin. Stacks of manure lay unused in his stable and littered the roads and approaches to his home-stead. The fact of the matter is, the country is far more pastoral than agricultural, and the people inhabiting it are better fitted for the former than the latter. Tent life, with its horse-breeding and cattle- and sheep-raising, is more to their taste than the cultivation of fields. Their agricultural implements are exceedingly primitive. There is the one-handled plough mentioned above; the flail is that of our forefathers, but more primitive; the fork is the forked branch of a tree; and the winnowing machine is the wind of heaven. Troughs and the like—even the grain measure—are carved from the trunks of trees, and very rough work at its best.

Any one who has seen Highland cattle will, by imagining clumsy animals about double the size, have a very fair idea of what yak are. If he will further imagine that they are nearly all black, that their black horns have a simple semicircular curve, and that they have long very bushy tails, his idea will be still nearer the mark. True, I have seen coloured yak, black yak with white faces and white tails, but these are the exceptions to the general jet-blackness of the animal. They are very hairy animals, their coats in winter being many inches long. The males become pack animals, and on the way back from the frontier I met two tea caravans, each of about 200 animals, entirely composed of yak. They are slow, plodding animals, but well-fitted for work on these mountain roads. Yak milk is the milk of the country, and provides butter and curds. The dzo, or Chinese Pien Niu, the cross between the yak and the cow, is also used as a pack animal, and is noted for its strength and endurance. It is, however, much rarer than the yak.

As regards the fauna of the country, I am not a mighty hunter; the animals did not come to me, and I did not go in search of them. I saw two tame wapiti, three musk deer in captivity, a herd of wild sheep on a mountain slope several thousand yards away, a wild pig, a few squirrels, a young fox on a chain, and the skin of a lynx; but bear are quite common, and I noticed their paws for sale in a shop in Ta-chien-lu.

If, as a mere amateur, I hazard an opinion as to the flora, it is that at the time of my visit it was more profuse than varied. I have made a small collection, and hope to have an opportunity of submitting the specimens to a competent authority later.

Tibetan religion and education

The religion of the people may be described as mechanical. They have their lamaserics, where, or on the street, they may engage priests to perform their religious duties—chant the sacred books, beat drums, and turn prayer cylinders or wheels. The latter are always turned from right to left, whether by hand, water, or air. They vary in size. In the house of a headman I counted over 20 let upright into different walls. They were made of raw-hide from 3 feet to a foot in length, and from a foot to several inches in diameter. They are filled with written or printed prayers, and the turn of a cylinder by hand is equivalent to uttering a prayer. Small cylinders for hand use are made of silver, copper, or white metal, some of them of beautiful workmanship. I found it difficult to purchase specimens of these, and the reason given me at Litang was that they are supposed to be cremated with their owners. Cylinders turned by water power are common, and I have seen them fitted to small windmills inserted in the apertures which do duty for chimneys on the house-tops. The draught was sufficient to turn mill and cylinder. On the road some of the members of my escort were always muttering what I took to be prayers, and even the women carrying water were, especially in Batang, usually reciting in a low voice something only intelligible to themselves.

The obo have also a religious significance. They are of two kinds: on the mountain passes they consist of mere conical heaps of stones thrown by passing travellers, and decked with prayer-flags on their summits. Each stone is a thank-offering to the gods for safety, while in the valleys they are more elaborate, usually oblong and built of stone, or alternate layers of turf and stone, some 3 feet or less in height, heaped like a sloping roof with slabs of slate or marble, inscribed with whole prayers or the single letters making up the invocation *Om Mani Padmé Hum*. Rising from the centre of this heap of prayers there is usually a rude carved pole some 6 feet high, but no prayer-flag, for the prayers carved in the lamaseries and sold to the people lie below. The letters, sometimes accompanied with figures of animals, fishes, snakes, and frogs, are common, and are not unfrequently painted in various colours.

Burial, cremation, exposure to the birds of the air, and throwing into the rivers are the methods employed in disposing of the dead in different parts of the country. In the case of cremation the ashes find a watery grave.

Education is at a discount. It is confined to the lamaseries, and even there few of the priests can do more than read their sacred literature, and that with the greatest difficulty. Writing is an art which few have learned. On the way to the frontier a lama attached himself for several days to my caravan, doing all sorts of menial duties in return for his food, and on the way back to Ta-chien-lu I had the company of another who was returning to his home north of the State of Pati from the Drébung lamasery, where he had spent eight years. Neither could write. The latter used to recount his experiences in Tibet, where he had seen the Dalai Lama, and his chief grievance was against the monastery, whose food was not at all to his liking. The tsamba, he said, was made of pea flour mixed with some substance that made it swell. It was filling, but not at all satisfying.

Administration

The States of Chala, Litang, and Batang are administered by native chiefs under the superintendence of the Chinese Commissaries at Ta-chien-lu, Litang, and Batang respectively. The chief of Chala has 49 deputies stationed throughout his jurisdiction—48 T'u-pai-hu (the head of 100 families) and one T'u-Ch'ien-hu (the head of a 1,000 families—the Tsa-li-t'u-ssŭ above referred to)—to assist him in carrying on the government of his kingdom. In Litang there are five chiefs and fewer Shelngo, and in Batang two chiefs and several Shelngo. The Shelngo (called Hsing-ngo in Chinese), occupies the same position as the head of a 100 families in the State of Chala.

The chiefs exercise control over Tibetans within their respective jurisdictions, but Chinese in the city and towns of Ta-chien-lu, Romi Chango, Litang, and Batang are dealt with solely by their own authorities. In cases between Tibetans and Chinese recourse is had to the chiefs or Chinese authorities according to the nationality of the plaintiff. The T'u-pai-hu are charged with the collection of rent and taxes payable by Tibetans and Chinese settlers, and with the arrangement of official transport. The Shelngo hold office for three years, when they return for duty to the headquarters of their chief, whence their successors are also drawn. The office of T'u-pai-hu, on the other hand, is hereditary.

There would appear, however, to be a system of village councils. I was witness of a fight between two Tibetans in a village in the interior in which from stones the combatants came to blows. When the parties to the affray had been separated by the by-standers, the headman at once summoned the men of the village, and a council was held at the end of the street. The decision I was unable to learn in detail, but some satisfactory arrangement was come to and peace was at once restored.

TA-CHIEN-LU TO CHENGTU BY WAY OF ROMI CHANGO AND MOU-KUNG T'ING

[*The reader is advised to refer to the map on page 8 for this stage of the journey.*]

10th October

I have already explained that two roads lead from Ta-chien-lu to Tibet. There is the official high road by way of Litang and Batang which I have just described, and the small but more important trade road which branches from the official route at the Cho To Pass, and then goes north and west, to Tai-ling, Dawo, Hor Chango, Chuwo, Kanzé, Rung-ba-tsa, Dergé, and Jyékundo, and from Dergé a branch road leads to Ch'amdo on the official road. The trader or traveller by the northern road need not, however, cross the Cho To Pass: he can leave Ta-chien-lu by the north gate, and proceed northwards for two days up the valley of the stream which joins the Lu or Ta-chien-lu River to the immediate east of that town, and from a few miles north of Hsin-tien-tzŭ, the end of the second day's stage, go west to Tai-ling, a long day's journey of about 30 miles (150 *li*).

Some caravans prefer this latter approach to the north-ern road, and over it a considerable traffic is conducted in the usual import and export trade of Tibet. The other great trade highway from Ssuchuan to Tibet passes through the city of Sung-p'an T'ing in the north-west of the province; but there is a third road which, crossing the bridge over the Min River at Kuan Hsien, 30 miles west by north of Chengtu, goes west to Tibet, and, as little or nothing is known regarding it, I resolved to proceed north from Ta-chien-lu as far as Romi Chango, the northern boundary of the state of Chala, and then proceed east to Kuan Hsien through the city of Mou-kung T'ing in the hope of being able to learn something of its capabilities.

As stated above, I returned to Ta-chien-lu from the Tibetan frontier on the 5th October, when the usual dif-ficulties of procuring fresh transport again presented themselves, and it was not till the evening of the 9th that I was able to have all the pack animals required safely secured in the yard of my inn. To have returned to Chengtu by the usual high road through Ya-chou would have been an easy matter, for transport is always available by it; but, having travelled it 21 years ago, I was unlikely, by taking it, to find anything new in a country where centuries show little change, and it was with pleasurable anticipations that I passed through the north gate of Ta-chien-lu at 8 a.m. on the 10th October, bent on a plunge into a practically unknown part of Ssuchuan.

I had exchanged friendly visits with the Sub-Prefect of Ta-chien-lu, who also holds the post of Commissary for the Chinese troops stationed in Tibet (Chün Liang Fu); the Assistant Imperial Resident for Tibet, who arrived at Ta-chien-lu from Chengtu *en route* for Ch'amdo half an hour after I returned from the Tibetan frontier; and the Ming Chêng Ssŭ, or native chief of the State of Chala, within which Ta-chien-lu lies. They all expressed themselves deeply interested in my travels, and the Assistant Imperial Resident was especially anxious to hear about the road he had to traverse to his post.

The Chinese authorities have the greatest dread of the mountain passes, and when I was starting westwards they recommended all sorts of nostrums, such as snuff, musk, sugar, and the like, to prevent my suffering the severest anguish if not death itself; but, thanks to the Tibetan pony, I was able to surmount each pass without even the slightest feeling of uneasiness. The native chief, a young man of 36, who succeeded on the death of his elder brother three years ago, showed me the greatest cordiality, and soon after leaving the north gate of Ta-chien-lu I was met by a bearer with his card, accompanied by his best wishes for a safe and successful journey.

On leaving Ta-chien-lu the road ascends the right bank of the stream along the west side of a narrow valley hemmed in on both sides by high hills covered with grass and brushwood, and opening here and there into side valleys and gullies each adding its quota to the stream. Sometimes the main valley is wide enough to allow of cultivation along both banks, and the hillsides are here and there easy enough to admit of cultivated terraces; at others they descend steeply to the banks of the stream and are the haunts of the firewood cutters for Ta-chien-lu, for that city is entirely dependent on wood for fuel, coal not having as yet been discovered in the neighbourhood, although signs of the existence of the mineral are by no means wanting. Other minerals are, however, present.

Several wooden bridges span the stream, and up a gully on the left bank just above the first bridge, which is 5 *li* north of Ta–chien–lu, silver was mined until last year at a place called P'ien–ai–tzŭ–kou, 40 *li* east of the stream. Gold was also worked at a place called Têng–chang–kou, 50 *li* inland from the second bridge, a mile or so above the first and on the left bank. I am given to understand that mining licences were issued by the Sub–Prefect of Ta–chien–lu, but that on his transfer to another post last year, which was not carried into effect, all mining was suspended, and it is further stated that the native chief and his people did not favour the extraction of the metals.

There are hot sulphur springs just above the second and third bridges on the right and left banks of the stream respectively, and my pony had a great aversion to the smell and warm water through which he had to wade. In some places only the stubble of barley, wheat, and peas remained on the cultivated plots; but buckwheat, oats, and a little maize mixed with beans were still standing or in the process of being harvested. In one place I noticed a small patch of poppy in full dark-red bloom.

The road, fairly good in places, was almost impassable for a chair in others, being narrow, full of boulders, and occasionally hemmed in on both sides by stone dikes over-grown with brushwood, such as rose and gooseberry bushes. It crossed to the left bank of the stream by the third bridge above Ta–chien–lu. An occasional prickly oak was to be seen, and here and there groups of small bamboos appeared by the roadside. Trees of any size, except in the vicinity of occasional farmhouses and rarer hamlets, were conspicuous by their absence. Those to be seen were prin-cipally poplars, with low birches on the hill slopes. There were many ruins telling the same old story of the original inhabitants being driven from their homes along the high road by the oppressive system of transport. On the roof of the Tibetan-built house in the hamlet of Yü-tzŭ-tung at which I breakfasted, I was surprised to find a winnowing machine; but the explanation is quite simple, for the valley, from which the Tibetans have fled, is now occupied by Chinese, on whom the system of transport does not press so heavily. They, like the Tibetans who have to supply transport, are exempt from rent, but the calls on them are less burdensome.

The valley follows a general northerly direction with a slight bend to the west, and the road on its east side creeps up the hillside high above the bottom of the valley. From its highest point a splendid view was obtained of the snowy range which runs east and west behind Ta-chien-lu. Wang-mu, 60 *li* from the city, is usually reckoned the end of the day's stage; but its accommodation did not possess sufficient attractions to induce us to spend the night, and we pushed on to the five-family hamlet of Niu-o-kou (9,503 feet), 5 *li* further north, where, although I am settled in a fairly decent room with the *lares et penates*, I fear my followers are not so comfortably housed. Some of them are sleeping on the roof, for the Chinese inhabitants retain the Tibetan style of architecture, even to the prayer-flags flying from the roofs. There was no sign of trade during the day; the only carriers we met were men, women, and animals, with loads of brushwood bound for Ta-chien-lu.

11th October

Rain overnight and a snowstorm on the morning of the 11th October were not a good beginning to our second stage from Ta-chien-lu. We got off at 6.30 a.m., however, and the snow, which was falling in huge flakes, soon ceased. The road followed up the left bank of the stream, rising high above the bottom of the valley, which gradually contracted and was quickly cooped up between steep hillsides clad with brushwood and a sprinkling of silver fir, prickly oak, mountain ash with bunches of beautiful waxy white berries, poplar, and other trees. Turning north-west, over the mountain ridge bounding the valley on the east side, the road descends into the same valley running north and south, and bounded on both sides by high hills white with snow. The valley, which had previously been very much contracted, now opens out, admitting of cultivation on both banks of the stream. The crops, with the exception of a field of oats, were all harvested. In the valley there was a new-looking Tibetan house. The hillsides sloping to the valley were clad with brushwood, young birches, and occasional silver firs, and prickly oaks turning russet at the approach of winter. In the valley bottom were a few poplars, and the mountain ash with gooseberry and currant bushes forming roadside hedges.

Crossing the stream by a wooden bridge, we breakfasted at the hamlet of Ch'i-mu-t'o, 20 *li* from Niu-o-kou. The valley continues to be inhabited by Chinese, and some of the houses, built in Tibetan style, have now sloping roofs of planks kept in position by stones. At Ch'i-mu-t'o I asked the owner of his house why he, a Chinese, still retained the prayer-flags and burned incense on his roof. He explained that by burning the branches of juniper or other trees in the roof-stove his flocks would be preserved from wild beasts when put out to graze on the mountain sides; but that, I think, is not the real reason. The fact is, that nearly all these Chinese are mated to Tibetan women, and they, as in other countries, have much to do with the religious services of the household.

Soon after leaving Ch'i-mu-t'o we re-crossed the stream and struck a hot spring on the left bank. To the immedi-

ate north of the hamlet of Jê-shui-t'ang, 10 *li* north of
Ch'i-mu-t'o, there is a similar spring on the the same bank
of the stream. A short distance beyond Ch'i-mu-t'o a
splendid snowy range showed itself to the north, the summits rising high above the clouds; but a lower range which
we approached soon obscured the view. It is this lower
range which blocks the valley and divides it into two side
valleys, one going south-west the other north, each sending down a rivulet to make up the stream we had been
following since leaving Ta-chien-lu.

The approach to the northern valley beyond the hamlet of Lung-pu, 25 *li* from Ch'i-mu-t'o, is over an
execrable road, over whose projecting boulders I had to
lead my pony for a long distance, riding being out of the
question, and my empty chair suffering very considerable
damage. The road improved on entering the valley, because
it has been left to nature and runs through a jungle of
juniper, prickly oak, rhododendrons, and scrub growing in
the valley bottom sloping from the east to the left bank of
the rivulet on the west side. This valley, like the sides of the
high, now snow-clad, hills which bound it, was once a forest, for stumps of trees are everywhere to be seen amid the
scrub, and the hill slopes are seamed with lumber shutes
now filled with snow. Side valleys open out, and rills hurry
from them to join the rivulet in the bottom of the valley.
Below its junction with the rivulet from the south-
western valley, the stream was choked with lumber, and at
Lung-pu I saw numbers of lumberers, armed with long
poles, who had been at work trying to clear the stream.
There was not a single house between Lung-pu and the
four houses of Hsin-tien-tzŭ—the end of the day's stage;
but at noon I was able to have a hot meal amid the snow
by the side of a disused charcoal burner's stone-built pit, in
which we found it possible to light a fire. Cultivation there
was none.

Hsin-tien-tzŭ belies its name of "New Inn". I am spending the night in a room in the best of its four houses, and
its wooden walls (it is, for a wonder, an attempt at a
Chinese house) are leaning in every possible direction, and
admit icy draughts from the snow-clad hills around that
make writing anything but a pleasant occupation. It lies at
the foot of a low spur, which projects into the valley from
the hills to the east, and appears to block it towards the
north, and at the mouth of a wild uninhabited valley
which pierces the hills on the west. It is distant 85 *li* from
our last night's quarters, and 30 *li* from the southern foot
of the Ta-p'ao range which we have to cross tomorrow—
the snow-clad range which we saw to the north earlier in
the day. I saw numerous traces of camp-fires along the
road; but the only semblance of trade was some 20 loads
of charcoal—a local trade—bound for Ta-chien-lu. It was
being carried by yak and oxen. The smoke from the charcoal pits was noticed high up on the hillsides in several
places during the day.

I have been trying to discover what the four families of
Hsin-tien-tzŭ do to earn a livelihood. With the exception
of a few goats they have neither flocks nor herds, nor do
they cultivate the land around them. The latter is only
10,265 feet above the level of the sea, so that wheat, barley, peas, and turnips could be grown; but all the hamlet
possesses are a few grass plots surrounded by stone dikes,
intended to yield hay for the goats during the winter
months.

12th October

The Ta-p'ao Shan, which we crossed today at an altitude
of 14,496 feet, has, like most high passes in this part of the
country, the reputation of being the haunt of robber
bands, and the fact was carefully drummed into me by my
followers. I accordingly gave instructions last night that we

were all to proceed in company on the morrow—pack animals, writer, servants, chairs and chair-bearers, and escort—so as to prevent the possibility of any raid upon stragglers of the caravan. The plan mostly in vogue among robbers is to cause a stampede and, during the disorder, try and cut off any straggling pack animals and their loads. I little anticipated, however, the difficulty of carrying out these instructions under the conditions which faced us this morning.

On getting up at 5 a.m., I found that snow had fallen silently and heavily during the night, and that the ground was covered to a depth of 4 or 5 inches. The mountain sides bounding the valley had received an additional coat, and the silver firs dotted thereon looked like large white cones. I have said that Hsin-tien-tzǔ lies at the foot of a spur which drops into the valley from the east; but room is still left for the stream at the foot of the western bounding hills. The spur slopes southwards from the foot of the Ta-p'ao Shan, and we ascended it through brushwood and small trees laden with snow, altogether concealing their identity. We arrived at the base of the mountain at 8 a.m., two hours after starting, where we all breakfasted. I purposely walked the whole way behind my chair to keep the caravan together and to save my pony for the coming ascent.

At the mountain foot the road divides, one branch going north by west up a gully to Tai-ling (90 *li*) on the little road to Tibet, the other north-east over the Ta-p'ao Shan to Romi Chango on our road to Mou-kung T'ing and Kuan Hsien. The line of the Tai-ling road was partly visible, but our road over the mountain was, with the exception of a short distance near the base, entirely obliterated by snow. The pack animals were sent ahead to clear a path, but they very soon outstripped the chair-bearers and some of the escort who were on foot. All went well as

long as the track of the road was discernible; when that
failed, a guide had to be sent ahead to find the path. Much
time was spent in this pursuit, and he ultimately led us on
to the pass by a series of very steep zigzags which proved
exceedingly tiring to the animals. Many a breathing space
was required, and I found myself alone many zigzags
below the pack animals. A long distance below me were
two mounted men of my escort on their sorry nags, and
still further below the chairs, chair-bearers, and sundry
stragglers were dark, creeping specks on the white mountain side. At one point, several hundred feet under the pass,
my pony slipped on the foot-wide path, and horse and
rider slid together down the mountain side for several
yards; but, as the snow was fortunately soft, we brought up
within a few feet of the head of a precipice. The latter was
not very deep—only some 30 or 40 feet; but it was quite
enough to end this narrative. The pony was more fright-
ened than hurt, and, dragging him back to the path, I
remounted and proceeded towards the pass, where black,
rocky points projected from the snowy ridge.

At the obo, which I reached at 11 a.m., I used my hypsometer, as I had done on all the passes west of
Ta-chien-lu, and found the altitude to be 14,496 feet
above the level of the sea. From the pass I had an excellent
view of the trough-like valley we had just left, and below
us to the north-east lay a similar valley along which lay our
way. Snow lay everywhere in the valley and on the mountain side. The only sound that broke the stillness of the
snowy scene was the howling of a wolf in the distance. The
descent on the north-east side was comparatively easy, but,
of course, necessitated walking. The guide, who preceded
the pack animals, had left his pole where the path makes a
sharp bend to the north. As we descended, the first vegetation to peep out from the snow was the dwarf
rhododendron, the hardiest of plants, and soon other

shrubs filled the valley on both sides of the inevitable rivulet. An hour below the pass I caught up my pack animals ferreting for grass under the snow in an open camping-ground surrounded by light-green larch, the first I had seen on the present journey, growing amid a jungle of brushwood. The mountain slopes on the opposite side of the valley were clad with a forest of larch which had suffered severely from fire. Grim rocky summits towered above the forest.

During the mid-day meal, served on the snow, the whole caravan, with the exception of my writer and his chair, turned up, and we proceeded down the valley through a forest of larch succeeded by silver fir, birch, dwarf bamboo, mountain ash, an occasional Scotch fir and a few maples. The road, in many places a mere forest track, was frequently execrable and seemed unending. Ahead lay a mountain range clad with snow to the verge of a precipitous face; but hour after hour seemed to bring it no nearer, and the forest became denser than ever. I have already referred to the moss drooping from the branches of the silver fir and prickly oak in the forests west of Ta-chien-lu; but in this valley it was far more abundant than I had hitherto seen. It clung in wreaths to silver fir, birch and larch, and small shrubs were not exempt from its ravages. "Fairies' Scarf" is undoubtedly a parasite that kills, and numerous silver firs were showing signs of the inevitable death-struggle. The road, such as it is, crossed the rivulet six times over rude plank bridges, and it was not till five p.m. that we emerged from the forest at the Tibetan six-family hamlet of Ku'ei-yung, where, after a journey of 120 *li*, we put up for the night.

It is a very hard day's work from Hsien-tien-tzŭ to Ku'ei-yung, but, unless one camps out, it has to be done, for there is not a single habitation between the two places. Of animal life I saw only a single squirrel, which crossed my path in the forest. On the Ta-p'ao Shan Pass I heard, as I have said, the howl of the wolf, and on leaving Hsin-tien-tzŭ at 6 a.m. a pheasant was crowing on the mountain side. The peasantry give a long catalogue of wild animals in the mountains, such as the bear, leopard, wild boar, hare, etc., and I have no doubt they are to be found. Bear's paws I priced in a shop in Ta-chien-lu. On crossing the Ta-p'ao Shan we were again amongst Tibetans and Tibetan houses of the proper architectural style.

At Ku'ei-yung I was quartered in the only available spare room—the family shrine—on the roof of the house. In this room towards night my eyes began to pain me very badly, and I put it down to the smoke from the rooms below. I was assured, however, that the fires had been out for some time, and in sheer despair, I had to bandage my eyes and go to bed. It was only next morning that I discovered the cause. Four of my chair-bearers were suffering, like myself, from severe inflammation of the eyes, three of them being practically snow-blind. I had suffered no inconvenience whatever while crossing the pass during the day. As my writer and his chair were still missing when darkness fell, I sent out men with lanterns to meet and bring them in. His story is that his bearers gave in soon after crossing the pass, and that he had the greatest difficulty in making them go on; that he ultimately left his chair and proceeded on foot, but that, hearing the barking of dogs, as he thought, in the forest, he hurried back to his chair and bearers. Before rescue arrived he had made up his mind to pass the night in a tree. He was a pitiable sight when he and his men turned up at 8 p.m.

During the evening the caravan drivers came and begged me to make a late start on the morrow. They said that, owing to the snow and the late arrival at Ku'ei-yung, their animals were in need of several hours' grazing before starting. Owing to the suffering of several of my men and my own, I willingly agreed to their request, and tomorrow's stage will be short.

I noticed that the drivers of the pack animals drew their hair forward and over their eyes to prevent the latter being affected by the snow.

Goitre is exceedingly common along this road. The great majority of the women and many of the men are afflicted by it. Women seem far more liable to be attacked by it than men.

13th October
On leaving the clearing round the hamlet of Ku'ei-yung (10,041 feet), from which the harvest of barley, wheat, peas, and turnips had been garnered, we again entered the forest at 9 a.m. on the 13th October in the seemingly vain attempt to find a way out of the valley and reach the snowy range that lies to the north of it. Our attempt has been unsuccessful, for, from a variety of causes, we have accomplished only 40 *li* during the day. With the exception of larch, we had the same uninhabited forest and the same forest track, the road crossing and re-crossing the stream six times, as it did yesterday.

We arrived at noon at the village and clearing of Mao-niu, which contains 30 odd families of Tibetans and Chinese, in the proportion of two to one. The importance of the village, which is purely Tibetan in style, and has several ruined watch-towers, may be gathered from the fact that it boasts of a lamasery, recently put in order, with some ten priests attached to it. This I visited, and walked all over the village, with its walnut and apricot trees. I found that it is when there are only Chinese in a hamlet or village in the native State of Chala that they are called upon to provide *ula* or transport. If the population is mixed, Chinese are exempt; but their rent payable to the native chief is heavier than in the case of Tibetans, and is levied in silver. Tibetans pay in kind, not according to the amount of land under cultivation, but what is practically the same thing, the amount of seed sown. In their case it ranges from 25 to 60 catties of wheat, against from 0.6 taels to 2 taels in the case of Chinese.

Mao-niu (9,308 feet) stands on rising ground on the west side of the valley, which breaks up into two branches, one to the west, along which runs a road to Tai-ling, 90 *li* distant, the other to the north, which we follow, leading to Romi Chango. A stream from the western valley joins the stream which we have been following since crossing the Ta-p'ao Shan, below and to the north of the village. We are still 150 *li* from Romi Chango, made up of two stages of 90 *li* and 60 *li* respectively. The road is said to be an improvement on the last two days, and the country, along the high road at least, to be well peopled, affording some accommodation for travellers.

14th October

Descending from Mao-niu at 6.30 a.m., we struck the left bank of the stream flowing northwards, down the never-ending valley, and crossed it by a plank bridge above its junction with a much smaller stream coming from the western valley leading to Tai-ling. Our road now lay along the right bank of the united waters, sometimes close to the stream, at others high above it, with nothing between us and destruction but a narrow footpath and confidence in the sure-footedness of the Tibetan pony. Not unfrequently the valley became a narrow gorge, not more than 50 yards across, with, at one place (Ta Tai), a sheer sandstone cliff rising hundreds of feet above the footpath. Where it was at all open there was some cultivation and a house here and there, but the people seemed poverty-stricken. They were mostly Chinese, and the crops on the ground were patches of maize (red and green or yellow), buckwheat, hemp, and tobacco (*Nicotiana rustica* L.). The tobacco had been harvested, but fresh shoots from the old stalks bore bunches of yellow flowers. This tobacco is called Lan-hua-yen, from a fancied resemblance the perfume of its blossoms bears to that of the Lan-hua, and to distinguish it from *Nicotiana tabacum* L., which has white, pinkish blossoms, and is called Liu-yeh-yen, i.e. "willow-leaf tobacco". The latter is growing in the garden of the house in which I am now writing. I have asked the people along the road where they dispose of their produce, and the invariable answer I have received is that they have none to dispose of, and that they require to purchase to supply their actual wants. Whence the funds to purchase? I enquired, and they stated that, in addition to farming, they hire themselves out as carriers, and can thus make ends meet.

We had crossed from the right to the left of the stream, now 30 yards wide, to reach the Chinese hamlet of T'ung-lu-fang with its seven or eight houses, 30 *li* from Mao-niu. Here we breakfasted, and kept to the left bank for another 30 *li*, when we arrived at the three houses of Ta Tai under the sandstone cliff above referred to. At Ta Tai we crossed to the right bank but re-crossed a few minutes later when the sandstone cliff ceased. At Ta Tai I got into my chair to have a rest, but had soon to abandon it, owing to the boulders strewing the path. At other places I preferred walking to riding for one prefers to walk a plank substituted for the road round a rocky corner high above the rushing stream to riding over it.

Twenty *li* north of Ta Tai the valley or gorge is blocked by a high mountain range, which shut out our view of the snowy range ahead which had been visible for days. The stream had now become too wide (about 50 yards) for a simple plank bridge, and before reaching the blocking range we crossed to the right bank over a one-arch bridge of planks laid on beams projecting upwards from stone piers. At the blocking range a valley to the west pays its not insignificant tribute to our stream, which now goes east and north-east. Following its right bank for a short distance we crossed to the left by a similar bridge, in which the narrow footway was patched in places with loose stone slabs. Its condition was so rickety and shaky that each pack animal was led across separately.

We had crossed the stream six times since morning, and this remained the total for the day, for the large white-washed lamasery of T'ung-ku soon came into view, and I was accommodated in the loft of a Tibetan-built house at 3.15 p.m., my companions being Indian corn-cobs—much preferable to the lively companions that, to judge from appearances, might be my fate on the ground floor. The lamasery of T'ung-ku has 12 or 13 priests. I say *priests* advisedly, for I have learned that not every inmate of a lamasery is a lama. The great majority are merely "trapa"—learners or acolytes—who have not and are never likely to reach the higher dignity. The village itself (7,489 feet), which occupies rising ground a short distance from the left bank of the stream, is well wooded, and buckwheat of both kinds seemed to occupy the greater part of the arable land around it. It has a population of over 100 families, 90 per cent of which are Tibetan.

The most noteworthy trees observed during the day's stage of 90 *li* were the birch, poplar, prickly oak, and maple; but the steep mountain slopes were exceedingly rocky, and were clad with little but grass and scrub. This refers especially to the latter half of the stage, for, as far as T'ung-lu-fang, birch was by no means uncommon on the mountain sides. We are still in the never-ending valley, and are distant 60 *li* from Romi Chango, the end of tomorrow's stage. Cultivation is becoming more general, and on the mountain slope on the opposite side of the valley from T'ung-ku there is much arable land reaching almost to the summit.

15th October

On leaving T'ung-ku the path, called a road, runs along the left bank of the stream for 10 *li*, when it crosses by the usual frail bridge, at which the greatest care was again exercised by our drivers. Mid-way and high up on the mountain side smoke was rising from the incense fires of a large Tibetan village surrounded by cultivated patches. This village bears the name of Chin-pi. A little beyond the bridge, our course being north-east with the stream, a valley opens out to the east and pays its small tribute to the main stream, which soon becomes a dashing white torrent with a boulder-strewn bed. At 15 *li* from T'ung-ku the path has to pass a cliff some 30 feet above the stream, and to effect this piles, supporting a narrow roadway of planks and loose stone slabs, have been driven into the rock for a distance of 20 yards. Here the drivers took the precaution of unloading the pack animals, carrying the loads, and leading the animals over one by one. The road then crossed to the left bank by another frail bridge, and here the animals were reloaded. This delayed us for an hour, and instead of breakfasting at the half-way village of Kung-ch'a as we had anticipated, we partook of that meal in one of two nameless houses opposite an 800-feet cliff, with the hamlet of La-chiao-shan perched on the top of it.

Except where the valley opens out, which is rare, there is room neither for cultivation nor houses, but all the mountain slopes are brought under cultivation where possible, and homesteads and hamlets in Tibetan style with numerous watch-towers are built in the most inaccessible places. I have not the least doubt that the latter have been chosen for safety. In some places the stream is cooped up between steep cliffs, not unlike the gorges of the Upper Yang-tsze; but the steep mountain slopes above the cliffs are well tilled, and dotted with houses and hamlets. Where there is room for cultivation in the valley, which continues in a north-easterly direction, there are houses and villages, such as Kung-ch'a and Kanda; but, although native in style, they are inhabited by Chinese, who, as a rule, count three generations of occupation. Enquiries along the road elicited the statement that most of their forefathers came from the Province of Shensi, but other provinces, such as Hupei and Honan, are also represented. The natives of Shensi are well known to be wandering traders, and they seem to have settled on the soil.

To reach Kanda we have again to cross the stream, and this, so far as we were concerned, was the last passage of what I shall now call the Hsi Ho or West River, for such it is named at Romi Chango, the end of the day's stage, where it enters the Ta-chin Ho, known in its lower waters as the T'ung or Ta-tu River, which joins the Min River at Chia-ting, and was crossed by us at Lu-ting-ch'iao on our way westward to Ta-chien-lu. About half a mile from the end of the day's stage a bridge, called the Hsi-ho-ch'iao, crosses the stream, and below the bridge on the north side high, bare, rocky cliffs are succeeded by a valley to the north, whence issues the Ta-chin Ho, which swallows up the blue waters of the Hsi Ho in its muddy embrace. The picture is exceedingly impressive—the Ta-chin Ho flowing southwards from between bare rocky banks towering high above it.

Up this valley, which is gained by crossing the bridge over the Hsi Ho, a road leads to the native states of Pa-wang and Pa-ti, 40 and 90 *li* distant respectively, which are at present in a somewhat disturbed state. The late chiefs of the two states were brothers, and they have a third brother, who entered the priesthood. When the chief of Pa-ti died, some time ago, his seal of office was transferred to his brother of Pa-wang for safety, as the heir is only a child. The chief of Pa-wang has since died, and the priest brother is credited with having stolen both seals and brought them to Pa-ti. Such is the story told me by the civil authority, who is a Hsien or Magistrate, at Romi Chango. He exercises, under the Prefect of Mou-kung T'ing, jurisdiction in the two states and the military authority, who is, curiously enough, under Ta-chien-lu, has gone to Pa-ti to settle matters at the point of the bayonet.

A rocky promontory, forming the east bank of the Hsi Ho at its mouth, lies opposite the valley leading to Pa-wang, and, on surmounting this, we looked down on the compact little town of Romi Chango (6,402 feet), with its purely Chinese houses, stone foundations, wooden reddish-brown walls, and sloping tiled roofs, lying on the right bank of the Ta-chin just below its junction with the Hsi Ho. It is the northern limit of the jurisdiction of the Ming-chêng Ssŭ, or chief of the State of Chala. It contains over 130 Chinese families, and here the women are also Chinese. It appears to be a busy little place, with numerous shops. It draws from the native states around it rhubarb, Pei-mu, Ch'ung ts'ao, Ch'iang-huo (*Peucedanum decursivum* Max.), and some musk, which it forwards to Ta-chien-lu and Kuan Hsien for export, and it supplies them with grain and spirits.

Maize and buckwheat are the principal crops around Romi Chango. The former is exceedingly cheap, costing only 12 cash a catty. In the valley of the Hsi Ho I also noticed during the day tobacco, *Amarantus* spp., turnips, capsicum, and onions. Every advantage is now taken of the warmer climatic conditions into which we have descended. Rice, however, is not grown, and the town draws its supplies through Kuan Hsien, the cost laid down being about 2,400 cash a bushel of 30 catties or 40 pounds.

From the Hsi Ho we have passed into the valley of the Ta-chin River. Five *li* below Romi Chango a bamboo suspension bridge spanned the river until July of the present year, when it was swept away by floods caused by excessive rains in the interior. Only three hide-coracles are now available to effect the passage, and in these our baggage has to be ferried across tomorrow, for the road to Mou-kung T'ing lies along the north bank. Our pack animals from Ta-chien-lu have also to be changed here, and I am assured that the necessary number will be waiting on the left bank of the river tomorrow.

We have now left the region of silver firs, birches, and the like, and although I noticed a few prickly oaks during the day, they were small and stunted. The willow was common towards the latter end of the stage. One peculiarity of the valley is the presence of mica in the soil. It fairly glittered with it, and every stone seemed to be full of it.

16th October
The 16th of October is a black-letter day in the journey. I was up early enough to see the Chinese housemaids, in the shape of women and girls with the usual cramped feet, sweeping the steps and streets in front of their doors—a somewhat rare occurrence; but the return of my followers to their own civilization, in the shape of a Chinese town, meant rejoicing overnight and a late and lazy appearance in the morning. I had arranged with the caravan drivers—what was not included in the agreement at Ta-chien-lu—to carry the loads to the ferry in the morning, and, with considerable trouble, and, I am afraid, loss of temper, I effected a start at 7.30 a.m.—much behind the usual time. The road runs east along the right bank of the Ta-chin Ho, 60 or 70 feet above the river, and all went

well until after we had passed the remains of the suspension bridge, with its cables dangling from the piers on either side. Here part of the road has disappeared down the precipice, and at the narrow part a boulder projected into the path. The leading pack animal, a nice black pony, unfortunately bumped its inside pannier against the boulder, and, having no room to recover itself, slipped over the precipice with its load and crashed among the rocks lying in the river bed. The animal lay as if dead, with its load still strapped to the pack saddle, but it gradually regained consciousness, and began moving its blood-stained head and neck. The drivers had to make a long detour to reach the base of the precipice, and it was a pitiful sight to see the four men shedding tears of grief as they tried to raise the mangled animal. The load had been removed, but all their efforts proved vain. The poor beast lay wedged in between two massive rocks, and had carried its last pack. The load, pack saddle, and bridle were brought up, and on examining the panniers it was found that the cooking pots and utensils in one had been smashed to pieces, while the filter in the other was uninjured. As I held myself responsible to some extent for bringing these animals beyond Romi Chango, for which the drivers had not bargained at Ta-chien-lu, I thought it my duty to make some compensation to the owner, and it was with no assumed quiver of the lip and crocodile tears that he and his companions standing round received my modest gift of 10 taels. I was very sorry for these Tibetans, for they love their animals; they live in the same house with them at home, and are exceedingly careful to save them unnecessary labour. The Tibetan takes a pride in his horse and his gun, dismounting at all difficult or steep places to spare his animal.

Beyond the scene of the accident two representatives of the Ming-chêng Ssǔ said good-bye, and assured us that pack animals awaited me on the opposite side of the river, and the civil official of Romi Chango awaited me above the ferry to speed me on my way. We had to scramble down the huge boulder bank to the river, where the hide-coracles were in waiting to carry my party across the Ta-chin Ho. The civil official had expressed some doubt as to the possibility of getting my Tibetan pony across, but he was one of the first to reach the left bank. A double rope was fastened to his halter and held by a man sitting in one of the coracles. The pony was suddenly pushed into the river from behind, the boatman in the coracle worked his single slightly curved paddle with all his might and the pony was soon swimming for dear life, as if he had done the same many a time. I followed, having a coracle allotted to myself and the boatman, and in a few minutes found my pony quietly grazing on the other side. The boatman strikes up river for a short distance, and then dashes across, landing on the other side several hundred yards below, and carries his coracle to the starting point. My followers had little confidence in this novel means of crossing a river, nor was it increased when a boatman, carrying across two of my escort, dropped his paddle near the landing-place, and with great difficulty reached the bank. One of the men came ashore crying like a child, and his companions had great difficulty in comforting him. My official chair was towed across in a larger coracle, with the loss of the water-proof cover. In two hours we were all on the left bank, bag and baggage, to find ourselves stranded between a large lamasery and the mouth of a small river—the Hsiao-chin Ho—which enters the Ta-chin Ho just below the ferry, without sign of transport of any kind.

The Ta-chin Ho is about a couple of hundred yards in breadth, and flows with a very swift current east and south. The Hsiao-chin Ho, along which our road lies, is some-what larger than the Hsi Ho, where it enters the Ta-chin

Ho above the town of Romi Chango. A polite message was sent to the representatives of the native chief to come across the river and explain the absence of transport. The reply came back that they were afraid to cross, but would send porters to carry my baggage until we met the pack animals, which were in the valley of the Hsiao-chin Ho higher up. These, men and women, came over in twos in the coracles, and it was noon before we effected a start. We followed the right bank of the Hsiao-chin Ho, flowing down a valley bounded by high, bare, rocky mountains. A mile from the mouth of the river we met part of the trans-port we had bargained for at Romi Chango, and transferred part of the loads to these animals, taking on the balance of porters to the Tibetan village of Pien-ku, where, after a great struggle, we secured three additional pack horses. We were still short, and I left the writer behind to secure other porters, for the porters change at every village, and bring on the balance of the baggage.

I pushed on to the village of Yo-tsa (6,904 feet), 15 *li* distant, to arrange for a full complement of pack animals on the morrow. This I reached at 4 p.m., and the writer did not turn up with the rest of the caravan until 5, too late to proceed further that day. The road, at one time at the water's edge, at another high above it, is for the most part a mere footpath running north-east with the valley along the right bank of the river and the country resembles the valley of the Hsi Ho, with the exception that the hill slopes are more extensively cultivated. There are the same Tibetan villages and farmhouses, with watch-towers resembling exaggerated chimneys of blast furnaces, perched high up in the most inaccessible-looking places; but there is this difference—the houses are nearly all white, and I learn that the exteriors are white-washed every year in the second moon. The crops included maize, *Amarantus* spp., and plots of tobacco and hemp. The sites of the villages were well wooded, and in the valley the willow and walnut were particularly abundant.

The village of Pien-ku, 20 *li* from Romi Chango, consists of one large Tibetan house, or agglomeration of houses, by the roadside, with two wretched houses to keep it company, and a fine wooded collection of Tibetan houses high up on the mountain side. There are altogether about 90 Tibetan families in and around this village, and three or four Chinese. A fine lamasery, with gilded pinnacles, and surrounded by a grove of willows, lies on the left bank of the river, just below the ten-family Chinese village of Yo-tsa, where I am spending the night in a room with 12 large bunches of *Capsicum longum* hanging from the rafters. The front of the house is adorned with a large number of similar bright-red bunches, hung out to dry.

I had been beginning to doubt whether I was not passing from Tibetan to some other race during the day, for the clothing of the people, although woollen and coloured, was beginning to lose the Tibetan cut; but I was reassured when I heard the driver answer *Laso* ("Certainly") to a message I had given them through an interpreter from the Romi Chango yamen. *Laso* and *Mari* ("No") are the two commonest words one hears among the Tibetans. The interpreter has been trying to explain to me that the Tibetan spoken at Ta-chien-lu is the *Kuan Hua*, or official language, as against the *T'u Hua*, or local dialect of this part of the country.

17th October

We spent 12 hours in the valley of the Hsiao-chin Ho today, accomplishing a distance of 85 *li*. They proved exceedingly long *li*, and it was quite dark when we made the eight-family Chinese village of Shêng-ko-tsung, situated on rising ground on the right bank. From Yo-tsa we followed the right bank of the river in a northerly direction till the valley was blocked by a range ahead, leaving a very narrow passage for the river, which dashed down a seething mass of whiteness between a steep rocky precipice on one side and huge boulders on the other. We passed the first bridge (Ka-ya), 15 *li* from Yo-tsa, on our right, and crossed the Tê-shêng bridge, 15 *li* higher up. The latter was in an exceedingly dangerous condition, and the pack animals were led over one by one, one man holding the bridle and another the tail to steady the animal. It was narrow; holes in the floor boards were patched with stones; the rails were hanging loose in several places; and it swayed in a very uncomfortable fashion.

Previous to this we had experienced great difficulty in passing our animals round a sharp, rocky bend in the road which a stone tablet informed us had been built in the year 1740. As a matter of fact, a great part of the day was spent on a pathway overhanging the river, with steep cliffs overhanging the pathway. I preferred walking to riding or sitting in a chair, with the uncomfortable feeling of being very near to destruction. Beyond the point where the river is cooped up to form dashing waterfalls, the valley turns from north to north-east, and keeping to the left bank we reached the hamlet of La-ma-ssǔ, where we had our mid-day meal at 1 p.m. The hamlet lies in a bend where the river, flowing from east, turns south-west. In the elbow on the opposite bank stands the fine large lamasery of Gi Lung, which accommodates over 100 priests. It has a private bridge for the use of its inmates.

Still keeping to the left bank along a precipitous path-way high above the river, we made, after 15 *li* from La-ma-ssǔ, the hamlet and bridge of T'ai-p'ing-ch'iao, the bridge of Great Peace. In its present condition, even worse than the Tê-shêng bridge we had crossed earlier in the day, its name is a sad misnomer, and it might far more appro-priately be called the bridge of Great Terror. The same tactics were employed by the drivers of our caravan as at the Tê-shêng bridge, and with success. Even to have to walk over this bridge, not to speak of taking pack animals across, was an experience which one would not care to repeat. After the passage of the T'ai-p'ing bridge we held by the right bank for the rest of the day, the road improving till the valley was completely blocked by hills to the east, leaving room for the passage of the river only when it ascends and descends projecting bluffs to reach Shêng-ko-tsung. The cultivated mountains bounding the valley have become rockier and steeper. The beautiful houses are also wanting, and the usual dingy buildings with occasional towers have taken their place. There is one exception—the large white house of a native steward or overseer situated in a hamlet on the left bank of the river a little to the west of Shêng-ko-tsung.

In the bottom of the valley, when the latter opens out, as it does occasionally, are nondescript, semi-Tibetan houses and cultivated patches of maize, buckwheat, Amarantus, millet, hemp, and beans, with tobacco, melons, and brinjals in their garden plots. The commoner trees seen during the day in the bottom of the valley were the willow, walnut, peach, and poplar. There was little or no wood on the mountain slopes. A few small cattle, goats, and pigs represent the livestock.

For the first time for some days have I seen any indication of trade along this road. There were several pack loads of Ch'iang-huo going with us from Romi Chango to Mou-kung T'ing, and we met one wooden tub of rape oil and two loads of water tobacco from Mou-kung. Salt finds its way here from the Wu-tung-ch'iao salt wells through the city of Chiung Chou by way of Mou-kung, and costs at the moment in Shêng-ko-tsung 110 cash a catty of $1\frac{1}{3}$ lb. There was a dearth in the supply last year, and the price ran up to over 200 cash.

We are now distant 60 *li* from the city of Mou-kung
T'ing (pronounced Mêng-kung T'ing), or as it is generally
called locally, Hsin-kai-tzǔ, and we hope to reach it
tomorrow. The hamlet of Shêng-ko-tsung (7,592 feet) is a
poor place. It has a single inn with a common room for all
comers, and I am quartered in a private house in which I
am allotted a windowless room permeated by the odour
from the pig-sty behind. Rain has just been falling, and as
the roof leaks, I am plentifully bespattered with a black
liquid composed of rain-water and the soft encrustation of
black smoke on the rafters of many years standing.

18th October

When one has to cross a mountain pass during the day one
is quite satisfied when it is over; but there is nothing more
exasperating than to have to ascend and descend steep hillsides with a minimum of level road. The latter was our fate
today between Shêng-ko-tsung and Mou-kung T'ing, a
distance of 60 *li*. We followed the right bank of the Hsiao-
chin Ho eastward the whole day until almost opposite the
city, when we crossed by a good bridge of the same old
type, but in excellent repair, even the railing being painted.
There was very little room for cultivation in the bottom
of the valley after leaving Shêng-ko-tsung, and the mountain sides soon became too steep and rocky to admit of
village. In fact, 30 *li* from Shêng-ko-tsung the valley
became a gorge with high rocky cliffs dropping sheer
down to the water's edge on both sides, with the roadway
cut from the solid rock. The hamlet of Hsin-ch'iao-t'ang
or "New Bridge Station" marks the eastern end of the
gorge, and derives its name from a bridge which crosses a
stream flowing into the main river from a northern valley.
The bridge may once have been new, but it was so patched
with stones that my pony would not look at it, preferring
to ford the stream higher up.

In some places the road in the gorge was positively dangerous, and even walking I was very glad when it was over. East of Hsin-ch'iao-t'ang cultivation reappeared on all available bottom land, where arable patches presented from a height a very pleasing picture, and on a long sloping bank stretching from the foot of the mountains to the south down to the left bank of the river. The mountain sides are too steep for the agriculturist, but sloping summits have been rendered arable. The mountains on the north bank are too rocky, and where there was sufficient soil they were clad with grass and brushwood.

In the valley itself the most prominent trees were poplar, ash, and cypress. Maize was the principal crop, harvested, it is true, but the withered stems still remained on the ground. There was some millet ungathered, and in the house where I breakfasted at Ts'ai-yüan-tzŭ the ears of *Setaria italica* L. were hanging over the rafters. Amarantus (red and yellow) and tobacco were also on the ground in small patches. There is only one crop a year. The houses seen during the day were very common and inconspicuous.

As Mou-kung T'ing is neared the road runs up a steep hillside, and a more gradual descent leads to the bridge, already mentioned, which spans the river to the immediate west of a rocky gorge from which the Hsiao-chin Ho emerges. The city (8,138 feet) stands on a terrace reached by a steep brae, which winds up from the south end of the bridge. Behind is sloping cultivated land, backed by mountains to the south. The city, which has neither wall nor gates, is very small, but well paved with stone and clean. It consists of three streets, and has a Chinese population of 317 families. It is well stocked with officials—a Sub-Prefect and a Commissary, and three military officers—a colonel, captain, and Hsün Kuan, as well as a native official holding the rank of and called a Shou-pei.

Noticing some non-Chinese (for convenience sake I will call them Man-chia, the term generally applied to Tibetans and the non-Chinese tribes in western Ssuchuan) in the street while passing to my inn, I sent for one, and was soon supplied with three. One was dressed in brown woollen stuff with round black felt hat and queue, while the other two wore the Chinese costume. The man with the woollen clothing was a native of a place called in Chinese Pa–chioh–t'un (Senamia in the native dialect), 80 *li* from Mou-kung T'ing while one of the other two called himself a Wokjé man. The former spoke little or no Chinese, the latter fluently. They belonged to distinct tribes. At the very first numeral, "One", I found my old friend "Ketig", I thereupon unearthed a note-book from my baggage and much to their surprise and amusement, I read out to them their numerals and easy sentences which they at once correctly translated into Chinese. These I had taken down from a native teacher from Tsa-ku-t'un, whom I had employed for a short time in Chengtu, and it came out that a large number of these tribes speak the same language with only slight variation. The man with the woollen clothing had a smattering of the written language and he was able to read several sentences correctly. The character was Tibetan. I had the same sentence written in Tibetan; but although he could read the words he failed to understand their meaning. I am under the impression that these tribes have borrowed the Tibetan alphabet as better suited than Chinese in which to reduce their language to writing, and I hope to have other opportunities of verifying this between Mou-kung T'ing and Kuan Hsien. It is well known that, in Tibetan writing, many consonants are used which are not sounded in speech, and that certain tribes on the frontier of India still exist who use the discarded consonants, and it has been suggested to me that these tribes in Ssuchuan may do the same. So far as I can judge such is not the case, for there are no superfluous letters in the writing representing the sounds taken down by me. They are pronounced as they are spelt.

I reproduce here some numerals in European dress:

1	Ketig	22	Ke nis shchi ke nis
2	Ke nis	30	Ke sŭm shchi
3	Ke sŭm	33	Ke sŭm shchi ke sŭm
4	Ke dé	40	Ke dé shchi
5	Ke möng	45	Ke dé schchi ke möng
6	Ke drög	50	Ke möng shchi
7	Ke shnis	58	Ke möng shchi warryad
8	Warryad	60	Ke drög shchi
9	Ke gu	69	Ke drög shchi ke gu
10	Shchi	70	Ke shnis shchi
11	Schatig	80	Warryad shchi
12	Scha nis	100	Peuria
13	Schasŭm	102	Peuria ke nis
14	Scha dé	103	Peuria ke sŭm
15	Schamöng	200	Ke nis peuria
20	Ke nis shchi	1,000	Stung tsu
21	Ke nis shchi ketig	1,300	Stung tsu ke sŭm peuria

19th October

Mou-kung T'ing I found a most inquisitive place, and the guards set over my inn by the Sub-Prefect seemed incapable of restraining the curiosity of the population. When I left at noon of the 19th October, the street in which I lived was simply crowded to catch a passing glimpse of the foreigner, and I was the recipient of that doubtful honour usually accorded to royalty. My sympathies are with royalty. I am, as a rule, astir and away before the bulk of the population are out of bed, but at Mou-kung T'ing I was delayed for half a day, owing to the fact that no arrangements for my future transport had been made by the authorities, in spite of due and timely warning and a request for a fresh relay of pack animals. I was asked to remain over a day to admit of something being done, but this I declined, as I had no guarantee that even then anything would be done.

The whole system of official transport is, as I have already explained, vexatious and detestable to me; but as I pay my way to the full, and private arrangements would mean undue delay, and would in this part of the country be practically futile, I have had to have recourse to the authorities ever since I left Ta-chien-lu for the Tibetan frontier. On a long journey like the present, animals are knocked up in a few days, and must frequently be changed, and without the necessary official order for relays travelling would be altogether impossible. At the last moment, I had perforce to be content with 12 of the animals which I have had for three days, and the balance made up locally. It was very unsatisfactory, as it is a long journey of anything from 8 to 12 or more days to Kuan Hsien before a fresh relay could be obtained. It was, however, preferable to delay.

Mou-kung seemed to know nothing outside Mou-kung, and the information I was able to get regarding roads leading anywhere was of the vaguest description. To the enquiry regarding a direct road to Sung-p'an T'ing, I was told that there was a difficult track somewhere or other, but that travellers and trade always made for the nearest point on the high road from Chengtu to Sung-p'an. This vagueness led to considerable trouble with several of my chair-bearers. Four of them insisted on being paid in advance for 12 stages to Kuan Hsien, while I was told that it could possibly be reached in eight. I declined to gratify them, offering payment for eight stages in advance, and promising full payment for each day beyond that time. This offer, knowing that it would be next to impossible to get other men in an out-of-the-way place like Mou-kung, they declined; but I was equally stubborn, and asked the Sub-Prefect if he could possibly procure men for me. As soon as my men heard what I had done, they came and said that they would agree to ten stages, if I would pay them then and there for that number. This I refused to accede to pending a reply from the Sub-Prefect; and to my intense surprise the latter sent me four men with whom, to judge from their capabilities today, I am thoroughly satisfied. I am perfectly sure the four recalcitrants regret being left behind in Mou-kung to find their way back to Chengtu; but it is a warning to others that there can be only one master of a caravan.

The city of Mou-kung is divided into two parts by a streamlet from the south, flowing northwards down a deep ravine to the main river. Going east, we crossed some high ground and descended to the streamlet and over the painted bridge spanning it. The road then skirts the left bank of the river for 15 *li*, a good road for the most part, till it strikes a cliff, which it has to round. Here it consists of a stone staircase, with the cliff on one side and a stone wall 6-feet high built on the outer edge, to prevent accidents and the passer-by from looking down a sheer precipice of several hundred feet into the river. Up to this point there was some cultivation, which ceased at this gorge, for both banks are very rocky and precipitous. Once round the gorge, the valley breaks up into two valleys, one to the north, and the other to the east. A snow-clad mountain showed itself up the eastern valley. From each valley issues a stream of about the same size, and the united waters make up the Hsiao-chin Ho. That from the north is called the Fu-pien River, because it passes a town of that name, that from the east is said to rise in the Pan-lan Shan mountains, which we have to cross the day after tomorrow.

Our course lay up the eastern valley, along the left bank of the stream, but high above along a mountain side over a fairly good pathway, with steep gradients here and there, and rendering the 45 *li* accomplished during the day rather tiresome by the great number of gullies that had to be rounded. The valley itself, somewhat open at first on the south side, is well cultivated deep down near the stream, and higher up there is a fine picture of cultivation on the right bank, with the village of Hsiao-kuan-chai, consisting of some 12 native non-Chinese houses and two very high brown-stone towers, like huge smoke-stacks, near the east end of the farmlands and a little to the west of a razor-edged bluff, which intrudes into the valley from the south, and leaves just room for the stream to find its way westwards. Hsiao-kuan-chai has a bridge to itself, and a small footpath winds up the steep hillside to the main road, which, crossing the neck of the bluff, zigzags by a stone staircase down the other side, crosses a bridge spanning a mountain torrent from the south about to join the stream in the valley, and a few hundred yards beyond enters the village, with some 15 families, of Kuan-chai (8,211 feet).

I had thought the village of Hsiao-kuan-chai a pretty picture, deep down in the valley, but, on descending from the bluff, something still more wonderful met my eye. Standing on the left bank of the stream, and connected with the right by a bridge, is a beautiful old building, like a castle of the Middle Ages. Encircled by a high stone wall about 20 feet high, are a curious collection of stone buildings several storeys high, with small windows resembling square open portholes, two of the buildings ending in two-storeyed square-windowed towers—the lower of wood, the upper coloured white and yellow—surmounted by conical roofs. In the centre rises the high common brown-stone tower, its summit coloured white, as are also some parts of the various stone buildings. It is the official residence, or yamen, as it is called by the Chinese, of the Wokjé chief (Wo-jih T'u Ssŭ).

In consequence of my enquiries into the question of languages, I had heard for the last day or two of the Wokjé, and on arrival at Kuan-chai I sent my card with greetings to the chief. He at once sent his headman, along with an interpreter, to see me, explaining that he himself was far from well, and begged to be excused paying me a visit. I took the opportunity of submitting my Tsa-ku-t'un vocabulary to the headman and found that my transcription of the language was perfectly intelligible to him, and he then gave me a list of the tribes speaking the same tongue, with only slight variations. They are the Tsa-ku-t'un, Wa-ssŭ, Mu-pin, Tsé-lung (Mou-kung T'ing), Pa-chioh, Pieh-ssŭ-man, So-mo, Han-niu, Kros-jia, 'Rzung-galo, and Chok-chieh. I can speak for Mu-pin, for several people from that district have been my companions on the road from Ta-chien-lu northwards, so that I can confidently state the Tsa-ku, Mu-pin, Tsé-lung, Pa-chioh, and Wokjé tribes speak the same language, and I have no doubt that the information regarding the others is correct. The Wokjé headman further stated that he did not speak Tibetan, or any language but his own, and that Tibetans did not understand him. In writing the Wokjé language the Tibetan alphabet is employed and nothing more. The Wokjé have no printed books of their own. Such printed books as they have come from Tibet, and have to be explained by those who have learned the language of that country.

I had a crowded reception by Wokjé and Chinese, who were inquisitively respectful, but a lama, with intolerable insolence written on his face, pushed his way through the crowd and swaggered into my room, sneering into my face. He left the room much quicker than he had entered it, passing through the crowd without looking or remaining to see what had happened to him. It would have been undignified for him to have examined the sore part in the presence of the crowd, who were highly amused, mimicking to each other the swagger and retreat of the learned man.

We are now on one of China's trade highways, and met during the day carriers from Kuan Hsien with native cloth and straw sandals, and with paper from Chiung Chou. One of the former told me that he had been 22 days on the way, having been delayed by rain and snow. He said that the Pan-lan Shan Pass was covered with snow to the depth of over 1 foot. These pack carriers travel at the rate of only from 20 *li* to 30 *li* a day. A considerable number of carriers with the medicinal roots of *Peucedanum decursivum* Max., are accompanying us.

20th October

News was brought to me at 5 a.m. that 11 of our pack animals that had been grazing overnight had disappeared, and I did not at all relish the idea of being delayed waiting for a fresh supply. The drivers were at once sent back to renew their search, and I sent word at the same time to the Wokjé chief, informing him of our misfortune. Luckily the animals had merely strayed from the grazing ground to the bank of the stream, and were found and brought in an hour later. Loading had then to commence, and we did not get away from Kuan-chai until 7 a.m.

I spent the interval in freely mixing with a group of Wokjé men and women, who crowded the entrance of the inn to see my caravan start. Some of the ladies were exceedingly good-looking, and, although a little shy, were amused at the interest I displayed in their dress. They wore loose dark-brown gowns, bound with several turns of a red sash. Their legs were bound with cotton cloth of a greyish colour, and most of them wore sandals of rather a fine make with uppers. One or two had long cloth or hide boots reaching to the knees. They all had queues, which were drawn once over a blue cloth scarf projecting a few inches over the forehead and falling a foot or so down the back. The end of the queue was then fastened underneath. For ornaments they wore silver ear-rings of rather stout make, each ring about an inch in diameter, and having one flat end near the join usually set with turquoise. A flat dull-red ring of glass or other material was threaded into each ear-ring. They wore long flat silver rings, one or more set with turquoise or coral, and strung on the queue on the top of the head were similar rings larger in size. On the centre of the queue amid the rings each had a silver minia-ture of a bird, such as a pigeon or eagle. On their wrists they had silver or copper bracelets nicely chased. The men wore similar brown gowns and sandals or boots. Their heads were shaved in front like Chinese and they wore queues, but some had the latter concealed under red or purple turbans. They had no ornaments or jewellery.

On leaving Kuan-chai the road rises and falls, and keeps on rising and falling, with a few level stretches along the mountain side in an easterly direction, turning south-east where we descended and crossed the stream to the right bank by a bridge 20 yards long, just beyond the seven- or eight-house village of Chiang-chün-pei, 28 *li* from Kuan-chai. We frequently looked on the roofs of houses deep down in the valley. They were usually covered with yellow maize cobs spread out to dry. With the exception of buck-wheat, with stems not more than a foot long, which was being harvested with reaping hook, the crops had already been garnered, and from below came the songs, with long-drawn notes, of the ploughmen as they turned the soil with a wooden plough shaped like a pick-axe with curved collar and one handle. The team usually consisted of one or a couple of yak, and the ploughman, with one hand on the collar and the other grasping the handle, sidled along the primitive plough as he trilled his long notes. Ploughing was everywhere in full swing, and the morning air resounded with the pleasant songs. Here and there one saw large herds of cattle, sheep, and goats browsing on the stubble. The mountain slopes and summits were cultivated where possible, and where too rocky or steep were covered with young larches in the sere and yellow leaf, and a russet-leaved shrub added warmth to the picture.

On the roofs of the houses, whether farmsteads or hamlets, were wooden frameworks, usually consisting of four upright poles with three or four rows, about 2 feet apart, of horizontal poles on which the grain and straw are suspended. The houses themselves—unlike Tibetan houses—had triangular turrets, about 3 feet high, at all the corners, and sometimes between with different patterns. These, like a rim at the summit of the house wall, the edges of the windows, and the base and base angles of the walls were washed white, and in some cases various white devices were painted on the walls. I noticed that, as in the case of Tibetan houses, access was had to the roof by the usual notched log.

From Chiang-chün-pei to Ta-wei, a distance of 28 *li*, the road follows in a south-east direction the right bank of the stream, which receives a considerable addition from each side of the bend in which Chiang-chün-pei lies. The next considerable addition is from a valley to the immediate east of Ta-wei, opening out to the south on the left bank of the stream. This village, with two towers, stands on rising ground on the right bank, and is connected with the opposite bank by a wooden bridge, over which and up the valley just mentioned runs the road to Mu-pin and Chiung Chou. Some distance above this addition the stream narrows till, at one place, it is not more than 10 yards across. From Ta-wei the valley runs direct east. Soon the snowy range—the Pan-lan Shan—comes into view right ahead, but is quickly lost as the valley narrows. There is now very little cultivation, and the mountain slopes here and there show a sprinkling of silver fir, dark green amid the yellow birches and russet scrub. There are few trees in the valley. A few birches and poplars almost complete the list.

Ta-wei ought to have been our first day's resting place east of Mou-kung T'ing, but having failed to make that place yesterday, we have lost the run of the stages, and have been obliged to put up for the night in the four-house hamlet of Ti-shui-ngai, 75 *li* from Kuan-chai.

21st October

Leaving Ti-shui-ngai the road runs east along the right bank of the stream past several excellent farmhouses with various white-washed devices. The frameworks on the roof were in many cases stacked with grain. The stacking is effected by fixing the sheaves to pieces of wood, usually saplings, interlaced vertically in the horizontal bars. The road soon rises, but has to descend 13 *li* from Ti-shui-ngai to cross a stream issuing from a high, rocky, narrow gorge to the north. This affluent is as big as the stream itself above the junction at Shuang-ch'iao-k'ou. There is now a steep ascent up the mountain side covered with brush-wood, while the slopes on the opposite side of the valley are covered with silver fir and beautiful yellow larches. At the highest point there is a tunnel into the mountain side—a disused gold mine. I had noticed several short tunnels yesterday, and only discovered today that gold had been worked in the district. I understand from an official proclamation that work will be recommenced next year in the neighbourhood of Ti-shui-ngai and Sha-pa, which are 10 *li* apart.

The song of the ploughman was heard early in the morning, and I imagine it is intended to encourage the yak in their work. The coulter of the plough was, I observed, sheathed with iron. If the ploughing happened to be taking place near the road, a rush was made by the field hands to watch our caravan pass, and as I rode by I was an object of very considerable curiosity. Up the valley the snow-clad summits of the Pan-lan Shan were becoming nearer and nearer, and a breeze from the snowy heights tempered the warm sunshine. The road, or gravel path, was exceptionally good for a Chinese road. I rode ahead, out of the way of my chair-bearers and pack-animal drivers, for they are grumbling at the poor accommodation (sometimes a miserable solitary inn with the poorest possible quarters) at the end of each day's stage. Their heart's desire is to put up at only the larger places on the road, but that does not fit in with my plan of doing a good day's work and reaching Chengtu in the time I have mapped out for myself.

At Rih-lung-kuan (10,552 feet), a comparatively large village 25 *li* from Ti-shui-ngai, the valley proper ends and divides up into two valleys, one going north and the other east. Two streams of about equal size flow down these valleys and unite at Rih-lung-kuan. They come from the snows behind, and are the sources of this eastern branch of the Hsiao-chin Ho, which we have now been following for days. We crossed both streams above their junction and entered the valley going east, soon to leave it, however, for a side valley leading south-east. This we ascended, rising steadily but gradually till we reached the solitary stone hut, called Wan-jên-fên ("The grave of 10,000 men"), which lies just under the snowy slope of the Pan-lan Shan. Cultivation ceased at Rih-lung-kuan, and the road up the valley soon became a stone road in glorious disorder, and exceedingly trying for our animals.

It first crossed and re-crossed a brook from the snows, then passed through a small forest of scrub, with here and there a prickly oak and silver fir and larch on the mountain sides bounding the valley, and ultimately through grass-covered, marshy ground, vegetation practically ceasing on the snow-clad slopes. On ascending a small plateau, we found the hut of Wan-jên-fên (13,546 feet) and ourselves in a horseshoe of snow-clad ranges, with Pan-lan Shan forming the front of the shoe to the south-east. Looking back down the valley we could see what had been concealed from us in our valley wanderings—a massive snowy mountain to the north-west, with a bare rocky cone towering to the north of it. The cone is called Niu-hsin-tzŭ Shan, according to the landlord of the hut, and it lies to the north of Tsa-ku-lao. We cross the Pan-lan Shan tomorrow.

Carriers with cloth, paper, and straw sandals on the road today told me that they had been from 16 to 20 odd days out from Kuan Hsien, but I hope by pushing on day after day to reach it in six. They all speak of heavy rains and consequent delay on the road.

There is one omission I have made in regard to the native (non-Chinese) houses. It is this; they are more plentifully decorated with prayer-flags than even Tibetan houses. Not content with long flag-poles outside, the roof and each turret has its floating prayers. Obo or Hladzi have been common enough all the way from Ta-chien-lu, but much inferior to those on the road to the Tibetan frontier. Today I noticed quite a new style. A white oblong building with sloping roof was erected by the roadside, and was fitted on its four sides with stone shelves like a large bookcase for the reception of the stone offerings of passers by. Stone slabs with inscriptions in Tibetan characters were set between the shelves, which were about a couple of feet apart. Wan-jên-fên derives its name from being the burial place of the Chinese who were killed in the war with these tribes, and, it is said, interred in a large pit at the base of Pan-lan Shan.

22nd October

The name Wan-jên-fên is a slight exaggeration of facts. A small pavilion, so dilapidated that it leans against the stone hut, contains a tablet giving the names of the soldiers who fell or died during the war, and who found their last resting-place at the foot of Pan-lan Shan (pronounced Pa-la Shan in the neighourhood). I should say, from a cursory glance at the list, that it did not contain more than 50; but the Chinese character *wan* (10,000) means frequently nothing more than *many*, and this is, no doubt, the correct interpretation in this case.

We left the hut a few minutes before 6 a.m. The pools had a thick coating of ice, and grass and withered wild flowers were white with frost crystals. Snow lay to a depth of 3 inches on the ground, for some had fallen during the night, and was hard and slippery. This would have mattered little had it covered a good road; but we soon came to a stone road evidently not made by a Macadam. It resembled far more the effect of an earthquake. Chairing is always out of the question in crossing these passes, and riding was impossible. The pack animals were sliding about, and the drivers doing their best to keep them on their feet. Fortunately there were no steep gradients, and only one or two zigzags had to be made to reach the summit of the pass with a couple of poor square obo heaped with stones. I have taken the height of each pass crossed by hypsometer corrected for temperature, and the height of the Pan-lan Pass is 14,104 feet.

From the pass an excellent view was obtained of the mountain mass and bare stone cone referred to yesterday.

In yesterday's evening light, and at a lower altitude, the cone seemed to be higher than the mass, but it is undoubtedly lower. Looking south-east, on the other side of the pass, I looked down into a white sea of clouds from which stood out a range of black, rocky peaks slightly clad with snow, and beyond the range a second sea of whiteness. The south-east side of the mountain is for a considerable distance a counterpart of the north-western but steeper, and it was difficult to find the road amid the sea of boulders. Creeping up among these were a man and his wife. The latter had an infant on her back, and a child of three was trying to toddle by his father's side. I have pitied the children accompanying the annual immigrants into Manchuria in summer; but my heart went out to this poor child on its way up a mountain pass clad with snow, and over a road which no fitting words can describe. What a picture of misery! The family were bound for Mou-kung T'ing.

Sliding down among the snow and boulders called a road we soon entered the clouds, coming finally to a fairly good path going south-east into a valley whose opposite rocky side was almost obscured. At a solitary house called T'ang-fang, on the mountain side, my men began to bargain for a young wild pig, called a Hsüeh Chu or Snow Pig, which was being skinned, but the price was to them prohibitive. It had the usual brown hair and bristles and weighed about 20 lb.

At 9 a.m., three hours after starting, we had reached the bottom of the valley going south-east and breakfasted at the lonely house, a guard station, called Hsiang-yang-p'ing. Here a garrulous old soldier took the place of one of the men who had come with me from Rih-lung-kuan, and I started him on the question of Chinese roads. I asked why they were left in such a fearful condition. He replied, "Who should repair them?" I naturally replied the

Chinese authorities. He shook his head at this and said, what everyone knows, that the people subscribe from time to time to keep roads and bridges in repair, but that, considering the number and mileage of roads in China, such a voluntary system was incapable of dealing with the task. I quite agreed with him, and suggested that the authorities might find money for such a good purpose and carry out the work, but he summed up the argument by saying that the officials would have to find the money from the people, who were too poor to pay for the repair of roads. He added that it would be an excellent thing if people would make donations of stone slabs for the work, but I did not carry the matter further, for stone roads in China without constant repair are much worse than no roads. Such has been my experience in these western provinces.

Stone roads were, however, to be with us the greater part of the day, for on leaving Hsiang-yang-p'ing what had once been a paved road runs south-east down the valley with its brook, rising higher and higher along a grassy mountain side. It lay along the north-east side, the south side being steep and rocky. The summits of the latter were white with snow, but the lower slopes were well wooded, for we had now descended to the altitude of silver fir and larch. The valley soon turns east, and becomes still more densely wooded.

At the bend a valley opens out to the west and adds its tribute to the brook. Mud an inch or two deep now took the place of stone on our path, which, after rounding the bend to the east, commenced to descend by a series of steep zigzags to the bottom of the valley and the left bank of the streamlet now 10 yards wide. It is one of the steepest descents I have met with in western China, and my sympathy for the porters who were labouring upwards with packs and loads of cottons, straw sandals, and sundries from Kuan Hsien was real. Here we also met the first caravan of 38 ponies laden with tea from Kuan Hsien bound for the Hsiao-chin-ch'uan—the country to the north and west of Mou-kung T'ing. Each pony had a load of two square packages cased with split bamboo, each weighing 60 catties or 80 lb.

After the descent we followed the left bank of the stream through dense shrubbery and scrub, passing several solitary houses, each with a patch or two of cultivated land. The mountain sides, whose summits were buried in clouds, were densely wooded. The valley contracts as the two inns known as Yü-yü-tien (8,695 feet) are neared, and we were not sorry to take up our quarters in one of them for the night. The inns on this road are of a very poor description; they are intended for the accommodation of porters, and are not extravagantly furnished. We have done only 63 *li* during the day, but we have gone through the various kinds of roads held in particular detestation by chair-bearers—the *Luan-shih Lu* and the *Hsi-pa Lu*—the "Gloriously stony" and the "Abominably muddy."

On crossing the Pan-lan Shan we passed from the jurisdiction of the chief of the Wokjé to that of the Wa-ssŭ or State of Chia Rong.

23rd October

Snow was falling on the forest-clad summits and slopes of the mountains and rain in the valley when we left Yü-yü-tien at 7.30 a.m. The cheery voice of the innkeeper, who repeated several times at parting, "The road is good and will be good going", animated for a moment the faces of my followers, who had held back, hoping that I would delay my departure for a day on account of the bad weather; but I am too near the end of my journey to allow weather to interfere with my further progress.

We had good reason to recall during the day the innkeeper's parting words, for of all the atrocious roads I have traversed today's was, I think, the worst. Soon after starting, the valley, which has maintained a general north-easterly course with many windings, contracts, leaving room for the stream only, and it has been found necessary to build a road through the rocky gorge. This has been done by driving holes in the cliff on the left bank some 8 feet above the level of the stream, inserting poles kept in position by wooden wedges, and laying planks for the road, which was not more than 4 feet wide. This wooden path, about 100 yards long, was in very bad condition, and the planks were slippery and wet. A wooden rail had once graced the outside edge, but the near half was now missing. My drivers, who come from Romi Chango, are new to the road, and, without realizing the danger, allowed the pack animals to proceed. The leading mule slipped within the first 2 or 3 yards, and dropped load and all into the stream below. It regained its footing almost immediately and made for a shingle island, where it stood and shook itself, evidently astonished at its performance. One of the drivers followed the mule and induced it somewhat reluctantly to ford the stream at the other end of the wooden cliff-pathway. Meantime, the other drivers, after trying to hide all holes with the loose planks, led each animal across, one at the halter and the other holding on by the tail. The passage was successfully accomplished, and we proceeded on our journey. Half an hour later we crossed to the right bank, and here the same care was taken in passing the animals across. Another cliff with propped pathway immediately appeared, and the same performance had to be gone through.

We breakfasted at the solitary Chinese hostel of Wên-hsien-kai, consisting of one common room, which was crowded with porters, whose packs were standing all round. They were all busy devouring a meal of cakes and boiled turnips. The good lady of the hostel explained to me that the small earthenware bottle hanging in front of the doorway contained water, and was intended to appease the gods.

Beyond Wên-hsien-kai the state of the road defies description. It runs by very steep gradients up and down the mountain side, and sharp, pointed blocks of stone rose at all angles from the pathway through the forest. The interstices between the stones were full of water, and the ponies slipped and steadied themselves in a most marvellous way, all the time hanging, so to speak, over the stream below. My own Tibetan pony fell completely over on his side, but managed to save himself from the brink of one continuous precipice. He was being led, for riding was out of the question, and when I did take refuge in my chair late in the afternoon to escape the rain which had begun to fall, the chair had to be tilted so far to avoid a huge boulder in the path that the chair-coolies lost their balance and all fell together, the chair on its side. I scrambled out and continued my walk.

Ten *li* from Wên-hsien-kai I crossed the stream, now a deafening, roaring torrent, swollen by additions from valleys on both sides, by a foot-bridge and walked along the left bank for about a couple of miles, regaining the right bank and the caravan over a fairly good plank bridge. Two more propped wooden pathways along cliffs, about 70 yards in length, one of them rounding a corner at a very sharp angle with several poles hanging loose, had now to be passed, and exceptional care was here taken by the drivers, who patched up the roadway after the passage of each animal.

The bridge of Ta-ngai-tung, 30 *li* from Wên-hsien-kai, had lately been rendered impassable by floods, and a temporary bridge, 5 *li* further down river, had been erected by utilizing a large rock in the middle of the torrent as a pier and throwing across a couple of spans of rounded poles lashed together. Here was a serious difficulty. Animals could not cross it, and the caravan had to be unloaded and the packs carried across the bridge. The animals had to be got across, however, and one of the drivers, riding my pony, selected a spot higher up and led the way across. The water, rushing with great force, reached the pony's girths. The others followed, but several, trying to take a short cut across the stream, were carried off their feet and succeeded in crossing with the greatest difficulty. After this the stream had to be crossed and re-crossed by the same dangerous bridges, 20 and 17 *li* respectively from the four-house hamlet of Wo-lung-kuan on the left bank, the end of the day's stage of 72 *li*.

These dangerous bridges and cliffways caused great delay, and we did not reach Wo-lung-kuan (6,620 feet) until 5 p.m., when darkness and rain were setting in. The whole day's journey may be described as threading in a north-easterly direction the valley of this stream, which enters the Min River at a place called Hsüan-k'ou, 60 *li* from Kuan Hsien. The valley does not lack great beauty. From time to time it becomes a gorge with here and there level spots of ground with room for a house and a few plots of cultivated land. These houses are simply intended for the accommodation and entertainment of porters on the road, the plots of land growing the vegetables for the purpose. Once or twice, however, I noticed the poppy in full bloom. The hillsides were clothed high up with silver fir, now, however, becoming less conspicuous as we descend, and, lower down, with various trees whose leaves showed tints from yellow to blood-red. I noticed the maple again, and the tree named Hung Sha, a fragrant pine with red wood, in much demand for the manufacture of coffins. This wood, discovered here about four years ago, is floated down to Kuan Hsien. The stream near Wo-lung-kuan was full of the dressed planking.

We met about a hundred porters from Kuan Hsien during the day with the usual loads of native cloth and straw
sandals. I am informed by the landlord of the inn in which
I am passing the night that from 7,000 to 8,000 cases of
tea from Kuan Hsien pass over this road annually, each case
weighing about 60 catties; but I hope his estimate, which
requires corroboration, is more accurate than the statement regarding the road made by the innkeeper this
morning.

24th October

Immediately to the east of Wo-lung-kuan, which we left
at 6.30 a.m., the valley divides up into two branches, separated by a range of hills approaching to the east end of the
village. The northern branch is densely wooded on its hill
slopes, and a goodly stream flows down to join the main
stream, which continues its course north-east down the
other branch, whose hill slopes are now less densely
wooded. Scrub and grass have taken the place of the silver
fir and other trees of yesterday.

The road follows the left bank of the stream, and things
were going well at the start, when we suddenly learned
that a part of the roadway passing under a rocky bluff projecting into the valley had been washed away by floods,
and that we must take to the hillside. This we did, circum-
venting the bluff by ascending and descending a steep,
newly made path. That the stream has recently been in
flood is evident from the number of large heavy logs
stranded on shingle banks and left there high and dry. Fine
bramble bushes (*Wu-pao'rh*), with tendrils several yards
long and in full fruit, lined the roadway. On a single bunch
I counted 29 black full-sized brambles. I omitted to mention that these brambles were also very common yesterday,
and that the bamboo had put in an appearance. Today I
saw bamboo at least 20 feet high. The valley occasionally

opens out, giving a little room for cultivation and a few houses and hamlets. Maize had been harvested, but Amarantus, beans, and hemp were still on the ground, and I noticed a small patch of *Perilla ocymoides* L. Peach, cypress, and poplar were common in the valley.

Just beyond the single house known as Chioh-mo-kou, 24 *li* from Wo-lung-kuan, the valley again splits up into a north and north-eastern branch, the road following the latter. Another *li* brought us to the hamlet of P'i-tiao-ho, where we crossed the stream by a bridge in fair condition, the pack animals not requiring any special care on the part of the drivers. Thirty *li* from Wo-lung-kuan we left the stream at Kou-k'ou or Erh-tao-ch'iao, and struck eastward up a gully, whence rushed a mountain torrent which obtruded itself on us for many hours, for it winds from side to side of the gully, and if we crossed or forded it once, we must have done so between 20 and 30 times. I gave up the tally in sheer despair. Riding or chairing was quite impossible, the bridges consisting for the most part of a single plank, while the pack animals had to wade.

Half-way up the gully, which is densely wooded, one of the pack horses gave in and had to be left behind in charge of one of the drivers, his load being distributed over the other unfortunate animals. He was a very wise animal to give in when he did. He may have looked up the gully, seen the high mountain range that lay before him, and made up his mind that he could not do it. We are apt to credit horses with too little sense, and we sometimes ask them to do the impossible; but my experience of the Tibetan pony is that he is very level-headed, and nothing in the world will induce him to undertake, say, a very steep descent (and it must be very steep indeed for him to refuse) with his rider. He stops dead, and refuses to budge until the latter dismounts. As it turned out, his comrades were very sorely pressed to reach the pass (9,988 feet) over the Niu-t'ou Shan, the serious ascent of which began at the head of the gully. The zigzags were unending, and the stone road near the summit was simply atrocious. So bad is it indeed that a branch road is taken by animals, and I followed the caravan winding backwards and forwards up the mountain side, slipping and resting every few yards. It is a painful sight in this 20th century, but it is of every-day occurrence in western China. It has often struck me that the manufacturer of foreign goods would be not a little surprised and pained if he could see the immense labour and suffering required and caused in the distribution of his goods.

If the west side of the Niu-t'ou Shan, which ends in a narrow ridge, is steep, the eastern face appeared to me to be steeper still; and as I followed my pony down to the resting-place for the night—a solitary house called Shao-ch'a-p'ing, 1,295 feet under the pass—I was momentarily afraid that he would fall and break his legs. It seemed to me that any animal but a cat must come to utter grief. We were enveloped in clouds during the upper part of the ascent, and nothing but whiteness was visible around us. I noticed near the summit, however, a few goodly sized red pines rising ghost-like from the gloom, and dwarf bamboos occasionally lined the pathway. We have accomplished only 66 *li*, but it has been one of our hardest days.

This road, bad as it is, is one of considerable commercial importance, and the exchange of commodities between Kuan Hsien and Mou-kung T'ing is, to judge from the large number of carriers, far from trifling. Native cottons, paper, straw sandals, and sundries are going west in ever-increasing quantities, and rhubarb, *Peucedanum decursivum, Astragalus hoantchy* Franch. and other medicines accompany us. Tea I have already mentioned, but we met none during the day.

25th October

If one were to give credence to all the statements one hears along the road, the Chinese in this part of the country must lead a very precarious existence, and be always on the verge of starvation. I say Chinese, because since crossing the Pan-lan Shan I have seen nothing but Chinese. The country of the Wa-ssŭ might have no existence, for the few houses one sees are of Chinese type and occupied by Chinese. It was different in the land of the Wokjé, who were always to be seen, and whose houses were dotted about in valley and on mountain side. Here we have simply Chinese squatters, who have built solitary refreshment houses for the accommodation of carriers.

When we were on the point of starting this morning the landlady of the inn known as Shao-ch'a-p'ing came to the door and began bewailing the badness of the times. She said that the crops had been bad, and that trade was consequently dull; that she kept the inn going; and that her husband did a little lumbering to keep the roof over their heads. There certainly was a roof of boards, weighted with stones; but I heard the rain dropping all round me overnight. Her object was, of course, to wheedle something out of me in addition to the ample payment already made, and she was delighted when I ordered an additional 200 cash to be presented to her. She said she came from Kuan Hsien about 20 years ago, and when I remarked that she must have been a mere infant at the time, she accepted the compliment and admitted to have been barely 10. She had left her home only once or twice during these 20 years, and had rarely seen the sun during that time; for the sun to shine on her home presaged bad harvests down below.

The morning of our departure was no exception to the usual condition of things at Shao-ch'a-p'ing, and we began the descent amid clouds and gloom, a red pine showing here and there, with brushwood and scrub lining the frightful stone road, slippery enough when at all dry, but in a positively dangerous condition when wet. We scrambled and slipped down as best we could till we reached a narrow valley or gorge, the entrance to which is marked by a waterfall dropping from the heights above. This valley resembles the valley on the other side of the mountain, even to the brook which had to be crossed and forded many times on the way down. On the road itself the pack animals had to be held back by their tails to prevent their falling, and they were frequently passed round rocky corners by one driver to another. In several places the road had been washed away, and very precarious paths had been selected by the first caravans appearing after the accidents. I was frequently over the ankles in mud as I tried to guide my pony over the best part of the road. Everything comes to an end, however, and it was a great relief, after sliding and stumbling for two hours, to reach level ground on the right bank of what had swollen from brook to stream in the interval, in the bed of a narrow valley bounded by low grassy hills leading south. Half a mile beyond we forded it at the solitary inn called Hao-tzŭ-p'ing, and followed its left bank down the valley which changes its course from south to south-east.

The road now continued fairly level for 20 *li*, and would have been classed as good in China had it been dry. At this distance, however, it was blocked by a rocky cone-shaped hill and turned south-west. At this point stands the two-house hamlet of An-chia p'ing through which we passed, and parting company with the valley commenced the ascent of a ridge thickly wooded, on the summit and called the Chiu-lung-shan. The ascent on the west side was easy enough, and from the crest we looked down into a deep valley running south-east and the usual brook going in the same direction. The eastern face of the

Chiu-lung-shan is very precipitous, and the road performs a series of steep zigzags. The south-west side of this new valley is bounded by high mountains, rocky and clad with scrub, while on the north-east the hills are rounded and partly brought under cultivation.

The road, instead of descending to the bottom of the valley, keeps to the hills on the north-east side, ascending and descending and skirting numerous valleys opening off the main valley. At last it rises to the crest of the Ch'i Shan, or "Varnish Hill", turns north-east, and by a steep gradient, descends south-east into a narrow valley, with the usual brook flowing north-west. In the middle of this narrow valley lies the two-house hamlet of Hei-shih-chiang (3,870 feet), which we entered over a covered-in bridge, and where we occupy the inn, one of its two houses. In the main valley we saw at a distance the village of San-chiang-k'ou, of which I shall speak later.

On crossing the Chiu-lung-shan we came on a number of new trees. The *Cunninghamia sinensis* was common, and the varnish tree—*Rhus vernicifera* D.C.—just shedding its leaves, was particularly abundant along the hillsides. The presence of this tree gives its name to the hill. The diagonal incisions in the bark, some 9 inches apart, were to be seen on the larger trees, while the young trees had not been tapped. The older trees stood from 25 feet to 30 feet high, and had short cross-pieces of wood lashed to stem and branches, to facilitate the ascent of the varnish collector. I am told that the amount of crude varnish annually produced here is from 700 catties to 800 catties, worth from 700 cash to 800 cash a catty; it is taken to San-chiang-k'ou, which is annually visited by agents from Kuan Hsien.

Soda is also manufactured in the mountains east and west of the Chiu-lung-shan, and the large wooden tubs used for drawing the soda from the ashes were seen at every house door during the day. When evaporated, it is packed in wooden tubs and carried to Kuan Hsien for sale. A full tub contains about 120 catties, or 160 lb, and constitutes a man's load.

Maize is the staple food of the people along this road. In the inn where I had my mid-day meal at Ts'ao-p'ing maize was being dried, preparatory to being ground into meal, over a slow fire of charcoal in a high bamboo basket, the maize being piled on a sieve on the top, and frequently turned during the process. An old woman of 78 was turning over the pile when I appeared, and began to grumble at my intrusion. Most reluctantly did she part with some of the maize for my pony, and it was only after I had paid for the maize and left her a handsome surplus that she left off grumbling. The by-standers, who are always numerous on such occasions, were amused at the old woman's attitude, and from their friendliness towards myself, I gathered that she was in her dotage. One of my followers asked for rice, and she indignantly replied that she had no rice, and that outsiders must be satisfied with all they had to eat— maize. I remarked that Kuan Hsien, where rice is plentiful, was only two days distant, but she closed the argument by saying, "Rice is too dear for us".

Maize, of course, was already harvested, but Amarantus, Perilla, and tobacco were still on the ground. The bramble was again common by the roadside, and one of my escort seemed particularly fond of the fruit, as well as of the succulent stalks of maize. The peach tree was very common in the vicinity of houses, and vegetables of various kinds, such as turnips and capsicum, occupied the garden patches.

26th October

We left Hei-shih-chiang at 6.30 a.m., in the hope of accomplishing a stage of 80 *li*, thus leaving only 40 *li* to reach Kuan Hsien the following day, in good time to arrange for change of transport for Chengtu. As will be seen, however, that hope was frustrated, and I am settled for the night in the market town of Hsüan-k'ou, after covering only 60 *li*. On leaving Hei-shih-chiang, the road commences a series of steep zigzags eastward up a mountain side—Yao-tzǔ Shan—and it is not till nearing the summit that there is any lessening of the precipitous ascent. We were buried in white gloom on the summit, which is 1,500 feet above Hei-shih-chiang. Yao-tzǔ Shan is the boundary of the Wên-ch'uan and Kuan Hsien districts, the former including the Wa-ssǔ territory from Pan-lan Shan eastwards.

Descending out of the gloom, a fair picture of Ssuchuan country life lay below us. To the north-east is a basin, 2,000 feet under the summit of Yao-tzǔ Shan, and the mountain slopes which appear to hem it in are well wooded, dotted with straw-thatched farmhouses, and under terrace cultivation. The scene was changed as if by the magician's wand. From silver fir, prickly oak, larch, birch, and trees suited to high altitudes, the road runs along the north-west side of the basin, through tea plantations in blossom and a country studded with the varnish tree, *Rhus semialata* Murr.—the source of nutgalls used in dyeing— *Cunninghamia sinensis*, the large-leaved privet, palms, loquat, peach, and clumps of bamboo. The box was also to be seen, and a few specimens of the *Sterculia platanifolia* L.f., with its fine large leaves. In the basin itself the stubble and straw of the rice crop still remained on the ground.

Shui-mo-kou, 30 *li* from Hei-shih-chiang, lying in the basin at the entrance to a valley running north-east, also brought us forcibly back to Ssuchuan life. It is a one-streeted market town, the type of so many scattered about the Chinese part of the province, with a population of from 360 to 370 families. The town lies on the left bank of a considerable stream, a combination of three streams, some of which had been our companions a day or two ago, meeting at San-chiang-k'ou, already mentioned, flowing north-east down the valley to join the Min River. It is connected with the opposite bank by two bamboo cable bridges, the upper leading into the country districts, the lower to Ch'ung-ch'ing Chou, on the Chengtu plain, a two-and-a-half days' journey, the road passing on its way the important market town of T'ai-p'ing-ch'ang. It is the centre of a considerable tea trade with the non-Chinese tribes to the west, and it is from it, and not from Kuan Hsien, that the tea packages start on their journey. The trade was until lately in official hands, but it is now a monopoly of a single tea establishment, which takes out tea licences from the Salt and Tea Commissioner at Chengtu. This establishment stated that its annual trade amounted to about 6,000 packages, each weighing 60 catties, an estimate which is not far short of the 7,000 to 8,000 given by an innkeeper on the road.

The stream, whose left bank we now followed for the rest of the day, is here and there obstructed by huge boulders, but there is sufficient volume of water to carry down bamboo rafts to Hsüan-k'ou, where they are made up into larger rafts and used for the carriage to Kuan Hsien, 60 *li* distant, of coal and coke which are found and manufactured at three places in the neighbourhood. The stream joins the Min immediately to the north-east of the town. On arrival on the left bank of the stream opposite Hsüan-k'ou, a market town with about 200 families, we found that our animals could not cross by the bamboo cable bridge. The latter consisted of 12 stout cables of split bamboo stretched between the two banks with boards laid cross-wise on the top to form the roadway, and five rows of similar cables on each side formed the rails. The boards were here and there lashed to the floor cables, but many of them were very loose, and some of the boards had disappeared altogether, making the passage too dangerous for animals. Moreover, three of the floor cables had given way, and the bridge formed a deep curve with considerable oscillation. Our animals had to be unloaded, and forded the stream higher up. All this entailed great delay, and we had to be content to remain for the night in Hsüan-k'ou (2,650 feet), instead of completing our programme of 20 more *li*. There was a herd of yak on the right bank of the stream at the ford. The bridge is about 70 yards long by some 8 feet wide.

Our arrival at Shui-mo-kou and Hsüan-k'ou created no little sensation, but the people were very respectful. I had a long conversation on the street with the small military official of the former place in the hearing of an immense crowd. He had visited Hong Kong, Canton, and Macao, and was loud in his praises of the British Colony. The soldiers sent by him as local escort to Hsüan-k'ou had never seen a breech-loader, and when I explained to them the mechanism of my fowling-piece they were utterly lost in admiration. Their only fear was that it might be loaded when they were carrying it, for this they did in turn as if it were a thing to be proud of.

We are promised an easy stage of 60 *li* tomorrow along the right bank of the Min River to Kuan Hsien.

27th October

We got away from Hsüan-k'ou at 6 a.m., and at the eastern end of the town struck the junction of the tributary with the Min River, where the latter, obstructed by rocks, sweeps with a very strong current from a mountain gorge to the north-west and bends north-east. A red pagoda stands on the spit of land just above the junction. The Min goes north-east, east, and south by south-west to the Chengtu plain, and the road follows its right bank, occasionally cutting off a bend by crossing a low ridge and again skirting high up the mountain side, where it flows through a gorge. Shingle islands and rocks are common, and the rapids caused by them bar any attempt at navigation. Bamboo rafts were descending, but there was no boat traffic up or down. The mountain sides bounding the river valley are well wooded, especially with the conifer *Cunninghamia sinensis*, and here it is, and in side valleys, that the plain of Chengtu finds its supply of building timber.

A mile or two north of Kuan Hsien, and below the junction of the Min with an affluent, on the left bank, called the Pai-sha Ho, lime and coal were being mined and coke pits were blazing close to the water's edge. Half a mile above the city the Min is crossed by a bamboo cable bridge of five spans, with a total length of about 250 yards. Ten stout cables support the plank floor, and five cables on each side form the rails, which have each its place in four-sided open woodwork columns, dotted at short intervals along the bridge and attached to the floor. The ends of the cables are kept taut by vertical wooden windlasses built into solid roofed structures on both banks. The plank floor was in excellent repair, and, although there was some oscillation, the pack animals had no difficulty in crossing it one by one with their loads. Across the bridge we stood on the other great trade highway from Ssuchuan to Tibet, which runs from Kuan Hsien to Sung-p'an, following in the main the valley of the Min River. On the very first stage, however, from Kuan Hsien, the road cuts off the bend we have just rounded by ascending a side valley, crossing the Niang-tzŭ-ling Pass, and descending to the river again at Ying-shui-wan. One of the piers of the cable bridge is built on a spit of land which begins just above the bridge and divides the river into two branches, but that on the right has a much smaller volume of water than the other.

Between the bridge and the city of Kuan Hsien there is a high ridge, with a wall and gateway along its crest, strik-

ing the river at right angles, and continued on the opposite bank, for the channel along the south wall of the city
is the work of that famous engineer, Li Ping, whose name
is justly held in honour throughout the province of
Ssuchuan, and to whom the temple lying on the wooded
hillside between the bridge and the foot of the ridge is
dedicated. This Taoist temple is undoubtedly the finest and
cleanest I have seen in China, and well may it be kept in
order, for Li Ping has, by his work and his teaching,
brought comparative affluence to the plain of Chengtu,
whose inhabitants are, in return for easy payments, entitled
to an abundant and fertilizing water supply.

Opposite the south-west angle of the city wall flows
the main channel of the river southwards; but a rocky
bluff, a continuation of the ridge, on which stands a less
gorgeous temple to Li Ping's son, lying on the left bank
of the main channel, throws a part of the river into the
artificial channel eastward along the south wall, and is the
commencement of that great system of irrigation which
makes the plain of Chengtu the granary of Ssuchuan.
And not only has Li Ping's engineering skill made the
plain more productive: it has likewise rendered possible
the transport of its wealth, for many of these waterways
are navigable by boats of light draught, and rafts of
timber, sometimes laden with coal and coke, are floated
from the mountains in the west to populous centres on
the plain. It is unnecessary for me to enter into details
regarding Li Ping's engineering feat. The subject has been
fully dealt with by other writers, but it is a pleasure to
call attention to a public work which, so rare a thing in
China, has not been neglected by the passing of centuries. Every winter Li Ping's advice is followed: "Dig the
channels deep, and keep the dikes low." By means of a
movable barrage erected above the bridge the water is
thrown first to one then to the other side of the river,

allowing the silt to be removed annually from the various channels. The dikes are, at the same time, put in order and kept low enough to allow the water to overflow from one channel into another, and prevent flooding of the surrounding country.

A Prefect, called the Shui Li Fu, who resides at Kuan Hsien, is in charge of the work, and in March every year the duty of opening the barrage and diverting the water on to the plain is carried out with great ceremony by the Taotai of Chengtu, who proceeds to Kuan Hsien for the purpose. A good view of Li Ping's skilful workmanship may be obtained from the platform built on the bluff behind the temple dedicated to his son.

The city of Kuan Hsien (2,280 feet) lies to the east of the ridge. It is a small place with four walls and three gates in the west, south, and east walls respectively. Its population amounts to about 30,000, and its main thoroughfares are scenes of busy life.

To the south and south-west the mountains recede some distance from the river. To the north it is backed by a range of high hills, and to the north-east they fade away into the Chengtu plain. It is the place whence porters and pack animals start on their journeys northwards to Sung-p'an, and westwards to the Tibetan border lands, and is a depôt of trade between Ssuchuan and Tibet.

28th October

On arrival at Kuan Hsien at 1.30 p.m. yesterday I immediately set about arranging transport, for although I knew that pack animals would no longer be procurable, I had resolved to make Chengtu (120 *li*, or about 30 miles) in one day, and allow my baggage to be brought on in two stages by wheelbarrows and porters. Every arrangement was made by nightfall, and we started at 5 a.m., practically before daylight.

My followers were as eager as I was to be home after the wear and tear of a three-month journey, and there was no dilly-dallying on the road. We reached the small city of Pi Hsien a little after noon, and at 5 p.m. we entered the west gate of Chengtu. The road between Pi Hsien and the capital was busy as ever. It was one string of foot passengers, porters, chairs, and wheelbarrows moving in both directions. The country was, of course, hidden by clumps of trees and bamboos, and the yellow stubble of the rice crop was broken occasionally by dark green plots of indigo and the light green sprouts of winter wheat. We had, however, exchanged the clear, sunny, buoyant atmosphere of the western highlands for the dark, cloudy, depressing climate of the Chengtu plain.

TA-CHIEN-LU AND THE TRADE OF TIBET

In dealing with the trade passing through the city of Ta-chien-lu, it should be borne in mind that no distinction is made between the country extending from Ta-chien-lu to the Tibetan frontier and Tibet proper. The former is, of course, part of the province of Ssuchuan; but, as its inhabitants are Tibetans, trade west of Ta-chien-lu is, in Chinese eyes, trade with Tibet. The following statistics, therefore, refer to the whole of the country served by the official and northern roads leading from Ta-chien-lu to Tibet. They were compiled in Ta-chien-lu from official and commercial sources, and, in the absence of exact data, may be looked upon as fairly approximate.

I have already stated that the commercial quarter of Ta-chien-lu does not impress one with the idea that the city is the chief depôt of Tibetan trade, but the daily traffic at the gates, as caravan after caravan passes out and in, shows that a comparatively large trade exists, and one soon learns that it is conducted not in the ordinary street shops, but in back offices without frontal display, and in the 48 "Ko Chuang", or Tibetan caravansaries, where buyers and sellers are lodged, and, in return for a commission, assisted in carrying on their business transactions. There are, in addition, a few Chinese inns, but the share which they take in the trade is insignificant.

I shall treat as exports what is sent from and through China to Ta-chien-lu for consumption in, and as imports what reaches Ta-chien-lu from, the west.

EXPORTS

Brick tea is the great export. I have already described the preparation of an ordinary Tibetan meal, whose ingredients are tea, butter, tsamba, and a little salt; but buttered tea without tsamba is made at all odd times as a refreshing drink as well as a food. Tea, therefore, is the first necessity of every Tibetan household. The trade in this article is carried on under a system of Government and provincial licences held by tea establishments in the districts of Ya-an, Jung-ching, Ming-shan, the department of T'ien-ch'üan—all in the Prefecture of Ya-chou Fu—and the independent department of Chiung Chou. Each licence covers five packages (not bricks), irrespective of quality, weight, and value. The number of licences held by Ya-an is 38,000; by Jung-ching, 30,000; by Ming-shan and T'ien-ch'üan together, 28,000; and by Chiung Chou, 20,300. But Chiung Chou, whose licences are entirely Government (not provincial), being unable to fill more than 8,000, disposes of the balance of 12,300 to Ya-an and Jung-ching, the former taking up 6,300 and the latter 6,000, and they have recourse to Chien-wei, O-mei, and P'ing-shan districts and Ma-pien Sub-Prefecture to enable them to fill their additional licences. The total number of licences, however, remain the same—namely, 116,300.

Now, did the manufacturing centres prepare the bricks of the same size and weight and pack them uniformly, we should be able by simple multiplication to arrive at the total quantity of brick tea sent annually to Ta-chien-lu, and a question which has engaged the attention of many minds would be set at rest. Unfortunately, this is not the case, and the output of each centre has to be treated separately. In Ya-an district alone is there uniformity of weight and packing of the four qualities of bricks manufactured.

In Ta-chien-lu I dissected a package of Ya-an second-quality brick tea known as *Chin Yü* intended for Tibet proper, with the following result. Opening one end of the split-bamboo casing of the package, which weighed 18 catties, or 24 lb, I drew out from a single row four flattish cylinders, each wrapped separately in two sheets of yellowish, slightly waterproofed paper made specially for this purpose in the department of Chiung Chou. Each wrapper had stamped on it in black ink, in a circle slightly larger than a 20-cent piece, a single Chinese character—one of the characters of the name of the manufacturing firm. Removing the paper wrapper, I disclosed a red paper label $10\frac{1}{2}$ inches long by $6\frac{3}{8}$ inches wide, half-concealed by half of a sheet of red paper, whose other half was drawn under one end of something hard below the label. Folding down the upper half of the red sheet and removing the label, I found a brown flat cylinder or brick of tea-leaves and twigs well compressed. In the centre of one of the convex sides was a patch of thin gold-leaf, less than an inch square, and a few inches above it a stamp similar to that on the paper wrapper, but in this case the ink was red. The red sheet of paper enveloped little more than half the brick, which measured $10\frac{1}{2}$ inches high and $19\frac{1}{8}$ inches in circumference, while the short and long diameters at each end were respectively 4 inches and 9 inches. The weight of the brick was $5\frac{2}{3}$ lb. The red label had printed in the centre the figure of Old Age riding a spotted deer, with the name of the manufacturing firm in Chinese and Tibetan on the top, with three lines of Tibetan writing under the central figure and the name of the tea in Chinese at the foot.

All Ya-an teas are similarly packed and stamped with the exception of the fourth or worst quality, which, instead of one square of gold-leaf, has four tiny four-sided pieces arranged to form the corners of a small square and a similar piece in the centre of the square. The first and second qualities of Ya-an tea go to Tibet, while the third and fourth are mostly consumed along the frontier.

Jung-ching teas are also packed in four qualities, the first weighing 14, and the second 14 and 15 catties to the package, each of four bricks, with five small pieces of gold-leaf on one side. A package of the third quality, weighing 16 and 17 catties, contains only three bricks, each of which has five pieces of gold-leaf on either side. The first and second qualities are intended for the Tibetan market.

Ming-shan and T'ien-ch'üan teas are packed in three qualities in 15 and 16, 13 and 14, and 12 and 13 catty four-brick packages respectively. Some of the first and most of the third quality go to Tibet, and the latter is used in paying caravan freight, being taken on with the finer tea for that purpose. Each brick has only one patch of leaf which, however, is not gold but tin.

Chiung Chou teas are packed in two qualities with 13 and 14 catty packages for the first, and 15 catty for the second. Each package contains four bricks, with one patch of tin-leaf. Most of the first quality goes to lamaseries in

Tibet, and the bulk of the second quality to Litang and Batang.

In this form the tea is carried on the backs of porters of all ages from the manufacturing centres to Ta-chien-lu, where it changes from Chinese to Tibetan hands. The sum of 50 taels is the standard of sale, and the following table shows the fluctuations that take place in the market in exchange for that sum:

Place of production	Net weight of package	Number of packages purchasable for 50 taels			
		First quality	Second quality	Third quality	Fourth quality
Ya-an	17	12–15	22–28	28–32	45–50
Jung-ching	13	20			
Jung-ching	13–14		30		
Jung-ching	15–16			51–52	
Jung-ching	13				55–60
T'ien-ch'üan } Ming-shan }	14–15	30–32			
Ming-shan	12		38–42	55–60	
Chiung Chou	12–13	12–14			
Chiung Chou	14		55–60		

The finer teas are now removed from their bamboo casings, and neatly packed and sewed in yak-hide cases, each containing 12 bricks. This is done to prevent the bricks from being crushed by collision with other loads or with forest trees. The precaution is very necessary, for stampeding is common among the yak and ponies which make up the caravans, and trees frequently encroach on the roadway, while the animals will scatter all over a forest to graze should they chance to make a halt in it. The coarser teas, which have usually a less distance to travel, are left to their fate in the original packages.

The licences are distributed as follows over the various classes of teas:

Place of production	First quality	Second quality	Third quality	Fourth quality
Ya-an	2,000	32,300	6,000	4,000
Jung-ching	1,400	20,000	10,600	4,000
T'ien-ch'üan Ming-shan	} 4,000	2,000	22,000	
Chiung Chou	6,000	2,000		
	13,400	56,300	38,600	8,000
Total		116,300		

As, now, each licence represents five packages of tea, the following table gives the number of packages of the different qualities supplied by the various manufacturing centres:

Place of production	First quality	Second quality	Third quality	Fourth quality
Ya-an	10,000	161,500	30,000	20,000
Jung-ching	7,000	100,000	53,000	20,000
T'ien-ch'üan Ming-shan	} 20,000	10,000	110,000	
Chiung Chou	30,000	10,000		
	67,000	281,500	193,000	40,000
Total		581,500		

Applying to this table giving the net weight of each package of the four qualities of tea, and the average number of packages sold for 50 taels, we get the following table:

Annual quantity of brick tea exported through Ta-chien-lu for consumption in the west.

Place of production	First quality		Second quality		Third quality		Fourth quality	
	Catties	Taels	Catties	Taels	Catties	Taels	Catties	Taels
Ya-an	170,000	37,037	2,745,500	323,000	510,000	50,000	340,000	21,052
Jung-ching	91,000	17,500	1,350,000	166,666	821,500	51,456	260,000	17,391
T'ien-chüan Ming-shan }	290,000	32,258	120,000	12,500	1,320,000	95,652		
Chiung Chou	375,000	115,384	140,000	8,695				
	926,000	202,179	4,355,500	510,861	2,651,500	197,108	600,000	38,443
Total			8,533,000 catties 948,591 taels					

That is to say, the total annual quantity of brick tea carried to Ta-chien-lu for consumption to the west of that city is approximately 8,533,000 catties, or 11,377,333 lb to the value of 948,591 taels. In the above tables I have, for the sake of convenience, grouped the different grades of tea manufactured in the various centres together as if they were of equal quality. This, however, is not the case, as may be seen from the disparity in values.

Native cotton goods from Shashih in Hupei, and from Ta-yi Hsien on the south-western border of the Chengtu plain, the latter manufactured from foreign yarn, are annually laid down in Ta-chien-lu to the value of about 46,500 taels.

Only a small quantity of silks and satins is sent to Tibet, and the value is said to amount to no more than 1,500 taels, but silk *khata*, the coarse scarves manufactured in Chengtu for ceremonial purposes, are valued at 20,000 taels. On only one occasion did I see the *khata* used, and that was when an old lady was sent by the family of a headman, who was himself absent, to beg me not to press for fresh transport at once, and to delay my departure from the village until next morning. Before presenting the request she handed me a *khata*.

About 2,750 bundles, each weighing 25 catties, of tobacco of a value of 6,000 taels are annually sent from the Chengtu plain, principally from Shih-fang Hsien and Chung-ning Hsien, to Ta-chien-lu. I have already explained that Tibetans rarely smoke, and the leaves are ground down into snuff.

A little raw cotton of the value of about 1,000 taels finds its way to Ta-chien-lu, but it is for local consumption only.

The above are the native goods sent to Ta-chien-lu for consumption in the west. Their value is 1,022,591 taels, but foreign goods, such as shirtings (23,000 taels), satinet

(1,500 taels), long ells (400 taels), and foreign sundries (6,000 taels) of a total value of 30,900 taels, also cross this province to Ta-chien-lu, so that the total value of native and foreign goods annually consumed to the west of that city may be placed at 1,053,491 taels.

IMPORTS

The principal import into Ta-chien-lu from Tibet and the intervening country is musk. The pods, with an inch-wide fringe of skin and hair, are brought to the city, where they are trimmed, cleaned, and made ready for the Chinese and foreign market. An ordinary pod in this raw state weighs about an ounce. The fringe of skin and hair is removed by scissors, and, in the case of musk intended for the Japanese market, the hair round the trimmed pod is carefully singed. There are several tests for adulteration. If the smell is not satisfactory and any doubt exists as to the genuineness of the contents, a small sharp scoop is thrust into the pod and a few grains extracted. The grains are put in a cup of water. If they remain granular the musk is genuine; if they melt it is false. Another test is to place a few grains on a live piece of charcoal. If they melt and bubble on the red surface the musk is good; if they at once harden and become cinder, the musk is adulterated.

The trimmed and clean musk pods are valued at from 15 taels to 16 taels per Chinese ounce (1⅓ oz English), and the total amount annually cleaned at Ta-chien-lu for the Chinese and foreign market is estimated at 1,100 to 1,200 catties, to the value of 300,000 taels.

Gold dust to the amount of 6,000 Chinese ounces (8,000 oz English), to the value of 192,000 taels—that is, 32 taels per Chinese ounce—is said to be the present annual import into Ta-chien-lu from the Litang district and from the Tibetan State of Chantui, the amount being equally divided between the two. I have stated elsewhere that the banks of the Li Chŭ in the Litang plain are exceedingly rich in gold, but that the lamas of the Litang lamasery are opposed to and prevent its exploitation.

I saw large flocks of sheep between Ta–chien–lu and the frontier of Tibet, and I anticipated that the annual import of wool into the former, even from that part of the country, must be enormous. This anticipation was strengthened by the high figures given by others; but very careful inquiries at Ta–chien–lu resulted in the total import being placed at only 400,000 catties, to the value of 48,000 taels.

Sheep-skins, numbering from 140,000 to 150,000 annually, reach Ta–chien–lu. They are valued at 1 mace to 3 mace, according to size and quality, and the total value is about 30,000 taels.

Tibet and the border-lands are famed for the production of certain medicines, animal and vegetable, including that mixture of animal and vegetable known as *Cordiceps sinensis*. Deer horns in the velvet are valued at 30,000 taels, and old deer horns, for the manufacture of medicinal glue, at 8,500 taels, the latter amounting in weight to 30,000 catties, worth 2 mace to 4 candareen a catty. Ch'ung–ts'ao (*Cordiceps*) is put at 5,000 to 6,000 catties, to the value of 15,000 taels, and the two quantities of Pei–mu (*Coelogyne Henryi* Rolfe), the inferior, also called Chih–mu, amounting each to 14,000 to 15,000 catties, worth 20,000 taels and 8,500 taels respectively. The dye known as *Rubia cordifolia* L., is also used medicinally; but the import amounts to not more than 2,000 catties, to the value of about 100 taels.

Raw borax comes from Tibet and the State of Dergé to the amount of 20,000 catties a year, worth 3,500 taels, and is converted into pure borax at Ta-chien-lu, whence it is exported for use in various industries.

Furs are represented by the fox and the lynx. Of the former, some 3,000 good skins are imported annually worth 5,000 taels, and 8,000 inferior, valued at 4,000 taels. I saw some excellent lynx skins in Ta-chien-lu. Some 600 are received every year, worth 2,000 taels.

A considerable number of yak-hides annually find their way to Ta-chien-lu, but they are nearly all used for packing tea and other articles, and return to Tibet.

Imports from Yünnan do not fall under the category of trade with Tibet; but it may be mentioned here that some 200 loads of Yünnan opium from Li-chiang Fu and Ho-ch'ing Chou, each load weighing 2,000 Chinese, or about 2,667 English, ounces, are annually brought by porters to Ta-chien-lu, the road followed being that which branches off at the Choto Pass. The total value of this opium is some 80,000 taels. There also come from Burma, through Yünnan, about 100 bales of cotton cloth, valued at 900 taels.

I have stated above that, so far as the tea trade is concerned, the standard of bargaining is the sum of 50 taels. In Ta-chien-lu itself silver (sycee), Indian and Chinese rupees, and copper cash are all current, but west of that city rupees—whole, halved, and quartered—are alone in use, and local transactions are very much hampered by the want of a smaller currency.

The bulk of the above trade follows the northern road from Ta-chien-lu, which is easier, safer, and passes through better grazing ground than the official road through Litang and Batang which has just been described.

SUMMARY

	Exports			Imports	
	Quantity	Value		Quantity	Value
		Taels			Taels
Brick tea	11,377,333 lb	948,591	Musk	24,533 oz	300,000
Cottons, native		46,500	Gold dust	8,000 oz	192,000
Silks and satins		1,500	Wool, sheeps	533,333 lb	48,000
Silk khata		20,000	Skins, sheep	145,000 pieces	30,000
Tobacco, leaf	68,750 lb	6,000	Medicines		84,600
Foreign goods		30,900	Borax	26,667 lb	3,500
			Furs—		
			Fox	11,000 pieces	9,000
			Lynx	600 pieces	2,000
Total		1,053,491	Total		669,100

Total of exports and imports 1,722,591 taels

ITINERARY

Chengtu to Ta-chien-lu

Date in 1904	Place	Distance in *li* between places	Height above sea level in feet	Remarks
July 28	Chengtu		1,700	Capital of Province of Ssuchuan
July 28	Ts'u-ch'iao	20		Large market town; about 1,000 houses
July 28	Shuang-liu Hsien	20		District city; 2,900 houses

Date in 1904	Place	Distance in *li* between places	Height above sea level in feet	Remarks
July 28	Huang-shui-ho	15		Market town; about 100 houses
July 28	Hua-ch'iao-tzŭ	25		Ditto; 300 houses
July 28	Têng-kung-ch'ang	15		Ditto; 100 houses
July 29	Ch'ing-lung-ch'ang	25		Ditto; 400 houses
July 29	Kuan-yin-p'u	15		Ditto; 160 houses
July 29	P'êng-shan Hsien	15	1,520	District city; 1,440 houses
July 29	Hsin-ch'iao-p'u	10		Ferry; about 30 houses
July 29	Lung-an-p'u	8		About 20 houses
July 29	Mei Chou	22	1,470	Department city; about 1,900 houses
July 30	Chang-chia-k'an	20		Market town; 270 houses
July 30	Hei-lung-ch'ang	20		About 10 houses
July 30	Ch'ing-shên Hsien	20		District city; 900 houses
July 30	Liu-chia-ch'ang	20		Market town; 90 houses
July 31	Hsi-lu-k'ou	15		Ferry across Min River; about 10 houses
July 31	Pan-ch'iao-ch'i	15		About 20 houses
July 31	Mêng-tzŭ-ch'ang	20		Market town; about 200 houses
July 31	Chia-ting Fu	20	1,350	Important Prefectural city; about 8,000 houses
Aug. 1	Su-ch'i	20		Market town; 400 houses

Date in 1904	Place	Distance in *li* between places	Height above sea level in feet	Remarks
Aug. 1	Kao-shan-p'u	15		About 20 houses
Aug. 1	Chên-tzŭ-ch'ang	15		Market town; 200 houses
Aug. 1	O-mei Hsien	20	1,740	District city; 1,400 houses
Aug. 2–6	O-mei Shan		10,158	Summit of Sacred Mountain
Aug. 7	Kuan-o-ch'ang	15		Market town; about 50 houses
Aug. 7	Kao-ch'iao-p'u	15		Ditto; 100 houses
Aug. 7	Huang-mao-kang	20	3,100	About 20 houses
Aug. 7	Yang-ts'un-p'u	20	3,100	About 40 houses
Aug. 7	Lung-ch'ih-ch'ang	20	2,900	Market town; 200 houses
Aug. 8	Ta-wei-ch'ang	15	2,550	Ditto; 40 houses
Aug. 8	Yü-lung-ch'ang	20	3,700	About 10 houses
Aug. 8	Ts'ai-kou	20		2 or 3 houses
Aug. 9	Ch'un-t'ien-p'ing	15	4,680	1 house
Aug. 9	Kuan-tou-shan	10		Ditto
Aug. 9	Fo Ngai	10		
Aug. 9	Lo-lo-p'ing	5	4,255	5 or 6 houses
Aug. 9	Chin-k'ou-ho	35		About 100 houses
Aug. 10	Pai-shih-kou	15		4 or 5 houses
Aug. 10	Nan-mu-yüan	15		About 40 houses
Aug. 10 {	Shou-p'ing-shan / Shou-yung-ch'ang }	20		Market town; 60 to 70 houses
Aug. 11	Ta-t'ien-ch'ih	15	6,050	About 10 houses
Aug. 11	Kao-liang-ch'ih	5		2 houses
Aug. 11	So-i-ling	10	9,146	Summit of pass

Date in 1904	Place	Distance in *li* between places	Height above sea level in feet	Remarks
Aug. 11	Hua-hsiang-kou	10		1 house
Aug. 11	Lêng-chu-p'ing	20	6,720	About 10 houses
Aug. 12	Ngai-wo-kai	5		
Aug. 12	Huang-mu-ch'ang	25		About 100 houses
Aug. 12	Ts'ai-tzŭ-ti	30		7 or 8 houses
Aug. 12	Ma-lieh Shan	5	7,850	Pass
Aug. 12	Ma-lieh Hsin-kai-tzŭ	25	5,500	60 to 70 houses
Aug. 13	T'ien-pa	10		About 10 houses
Aug. 13	Pai-ai-ho	5		8 or 9 houses
Aug. 13	Pai-ai-kang	5	4,150	
Aug. 13	Fu-lin	10	3,100	Important market town in Chien-ch'ang valley near left bank of T'ung River; over 500 houses
Aug. 14	Lung-tung-ying	15		About 10 houses
Aug. 14	T'ang-chia-pa Fu-hsing-ch'ang	15		About 100 houses
Aug. 14	Han-yüan-kai	15	3,600	Important market town; 300 houses. Junction of Chien-ch'ang and Ta-chien-lu roads
Aug. 14	Fu-chuang	25		Over 140 houses
Aug. 15	Pan-chiu-ai Tou-liu-tzŭ	25		About 20 houses

Date in 1904	Place	Distance in *li* between places	Height above sea level in feet	Remarks
Aug. 15	Ta-yang-kou	2		4 houses
Aug. 15	San-ch'i-k'ou	8		3 or 4 houses. Telegraph line and small tea road from Ya-chou join main road
Aug. 15	Ni-t'ou-yi Yi-t'ou	15	4,900	Important market town; over 400 houses
Aug. 16	Kao-ch'iao	15		About 20 houses
Aug. 16	San-ch'iao-p'ing	5	5,800	About 30 houses
Aug. 16	San-tao-ch'iao	15	6,975	About 10 houses
Aug. 16	Fu-lung-ssû	15	8,010	2 or 3 houses
Aug. 16	Fei-yüeh Ling	10	9,022	Summit of pass
Aug. 16	Hua-lin-p'ing	15	7,225	About 160 houses
Aug. 17	Lung-pa-p'u Hsing-lung-p'u	20	5,020	About 100 houses
Aug. 17	Lêng-chi	10	4,750	About 200 houses
Aug. 17	Wa-chioh	20		About 40 houses
Aug. 17	Ta-pa	10	5,100	About 10 houses
Aug. 17	Lu-ting-ch'iao	15	4,620	About 300 houses. Bridge across the T'ung River
Aug. 18	Tsa-li	15		About 10 houses
Aug. 18	Hsiao-p'êng-pa	10		About 10 houses
Aug. 18	Ta-p'êng-pa	10		About 20 houses
Aug. 18	Lêng-chu-kuan	10	5,220	About 30 houses
Aug. 18	Wa-ssŭ-kou	15	4,780	About 40 houses

Date in 1904	Place	Distance in *li* between places	Height above sea level in feet	Remarks
Aug. 19	Jih-ti	15		About 10 houses
Aug. 19	Liu-yang	20		About 8 houses
Aug. 19	Shên-k'ang	10		2 or 3 houses
Aug. 19–24	Ta-chien-lu Ting	15	8,349	Sub-Prefectural city; about 700 Tibetan and 400 Chinese houses
	Total	1,250		

Ta-chien-lu to Tibetan frontier and back

Aug. 25	Ta-chien-lu		8,349	
Aug. 25	Kung-chu-eh'iao	2		Bridge across Lu River ("Gate of Tibet")
Aug. 25	Ta-p'ing	18		Solitary house
Aug. 25	Cho-to	20	10,647	3 or 4 houses
Aug. 26	Cho-to Shan		13,923	Summit of pass
Aug. 26	Hsin-tien-tzŭ Jêh-shui-t'ang	60		Solitary house
Aug. 26	Ti-ju Ti-zu	10	12,451	3 houses
Aug. 26	An-niang-pa	30		About 10 houses
Aug. 27	Wa-chieh	30		1 or 2 houses
Aug. 27	Ying-kuan-chai	5		About 10 houses. Old Tibetan fort on hill top
Aug. 27	Tung-ngolo	25		About 40 houses
Aug. 28	La-tza Shan-kên	20		Solitary house
Aug. 28	Ka Ji La	10	13,958	Summit of pass
Aug. 28	Wo-lung-shih	40	11,329	About 10 houses

Date in 1904	Place	Distance in *li* between places	Height above sea level in feet	Remarks
Aug. 29	Ts'ao-pa / Ja-rih-ka	20		2 or 3 houses
Aug. 29	Ja-lĕng-ka	5		1 house
Aug. 29	Pa-ko-lou / Karimbo	20		2 or 3 houses
Aug. 29	Ho-k'ou / Nia-chŭ-ka	45	9,010	Village of over 20 houses on left bank of the Ya-lung or Nia-chŭ
Aug. 30	Ma-kai-chung / Mai-geh-drung	40	11,446	About 10 houses
Aug. 31	Shan-kên-tzŭ / Chan-pa-la-tza	20		
Aug. 31	Ra Ma La		14,948	Summit of pass
Aug. 31	Chien-tzŭ-wan / La-ni-ba	20		Hollow between passes
Aug. 31	Do-zé-la		15,041	Summit of pass
Aug. 31	Po-lang-kung	20		Post station
Aug. 31	Hsi-ngolo	25	11,715	13 houses
Sept. 1	Rih-kung-ta	25		Solitary post station
Sept. 1	Tsa-ma-la-tung	15		Solitary post station
Sept. 1	Dé-rih-ka La	20	14,137	Summit of pass
Sept. 1	Luan-shih-ch'iao	10		Solitary house; post station
Sept. 1	Wong-gi La / Chien-pa-ting		14,560	Summit of pass
Sept. 1	Ho-chŭ-ka	20	13,096	5 or 6 houses on left bank of Ho-chŭ
Sept. 2	Yao-cha-tzŭ	30		Solitary house

Date in 1904	Place	Distance in *li* between places	Height above sea level in feet	Remarks
Sept. 2	Hsieh Gi La ⎫ Litang Pass ⎭		14,165	Summit of pass
Sept. 3	Litang	30	13,234	Small town with large lamasery
Sept. 4	Ta-ch'iao	30		Bridge across the Li-chǔ. Solitary post station
Sept. 4	T'ou-t'ang ⎫ Jiom-bu-t'ang ⎭	30	14,555	Post station; 5 houses
Sept. 5	Huang-t'u-kang ⎫ Nga-ra-ka ⎭	25	15,429	Summit of pass
Sept. 5	Kan-hai-tzǔ ⎫ Tsamda ⎭	15		Solitary post station
Sept. 5	La-êrh-t'ang ⎫ La-tza ⎭	30		Post station; 5 houses
Sept. 6	La-ma-ya ⎫ Ranung ⎭	25	12,476	About 40 houses
Sept. 7	Yeh La Ka			Pass
Sept. 7	Dza Chǔ	20		Bridge across Dza Chǔ
Sept. 7	Mang-ga La			Pass
Sept. 7	Lei-kan-do	20	12,048	12 or 13 houses
Sept. 7	Erh-lang-wan ⎫ Nenda ⎭	20	12,767	Post station; 5 houses. Near foot of Mt Nenda
Sept. 8	Yünnan-ch'iao	30		Bridge; small road to Yünnan
Sept. 8	San-pa ⎫ Ra Ti ⎭	30	13,286	Post station; 5 houses
Sept. 9	San-pa Shan ⎫ Rung-sé La ⎭	30	15,437	Summit of pass

Date in 1904	Place	Distance in *li* between places	Height above sea level in feet	Remarks
Sept. 9	Ta-so Ta-ho	60	12,992	Post station; 6 houses
Sept. 10	Ta-so Shan J'rah La Ka		16,486	Summit of pass
Sept. 10	Pang-chai-mu Pang-cha-mu	60	12,875	Post station; 6 houses
Sept. 11	Hsiao-pa-chung Ma-chioh-hsi	30		4 or 5 houses
Sept. 12	Batang	30	9,184	Town of 400 houses, with large lamasery. Roads to Dergé, Yünnan, and Tibet
Sept. 13	T'ao-yüan-tzǔ Dza-hsü	15		Couple of houses
Sept. 13	Ch'a-shu Shan La-to Ting	5		Pass
Sept. 13	Chin-sha Chiang			Upper waters of the River Yang-tsze
Sept. 13	Niu-ku Ku-tu	15		Hamlet; 2 or 3 houses on left bank of the Chin-sha Chiang. Ferry and road to Ch'amdo

Date in 1904	Place	Distance in *li* between places	Height above sea level in feet	Remarks
Sept. 13	Shui-mo-kou ⎱ Lah ⎰	5		5 or 6 houses on left bank of Chin-sha Chiang
Sept. 14	Hê-t'ao-yüan-tzŭ ⎱ Tang-da ⎰	30		Solitary house
Sept. 14	Chu-pa-lung	20	8,430	Some 20 houses on left bank of Chin-sha Chiang
Sept. 14	Tsao-wu	5		Ferry
Sept. 14	Kung La ⎱ Go Ra ⎰	15		5 or 6 houses
Sept. 14	Ko-pu-lung	10		Small hamlet in valley after leaving the Chin-sha Chiang
Sept. 14	Ta-ko-ting	10		Some 10 houses
Sept. 15	K'ung-tzŭ-ka			Pass
Sept. 15	K'ung-tzŭ-ting ⎱ K'ung-tzŭ-ka ⎰	40	11,964	30 to 40 houses
Sept. 15	Mang-li	30		Some 10 houses
Sept. 15	Pang-mu-t'ang ⎱ Shang-mang-li ⎱ Trang-ba-la-tza ⎰	20	12,161	Some 10 houses
Sept. 16	Ning-ching Shan	15		The frontier of Ssuchuan and Tibet. Boundary stone on ridge
	Total	1,355		

Tibetan frontier to Ta-chien-lu

Date in 1904	Place	Distance in *li* between places	Height above sea level in feet	Remarks
Sept. 16	K'ung-tzŭ-ting	65	11,964	
Sept. 17	Chu-pa-lung	80	8,430	
Sept. 18–19	Batang	90	9,184	
Sept. 20	Pang-chai-mu	60	12,875	
Sept. 21	Ta-so	60	12,992	See Ta-chien-lu
Sept. 22	San-pa	90	13,286	to Tibetan
Sept. 23	Lei-kan-do	80	12,048	frontier.
Sept. 24–25	La-ma-ya	40	12,476	Distance
Sept. 26	T'ou-t'ang	95	14,555	from
Sept. 27	Litang	60	13,234	Ta-chien-lu
Sept. 28	Ho-chŭ-ka	60	13,096	to Tibetan
Sept. 29	Hsi-ngolo	90	11,715	frontier and
Sept. 30	Ma-kai-chung	85	11,446	back =
Oct. 1	Ho-k'ou	40	9,010	2,710 *li*
Oct. 2	Wo-lung-shih	90	11,329	
Oct. 3	Tung-ngolo	70		
Oct. 4	Ti-zu	90	12,451	
Oct. 5–9	Ta-chien-lu	110	8,349	
	Total	1,355		

Ta-chien-lu to Chengtu by way of Romi Chango and Mou-kung T'ing

Oct. 10	Ta-chien-lu			
Oct. 10	T'ou-tao-ch'iao	5	8,349	Bridge
Oct. 10	Erh-tao-ch'iao	5		Several houses
Oct. 10	San-tao-ch'iao	15		Several houses
Oct. 10	Yü-tzŭ-t'ung	5		8 houses
Oct. 10	Wang-mu	30		2 houses
Oct. 10	Niu-o-kou	5	9,503	5 houses
Oct. 11	Shih-t'ung-pa	15		2 houses
Oct. 11	Ch'i-mu-t'o	5		1 house
Oct. 11	Jê-shui-t'ang	10		5 or 6 houses

Date in 1904	Place	Distance in *li* between places	Height above sea level in feet	Remarks
Oct. 11	Chung-ku	5		2 houses
Oct. 11	Lung-pu	10		2 houses
Oct. 11	Hsin-tien-tzǔ	40	10,265	4 houses
Oct. 12	Shan-kên-tzǔ	30		Foot of Ta-p'ao Shan
Oct. 12	Ta-p'ao Shan	15	14,496	Summit of pass
Oct. 12	Shan-chioh	15		Foot of Ta-p'ao Shan
Oct. 12	Ku'ei-yung	60	10,041	6 houses
Oct. 13	Mao-niu	30	9,308	Village of 30 odd houses
Oct. 14	Hsiao-mao-niu	10		1 house
Oct. 14	T'ung-lu-fang	20		6 or 7 houses
Oct. 14	Ta Tai	30		3 houses
Oct. 14	T'ung-ku	30	7,489	Large village, about 100 houses
Oct. 15	Kung-ch'a	30		Over 10 houses
Oct. 15	Kanda	20		Hamlet
Oct. 15	Hsi-ho-ch'iao	8		Bridge leading to Pa-wang and Pa-ti
Oct. 15	Romi Chango } Romi-chang-ku }	2	6,402	Town of about 130 houses on the right bank of Ta-chin Ho—the T'ung River
Oct. 16	Ch'ien-ch'ang-pa	5		1 or 2 houses Remains of bamboo cable bridge
Oct. 16	Pien-ku	15		3 houses; village higher up on hillside
Oct. 16	Yo-tsa	15	6,904	12 houses

Date in 1904	Place	Distance in *li* between places	Height above sea level in feet	Remarks
Oct. 17	Pan-ku-ch'iao	20		8 houses
Oct. 17	Pan-shan-mên	20		20 houses
Oct. 17	La-ma-ssǔ	15		10 houses and large lamasery on opposite bank of stream
Oct. 17	T'ai-p'ing-ch'iao	15		2 houses
Oct. 17	{ Shêng-ko-tsung Shêng-ko-chung }	15	7,592	8 houses
Oct. 18	Ts'un-tu	15		1 house
Oct. 18	Ts'ai-yüan-tzǔ	10		1 house
Oct. 18	Hsin-ch'iao-t'ang	15		2 houses
Oct. 18	{ Mou-kung T'ing Hsin-kai-tzǔ }	20	8,138	Small Sub-Prefectural city; 317 houses
Oct. 19	P'a-chai-tzǔ	7		2 houses
Oct. 19	{ Mêng-mu-ch'ang Lao-ying }	8		Over 20 houses
Oct. 19	Ta-shui-kou	7		2 or 3 houses
Oct. 19	Kao-tien-tzǔ	8		3 or 4 houses
Oct. 19	Hsiao-shui-kou	5		2 houses
Oct. 19	Kuan-chai	10	8,211	10 houses, besides residence of chief of the Wokjé
Oct. 20	Mu-lan-pa	10		Some 10 houses
Oct. 20	Mu-lan-ch'a	2		1 house
Oct. 20	Yang-t'ien-wo	5		2 houses
Oct. 20	Chiang-chün-pei	10		2 houses
Oct. 20	{ Mo-ya-ch'iao Hsin-tien-tzǔ }	1		Bridge; 1 house
Oct. 20	Rih-êrh-chai	12		4 or 5 houses
Oct. 20	Ta-ying-p'an	5		4 or 5 houses

Date in 1904	Place	Distance in *li* between places	Height above sea level in feet	Remarks
Oct. 20	Mao-shui-k'ang	5		1 house
Oct. 20	Ta-wei	5		Over 10 houses and lamasery, branch road to Chiung Chou
Oct. 20	Kuang-chin-pa	12		2 houses
Oct. 20	Mao-êrh-chai	4		6 or 7 houses
Oct. 20	Ti-shui-ngai	4		3 houses
Oct. 21	Sha-pa	10		4 or 5 houses
Oct. 21	Shuang-ch'iao-k'ou	3		
Oct. 21	Ch'a-tien-tzû	2		1 house
Oct. 21	Shuang-tiao	5		3 or 4 houses
Oct. 21	Rih-lung-kuan	5	10,522	20 odd houses
Oct. 21	P'o-chai-tzŭ	12		1 house
Oct. 21	Kao-tien-tzŭ	8		1 house
Oct. 21	Sung-lin-k'ou	10		1 house
Oct. 21	Wan-jên-fên	20	13,546	1 house
Oct. 22	Pan-lan Shan	10	14,104	Summit of pass
Oct. 22	T'ang-fang	10		1 house
Oct. 22	Hsiang-yang-p'ing	5		Temple
Oct. 22	Kao-tien-tzŭ	15		1 house
Oct. 22	Ts'ai-yüan-tzŭ	12		1 house
Oct. 22	Têng-shêng-t'ang	3		3 or 4 houses
Oct. 22	Yü-yü-tien	8	8,695	2 houses
Oct. 23	San-shêng-kou	4		1 house and 1 temple
Oct. 23	Wên-hsien-kai	8		1 inn
Oct. 23	Sha-p'ing-wan	2		1 house
Oct. 23	Lung-ngai	8		1 inn
Oct. 23	Ma-t'ang	5		1 house
Oct. 23	T'zŭ-pa-kai	5		1 inn
Oct. 23	Hsin-tien-tzŭ	5		1 house
Oct. 23	Ta-ngai-tung	5		1 house
Oct. 23	San-tao-ch'iao	5		1 house
Oct. 23	Hsiao-ngai-tung	5		1 house

Date in 1904	Place	Distance in *li* between places	Height above sea level in feet	Remarks
Oct. 23	Hsin-tien-tzŭ	3		1 house
Oct. 23	T'ou-tao-ch'iao	5		2 houses and temple
Oct. 23	Wo-lung-kuan	12	6,620	2 houses and 2 inns
Oct. 24	Sung-p'an-ying	4		2 houses
Oct. 24	Ch'uan-pei-ying	3		4 or 5 houses
Oct. 24	Hua-hung-shu	8		7 or 8 houses
Oct. 24	Sha-wan	2		4 or 5 houses
Oct. 24	Chioh-mo-kou	7		1 house
Oct. 24	P'i-tiao-ho	1		7 or 8 houses
Oct. 24	Kou-k'ou } Erh-tao-ch'iao	5		1 inn
Oct. 24	Chuan-ching-lou	5		1 inn
Oct. 24	Hao-tzŭ-p'ing	5		1 inn
Oct. 24	Hsin-tien-tzŭ	5		1 inn
Oct. 24	K'ung-tung-shu	5		1 inn
Oct. 24	T'ang-fang	2		1 house
Oct. 24	Niu-t'ou Shan	6	9,988	Pass
Oct. 24	Shao-ch'a-p'ing	8	8,593	1 inn
Oct. 25	Ch'uan-hsin-tien	5		1 inn
Oct. 25	T'ung-ts'ao	5		1 inn
Oct. 25	Hao-tzŭ-p'ing	5		1 inn
Oct. 25	Ma-liu-p'ing	5		2 houses
Oct. 25	Pai-kuo-p'ing	5		3 or 4 houses
Oct. 25	An-chia-p'ing	5		2 inns
Oct. 25	Chiu-lung-shan	5		1 inn and temple
Oct. 25	Ch'uan-hsiang-p'ing	5		Some 10 thatched houses
Oct. 25	Ts'ao-p'ing	5		2 or 3 houses
Oct. 25	Pai-la-kou	2		1 house
Oct. 25	Shên-kou	5		2 or 3 houses
Oct. 25	Ch'i Shan	3		7 or 8 houses

Date in 1904	Place	Distance in *li* between places	Height above sea level in feet	Remarks
Oct. 25	Hê-t'ao p'ing	3		2 houses
Oct. 25	Hei-shih-chiang	2	3,870	2 houses
Oct. 26	Shih-pan-p'êng	5		1 house
Oct. 26	Wa-yao-p'ing	5		2 or 3 houses
Oct. 26	Yao-tzǔ Shan	3	5,370	Summit of pass
Oct. 26	T'ao-hua-tien	2		1 inn
Oct. 26	Hsin-tien-tzǔ	2		1 inn
Oct. 26	Wa-tuan-shan	3		1 inn
Oct. 26	Lien-san-p'o	3		4 or 5 houses
Oct. 26	An-tzǔ-p'ing	4		17 or 18 houses
Oct. 26	Shui-mo-kou	3		Market town; 360 to 370 houses
Oct. 26	Ts'ai-chia-nien	3		2 houses
Oct. 26	Ai-tzǔ-mo	2		2 houses
Oct. 26	Ch'a-pa-tien	3		5 or 6 houses
Oct. 26	Kuan-shan-p'ing	7		4 or 5 houses
Oct. 26	Fêng-chia-mo-tzǔ	4		2 houses
Oct. 26	Sun-chia-p'ing	8		3 or 4 houses
Oct. 26	Hsüan-k'ou	3	2,650	Market town on right bank of Min River; 300 houses
Oct. 27	Tao-liu-shui	1		1 house
Oct. 27	Fên-t'an-p'ing	1		Over 10 houses
Oct. 27	Chi-kung-chao	3		2 houses
Oct. 27	Lo-chia-hsüan	5		1 house
Oct. 27	Ngai-kou	2		Over 10 houses
Oct. 27	Liu-sha-p'o	3		1 house
Oct. 27	Ma-ch'i	5		Over 30 houses
Oct. 27	Jên-chia-k'an	5		3 or 4 houses
Oct. 27	Hou-tzǔ-p'o	5		Over 10 houses
Oct. 27	Ch'ing-yün-ying	1		Over 20 houses
Oct. 27	Sha-chin-pa	4		Over 10 houses

Date in 1904	Place	Distance in *li* between places	Height above sea level in feet	Remarks
Oct. 27	Shui-hsi-k'an	10		Over 10 houses
Oct. 27	Han-chia-pa	10		Over 20 houses
Oct. 27	An-lan-ch'iao	3		Bamboo cable bridge across Min River; over 10 houses
Oct. 27	Ho-kai-tzŭ			20 to 30 houses
Oct. 27	Erh-lang-miao			Temple dedicated to Li Ping
Oct. 27	Kuan Hsien	2	2,280	District city on western edge of Chengtu plain
Oct. 28	Hsin-ch'ang	20		Large market town
Oct. 28	Ch'ung-ning-p'u	10		Large market town
Oct. 28	Liang-lu-k'ou	25		Large market town
Oct. 28	Pi Hsien	15		District city
Oct. 28	Hsi-p'u	15		Large market town
Oct. 28	T'u-ch'iao	20		Large market town
Oct. 28	Chengtu	15	1,700	Capital of the Province of Ssuchuan
	Total	1,326		

Summary

	Distance in *li*
Chengtu to Ta–chien–lu	1,250
Ta–chien–lu to Tibetan frontier	1,355
Tibetan frontier to Ta–chien–lu	1,355
Ta–chien–lu to Chengtu	1,326
Total	5,286
	or about
	1,320 miles

New titles in the series

The War Facsimiles

The War Facsimiles are exact reproductions of illustrated books that were published during the war years. They were produced by the British government to inform people about the progress of the war and the home-defence operations.

The Battle of Britain, August–October 1940

On 8 August 1940, the Germans launched the first of a series of mass air attacks on Britain in broad daylight. For almost three months, British and German aircraft were locked in fierce and prolonged combat in what has become known as the Battle of Britain. In 1941 the government published *The Battle of Britain* to explain the strategy and tactics behind the fighting that had taken place over London and south-east England. Such was the public interest in this document, with its graphic maps and photographs, that sales had reached two million by the end of the war.

ISBN 0 11 702536 4   Price UK £4.99   US $8.95

The Battle of Egypt, 1942

Often referred to as the Battle of El Alamein, this battle was one of the major turning points for the Allies in World War II. The British, commanded by General Montgomery, were defending Egypt while the Germans under Rommel were attacking. This was a campaign the British could not afford to lose, because not only would it leave Egypt wide open for invasion, but it would also mean the loss of the Suez Canal and the oil fields. First published in 1943, *The Battle of Egypt* is an astonishing contemporary report of one of the most famous military victories in British history.

ISBN 0 11 702542 9   Price UK £5.99   US $10.95

Bomber Command: the Air Ministry account of Bomber Command's offensive against the Axis, September 1939–July 1941

Churchill declared on 22 June 1941:"We shall bomb Germany by day as well as by night in ever-increasing measure." Bomber Command of the RAF was to translate those words into action, beginning its attacks on Germany in May 1940, and steadily increasing its efforts as the war progressed. Published in 1941 at the height of World War II, *Bomber Command* tells the story of this fighting force during those early years.

ISBN 0 11 702540 2   Price UK £5.99   US $11.95

East of Malta, West of Suez: the Admiralty account of the naval war in the eastern Mediterranean, September 1939 to March 1941

This is the story of the British Navy in action in the eastern Mediterranean from September 1939 to March 1941 and their bid to seize control. During this time British supremacy was vig-orously asserted at Taranto and Matapan. This facsimile edition contains contemporary maps, air reconnaissance photographs of the fleets and photographs of them in action.

ISBN 0 11 702538 0   Price UK £4.99   US $8.95

Fleet Air Arm: the Admiralty account of naval air operations, 1943

The Fleet Air Arm was established in 1939 as the Royal Navy's own flying branch. With its vast aircraft carriers bearing squadrons of fighter pilots, its main role was to protect a fleet or convoy from attack, or to escort an air striking force into battle. In *Fleet Air Arm*, published in 1943, the public could read for the first time of the expeditions of these great ships as they pursued and sank enemy warships such as the *Bismarck*.

ISBN 0 11 702539 9   Price UK £5.99   US $11.95

Land at War: the official story of British farming 1939–1944

Land at War was published by the Ministry of Information in 1945 as a tribute to those who had contributed to the war effort at home. It explains how 300,000 farms, pinpointed by an extensive farm survey, had been expected to increase their production dramatically, putting an extra 6.5 million acres of grassland under the plough. This is a book not just about rural life, but of the determination of a people to survive the rigours of war.

ISBN 0 11 702537 2   Price UK £5.99   US $11.95

Ocean Front: the story of the war in the Pacific, 1941–44

Ocean Front tells the story of the Allies' war against Japan in the central and western Pacific. Starting with Pearl Harbor in December 1941, this fascinating book recounts the Allies' counter-offensive, from the battles of the Coral Sea and Midway, to the recapture of the Aleutian Islands and the final invasion of the Philippines. Illustrated throughout with amazing photographs of land and sea warfare, *Ocean Front* provides a unique record of the American, Australian and New Zealand fighting forces in action.

ISBN 0 11 702543 7   Price UK £5.99   US $11.95

Roof over Britain: the official story of Britain's anti-aircraft defences, 1939–1942

Largely untold, *Roof over Britain* is the story of Britain's ground defences against the attacks of the German air force during the Battle of Britain in the autumn of 1940. First published in 1943, it describes how the static defences – the AA guns, searchlights and balloons – were organised, manned and supplied in order to support the work of the RAF.

ISBN 0 11 702541 0   Price UK £5.99   US $11.95

Uncovered editions: how to order

FOR CUSTOMERS IN THE UK
Ordering is easy. Simply follow one of these five ways:

Online
Visit www.clicktso.com

By telephone
Please call 0870 600 5522, with book details to hand.

By fax
Fax details of the books you wish to order (title, ISBN, quantity and price) to: 0870 600 5533.
Please include details of your credit/debit card plus expiry date, your name and address and telephone number, and expect a handling charge of £3.00.

By post
Post the details listed above (under 'By fax') to:
The Stationery Office
PO Box 29
Norwich NR3 1GN
You can send a cheque if you prefer by this method (made payable to The Stationery Office). Please include a handling charge of £3 on the final amount.

TSO bookshops
Visit your local TSO bookshop (or any good bookshop).

FOR CUSTOMERS IN THE UNITED STATES
Uncovered editions are available through all major wholesalers and bookstores, and are distributed to the trade by Midpoint Trade Books.
Phone 913 831 2233 for single copy prepaid orders which can be fulfilled on the spot, or simply for more information.
Fax 913 362 7401